ATLANTIC OCEAN

Gulf of Mexico

MAINE

Duluth
Superior
St. Paul
MINNESOTA
olis
WISCONSIN
Milwaukee
Madison
IOWA
Des Moines
MISSOURI
Missouri
Jefferson City

Lake Superior
Lake Michigan
Lake Huron
Lake Ontario
Lake Erie
MICHIGAN
Lansing
Detroit
Chicago
ILLINOIS
Springfield
INDIANA
Indianapolis
Frankfort
KENTUCKY

Montpelier
VT
NH
Concord
Albany
MASS.
CT
RI
Boston
Providence
Hartford
NEW YORK
New York
Trenton
NJ
Augusta

PENNSYLVANIA
Harrisburg
Baltimore
MD
Washington D.C.
Annapolis
Dover
DEL
OHIO
Columbus
Charleston
Ohio
WV
Richmond
VIRGINIA
Norfolk
Durham
Raleigh
NORTH CAROLINA

Nashville
TENNESSEE
Tennessee
Memphis
ARKANSAS
Arkansas
Little Rock
MISSISSIPPI
Jackson
Birmingham
ALABAMA
Montgomery
GEORGIA
Atlanta
Columbia
SOUTH CAROLINA
Charlotte
Wilmington
Charleston
Savannah

LOUISIANA
Red
Baton Rouge
New Orleans
Biloxi
Pensacola
Tallahassee
Daytona Beach
Tampa
Orlando
FLORIDA
Miami

Mississippi

las
s Christi

Junior Worldmark Encyclopedia of the States

VOLUME 3

Junior Worldmark Encyclopedia of the States

States

VOLUME

Nevada to
South Dakota

AN IMPRINT OF GALE

an International Thomson Publishing company

JUNIOR WORLDMARK ENCYCLOPEDIA OF THE STATES

Timothy L. Gall and Susan Bevan Gall, *Editors*
Rosalie Wieder, *Senior Editor*
Deborah Baron and Daniel M. Lucas, *Associate Editors*
Brian Rajewski and Deborah Rutti, *Graphics and Layout*
Cordelia R. Heaney, *Editorial Assistant*
Dianne K. Daeg de Mott, Janet Fenn, Matthew Markovich,
   Ariana Ranson, and Craig Strasshofer, *Copy Editors*
Janet Fenn and Matthew Markovich, *Proofreaders*
University of Akron Laboratory for Cartographic and
   Spatial Analysis, Joseph W. Stoll, Supervisor;
   Scott Raypholtz, Mike Meger, *Cartographers*

U•X•L Staff

Jane Hoehner, *U•X•L Developmental Editor*
Carol DeKane Nagel, *Managing Editor*
Thomas L. Romig, *U•X•L Publisher*
Mary Beth Trimper, *Production Director*
Evi Seoud, *Assistant Production Manager*
Shanna Heilveil, *Production Associate*
Cynthia Baldwin, *Product Design Manager*
Barbara J. Yarrow, *Graphic Services Supervisor*
Mary Krzewinski, *Cover Designer*

∞™ This book is printed on acid-free paper that meets the minimum requirements of American National Standard for Information Sciences——Permanence Paper for Printed Library Materials, ANSI Z39.48-1984.

Library of Congress Cataloging-in-Publication Data
Junior Worldmark encyclopedia of the states / edited by Timothy Gall
   and Susan Gall.
      p.   cm.
   Includes bibliographical references and index.
   ISBN 0-7876-0736-3 (set)
   1. United States—Encyclopedia.   I. Gall, Susan B.   II. Title.
E156.G35 1996
973'.03—dc20
                                                95-36740
                                                CIP

ISBN 0-7876-0736-3 (set)
ISBN 0-7876-0737-1 (vol. 1)
ISBN 0-7876-0738-X (vol. 2)
ISBN 0-7876-0739-8 (vol. 3)
ISBN 0-7876-0740-1 (vol. 4)

U•X•L is an imprint of Gale Research
an International Thomson Publishing Company.
ITP logo is a trademark under license.

CONTENTS

READER'S GUIDE

Junior Worldmark Encyclopedia of the States presents profiles of the 50 states of the nation, the District of Columbia, Puerto Rico, and the U.S. dependencies, arranged alphabetically in four volumes. *Junior Worldmark* is based on the third edition of the reference work, *Worldmark Encyclopedia of the States*. The *Worldmark* design organizes facts and data about every state in a common structure. Every profile contains a map, showing the state and its location in the nation.

For this first *Junior* edition of *Worldmark*, facts were updated and many new graphical elements were added, including photographs. Recognition is due to the many tourist bureaus, convention centers, press offices, and state agencies that contributed the photographs that illustrate this encyclopedia. This edition also benefits from the work of the many article reviewers listed at the end of this Reader's Guide. The reviewers contributed insights, updates, and substantive additions that were instrumental to the creation of this work. The editors are extremely grateful for the time and effort these distinguished reviewers devoted to improving the quality of this encyclopedia.

Sources

Due to the broad scope of this encyclopedia many sources were consulted in compiling the information and statistics presented in these volumes. Of primary importance were the following publications from the U.S. Bureau of the Census: *1990 Census of Population, 1990 Census of Manufacturers, 1992 Census of Wholesale Trade, 1992 Census of Retail Trade, 1992 Census of Service Industries,* and the *1992 Census of Agriculture.* More recent economic statistics on the labor force, income, and earnings were obtained from files posted as of January 1996 by the Economics and Statistics Administration of the U.S. Department of Commerce on *The Economic Bulletin Board,* an electronic information retrieval service. The most recent agricultural statistics on crops and livestock were obtained from files posted by the U.S. Department of Agriculture on its gopher server and its world-wide web site at http://www.econ.ag.gov. Finally, many fact sheets, booklets, and state statistical abstracts were used to update data not collected by the federal government.

Profile Features

The *Junior Worldmark* structure—40 numbered headings—allows students to compare two or more states in a variety of ways.

Each state profile begins by listing the origin of the state name, its nickname, the capital, the date it entered the union, the state song and motto, and a description of the state coat of arms. The profile also presents a picture and textual description of both the state seal and the state flag (a key to the flag color symbols appears on page xii of each volume). Next, a listing of the official state animal, bird, fish, flower, tree, gem, etc. is given. The introductory information ends with the standard time given by time zone in relation to Greenwich mean time (GMT). The world is divided into 24 time zones, each one hour apart. The Greenwich meridian, which is 0 degrees, passes through Greenwich, England, a suburb of London. Greenwich is at the center of the initial time zone, known as Greenwich mean time (GMT). All times given are converted from noon in this zone. The time reported for the state is the official time zone.

The body of each country's profile is arranged in 40 numbered headings as follows:

1 LOCATION AND SIZE. The state is located on the North American continent. Statistics are given on area and boundary length. Size comparisons are made to the other 50 states of the United States.

2 TOPOGRAPHY. Dominant geographic features including terrain and major rivers and lakes are described.

3 CLIMATE. Temperature and rainfall are given for the various regions of the state in both English and metric units.

4 PLANTS AND ANIMALS. Described here are the plants and animals native to the state.

5 ENVIRONMENTAL PROTECTION. Destruction of natural resources—forests, water supply, air—is described here. Statistics on solid waste production, hazard-ous waste sites, and endangered and extinct species are also included.

6 POPULATION. 1990 Census statistics as well as 1995 state population estimates are provided. Population density and major urban populations are summarized.

7 ETHNIC GROUPS. The major ethnic groups are ranked in percentages. Where appropriate, some description of the influence or history of ethnicity is provided.

8 LANGUAGES. The regional dialects of the state are summarized as well as the number of people speaking languages other than English at home.

9 RELIGIONS. The population is broken down according to religion and/or denominations.

10 TRANSPORTATION. Statistics on roads, railways, waterways, and air traffic, along with a listing of key ports for trade and travel, are provided.

11 HISTORY. Includes a concise summary of the state's history from ancient times (where appropriate) to the present.

12 STATE GOVERNMENT. The form of government is described, and the process of governing is summarized.

13 POLITICAL PARTIES. Describes the significant political parties through history, where appropriate, and the influential parties in the mid-1990s.

14 LOCAL GOVERNMENT. The system of local government structure is summarized.

15 JUDICIAL SYSTEM. Structure of the court system and the jurisdiction of courts in each category is provided. Crime rates as reported by the Federal Bureau of Investigation (FBI) are also included.

16 MIGRATION. Population shifts since the end of World War II are summarized.

17 ECONOMY. This section presents the key elements of the economy. Major industries and employment figures are also summarized.

18 INCOME. Personal income and the poverty level are given as is the state's ranking among the 50 states in per person income.

19 INDUSTRY. Key industries are listed, and important aspects of industrial development are described.

20 LABOR. Statistics are given on the civilian labor force, including numbers of workers, leading areas of employment, and unemployment figures.

21 AGRICULTURE. Statistics on key agricultural crops, market share, and total farm income are provided.

22 DOMESTICATED ANIMALS. Statistics on livestock—cattle, hogs, sheep, etc.—and the land area devoted to raising them are given.

23 FISHING. The relative significance of fishing to the state is provided, with statistics on fish and seafood products.

24 FORESTRY. Land area classified as forest is given, along with a listing of key forest products and a description of government policy toward forest land.

25 MINING. Description of mineral deposits and statistics on related mining activity and export are provided.

26 ENERGY AND POWER. Description of the state's power resources, including electricity produced and oil reserves and production, are provided.

27 COMMERCE. A summary of the amount of wholesale trade, retail trade, and receipts of service establishments is given.

28 PUBLIC FINANCE. Revenues, expenditures, and total and per person debt are provided.

29 TAXATION. The state's tax system is explained.

30 HEALTH. Statistics on and description of such public health factors as disease and suicide rates, principal causes of death, numbers of hospitals and medical facilities appear here. Information is also provided on the percentage of citizens without health insurance within each state.

31 HOUSING. Housing shortages and government programs to build housing are described. Statistics on numbers of dwellings and median home values are provided.

32 EDUCATION. Statistical data on educational achievement and primary and secondary schools is given. Per person state spending on primary and secondary education is also given. Major universities are listed, and government programs to foster education are described.

33 ARTS. A summary of the state's major cultural institutions is provided together with the amount of federal and state funds designated to the arts.

34 **LIBRARIES AND MUSEUMS.** The number of libraries, their holdings, and their yearly circulation is provided. Major museums are listed.

35 **COMMUNICATIONS.** The state of telecommunications (television, radio, and telephone) is summarized.

36 **PRESS.** Major daily and Sunday newspapers are listed together with data on their circulations.

37 **TOURISM, TRAVEL, AND RECREATION.** Under this heading, the student will find a summary of the importance of tourism to the state, and factors affecting the tourism industry. Key tourist attractions are listed.

38 **SPORTS.** The major sports teams in the state, both professional and collegiate, are summarized.

39 **FAMOUS PEOPLE.** In this section, some of the best-known citizens of the state are listed. When a person is noted in a state that is not the state of his of her birth, the birthplace is given.

40 **BIBLIOGRAPHY.** The bibliographic listings at the end of each profile are provided as a guide for further reading.

Because many terms used in this encyclopedia will be new to students, each volume includes a glossary and a list of abbreviations and acronyms. A keyword index to all four volumes appears in Volume 4.

Acknowledgments

Junior Worldmark Encyclopedia of the States draws on the third edition of the *Worldmark Encyclopedia of the States*. Readers are directed to that work for a complete list of contributors, too numerous to list here. Special acknowledgment goes to the government officials throughout the nation who gave their cooperation to this project.

Reviewers

The following individuals reviewed state articles. In all cases the reviewers added important information and updated facts that might have gone unnoticed. The reviewers were also instrumental in suggesting changes and improvements.

Patricia L. Harris, Executive Director, Alabama Public Library Service
Patience Frederiksen, Head, Government Publications, Alaska State Library
Jacqueline L. Miller, Curator of Education, Arizona State Capitol Museum
John A. Murphey, Jr., State Librarian, Arkansas State Library
Eugene Hainer, School Library Media Consultant, Colorado State Library
Susan Cormier, Connecticut State Library
Dr. Annette Woolard, Director of Development, Historical Society of Delaware
Reference Staff, State Library of Florida
Cheryl Rogers, Consultant, Georgia Department of Education, Public Library Services
Lorna J. T. Peck, School Library Services, Specialist, State of Hawaii Department of Education

Marcia J. Beckwith, Director, Information Services/Library, Centennial High School, Boise, Idaho

Karen McIlrath-Muskopf, Youth Services Consultant, Illinois State Library

Cordell Svengalis, Social Science Consultant, Iowa Department of Education

Marc Galbraith, Director of Reference Services, Kansas State Library

James C. Klotter, State Historian, Kentucky Historical Society

Virginia R. Smith, Head, Louisiana Section, State Library of Louisiana

Ben Keating, Division Director, Maine State Library

Patricia V. Melville, Director of Reference Services, Maryland State Archives

Brian Donoghue, Reference Librarian, Massachusetts Board of Library Commissioners

Denise E. Carlson, Head of Reference, Minnesota Historical Society

Ronnie Smith, Reference Specialist, Mississippi Library Commission

Darlene Staffeldt, Director, Statewide Library Resources, Montana State Library

Rod Wagner, Director, Nebraska Library Commission

Reference Services and Archives Staff, Nevada State Library & Archives

Kendall F. Wiggin, State Librarian, New Hampshire State Library

John H. Livingstone, Acting Assistant Commissioner and State Librarian, New Jersey State Library

Robert J. Torrez, State Historian, New Mexico State Records and Archives

R. Allan Carter, Senior Librarian, New York State Library

Staff, Information Services and State Archives Research, State Library of North Carolina

Doris Daugherty, Assistant State Librarian, North Dakota State Library

Carol Brieck and Audrey Hall, Reference Librarians, State Library of Ohio

Audrey Wolfe-Clark, Edmond, Oklahoma

Paul Gregorio, Assistant Professor of Education, Portland State University, Portland, Oregon

Alice L. Lubrecht, Acting Bureau Director, State Library of Pennsylvania

Barbara Weaver, Director, Department of State Library Services, Rhode Island

Michele M. Reid, Director of Public Services, South Dakota State Library

Dr. Wayne C. Moore, Archivist, Tennessee State Library and Archives

Douglas E. Barnett, Managing Editor, New Handbook of Texas, Texas State Historical Association

Lou Reinwand, Director of Information Services, Utah State Library

Paul J. Donovan, Senior Reference Librarian, Vermont Department of Libraries

Catherine Mishler, Head, Reference, Library of Virginia

Gayle Palmer, Senior Library Information Specialist, Washington/Northwest Collections, Washington State Library

Karen Goff, Head of Reference, West Virginia Library Commission

Richard L. Roe, Research Analyst, Wisconsin Legislative Reference Bureau

Priscilla Golden, Principal Librarian, Wyoming State Library

Staff, Washingtoniana Division, Martin Luther King Memorial Library, Washington, D.C.

Advisors

The following persons were consulted on the content and structure of this encyclopedia. Their insights, opinions, and suggestions led to many enhancements and improvements in the presentation of the material.

Mary Alice Anderson, Media Specialist, Winona Middle School, Winona, Minnesota

Pat Baird, Library Media Specialist and Department Chair, Shaker Heights Middle School, Shaker Heights, Ohio

Pat Fagel, Library Media Specialist, Shaker Heights Middle School, Shaker Heights, Ohio

Nancy Guidry, Young Adult Librarian, Santa Monica Public Library, Santa Monica, California

Ann West LaPrise, Children's Librarian, Redford Branch, Detroit Public Library, Detroit, Michigan

Nancy C. Nieman, Teacher, U.S. History, Social Studies, Journalism, Delta Middle School, Muncie, Indiana

Madeleine Obrock, Library Media Specialist, Woodbury Elementary School, Shaker Heights, Ohio

Ernest L. O'Roark, Teacher, Social Studies, Martin Luther King Middle School, Germantown, Maryland

Ellen Stepanian, Director of Library Services, Shaker Heights Board of Education, Shaker Heights, Ohio

Mary Strouse, Library Media Specialist, Woodbury Elementary School, Shaker Heights, Ohio

Comments and Suggestions

We welcome your comments on the *Junior Worldmark Encyclopedia of the States* as well as your suggestions for features to be included in future editions. Please write: Editors, *Junior Worldmark Encyclopedia of the States,* U•X•L, 835 Penobscot Building, Detroit, Michigan 48226-4094; or call toll-free: 1-800-877-4253.

Guide to State Articles

All information contained within a state article is uniformly keyed by means of a boxed number to the left of the subject headings. A heading such as "Population," for example, carries the same key numeral (6) in every article. Therefore, to find information about the population of Alabama, consult the table of contents for the page number where the Alabama article begins and look for section 6.

Introductory matter for each state includes:
Origin of state name
Nickname
Capital
Date and order of statehood
Song
Motto
Flag
Official seal
Symbols (animal, tree, flower, etc.)
Time zone.

Flag color symbols

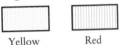

| Yellow | Red | Green | Blue | Orange | Brown | White | Black |

Sections listed numerically

1 Location and Size
2 Topography
3 Climate
4 Plants and Animals
5 Environmental Protection
6 Population
7 Ethnic Groups
8 Languages
9 Religions
10 Transportation
11 History
12 State Government
13 Political Parties
14 Local Government
15 Judicial System
16 Migration
17 Economy
18 Income
19 Industry
20 Labor
21 Agriculture
22 Domesticated Animals
23 Fishing
24 Forestry
25 Mining
26 Energy and Power
27 Commerce
28 Public Finance
29 Taxation
30 Health
31 Housing
32 Education
33 Arts
34 Libraries and Museums
35 Communications
36 Press
37 Tourism, Travel, and Recreation
38 Sports
39 Famous Persons
40 Bibliography

Alphabetical listing of sections

Explanation of symbols

A fiscal split year is indicated by a stroke (e.g. 1994/95).
Note that 1 billion = 1,000 million = 10^9.
The use of a small dash (e.g., 1990–94) normally signifies the full period of calendar years covered (including the end year indicated).

NEVADA

State of Nevada

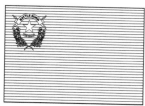

ORIGIN OF STATE NAME: Named for the Sierra Nevada mountain range, *nevada* meaning "snow-covered" in Spanish.

NICKNAME: The Sagebrush State. (Also: The Silver State.)

CAPITAL: Carson City.

ENTERED UNION: 31 October 1864 (36th).

SONG: "Home Means Nevada."

MOTTO: All for Our Country.

FLAG: On a blue field, two sprays of sagebrush and a golden scroll in the upper lefthand corner frame a silver star with the word "Nevada" below the star and above the sprays; the scroll, reading "Battle Born," recalls that Nevada was admitted to the Union during the Civil War.

OFFICIAL SEAL: A quartz mill, ore cart, and mine tunnel symbolize Nevada's mining industry. A plow, sickle, and sheaf of wheat represent its agricultural resources. In the background are a railroad, a telegraph line, and a sun rising over the snow-covered mountains. Encircling this scene are 36 stars and the state motto. The words "The Great Seal of the State of Nevada" surround the whole.

ANIMAL: Desert bighorn sheep.

REPTILE: Desert tortoise.

BIRD: Mountain bluebird.

FISH: Lahontan cutthroat trout.

FLOWER: Sagebrush.

TREE: Single-leaf piñon.

METAL: Silver.

GRASS: Indian ricegrass.

FOSSIL: Ichthyosaur.

ROCK: Sandstone.

TIME: 4 AM PST = noon GMT.

1 LOCATION AND SIZE

Situated between the Rocky Mountains and the Sierra Nevada in the western US, Nevada ranks seventh in size among the 50 states. Its total area is 109,806 square miles (284,396 square kilometers). Nevada extends 320 miles (515 kilometers) east-west. The maximum north-south extension is 483 miles (777 kilometers) and the total boundary length is 1,480 miles (2,382 kilometers).

2 TOPOGRAPHY

Almost all of Nevada belongs to the Great Basin, a plateau with isolated mountain ranges separated by arid basins. The state's highest point is Boundary Peak at 13,143 feet (4,006 meters). Nevada has a number of large lakes and several large saltwater marshes known as sinks. The state's longest river is the Humboldt. The Colorado River forms the southeastern boundary of the state.

3 CLIMATE

Nevada's climate is sunny and dry. The normal daily temperature at Reno ranges from 32°F (0°C) in January to 69°F (21°C) in July. Normal daily temperatures in Las Vegas are 44°F (7°C) in January and 85°F (29°C) in July. The all-time high, 122°F (50°C), was set in 1954; the record low was –50°F (–46°C), set in 1937. Nevada is the driest state in the US, with overall average annual precipitation of less than 4 inches (10 centimeters) in Las Vegas, and about 7 inches (17.8 centimeters) in Reno.

4 PLANTS AND ANIMALS

Various species of pine—among them the single-leaf piñon, the state tree—dominate Nevada's woodlands. Creosote bush is common in southern Nevada, as are many kinds of sagebrush throughout the state. Wildflowers include shooting star and white and yellow violets.

Native mammals include the black bear, cottontail rabbit, and river otter. Grouse and partridge are among the leading game birds, and trout, salmon, and whitefish thrive in Nevada waters. Listed as endangered are the Moapa dace, woundfin, and bonytail chub.

Nevada Population Profile

Estimated 1995 population:	1,477,000
Population change, 1980–90:	50.1%
Leading ancestry group:	German
Second leading group:	English
Foreign born population:	8.7%
Hispanic origin†:	10.4%
Population by race:	
White:	84.3%
Black:	6.6%
Native American:	1.6%
Asian/Pacific Islander:	3.2%
Other:	4.3%

Population by Age Group

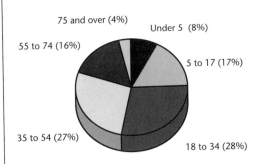

75 and over (4%)
Under 5 (8%)
55 to 74 (16%)
5 to 17 (17%)
35 to 54 (27%)
18 to 34 (28%)

Top Cities with Populations Over 25,000

City	Population	National rank	% change 1980–90
Las Vegas	295,516	54	56.9
Reno	139,884	129	32.8
Henderson	84,358	262	NA
Sparks	56,188	446	30.9
North Las Vegas	55,571	453	11.6
Carson City	42,839	622	26.3

Notes: †A person of Hispanic origin may be of any race. NA indicates that data are not available.
Sources: Economic and Statistics Administration, Bureau of the Census. *Statistical Abstract of the United States, 1994–95.* Washington, DC: Government Printing Office, 1995; Courtenay M. Slater and George E. Hall. *1995 County and City Extra: Annual Metro, City and County Data Book.* Lanham, MD: Bernan Press, 1995.

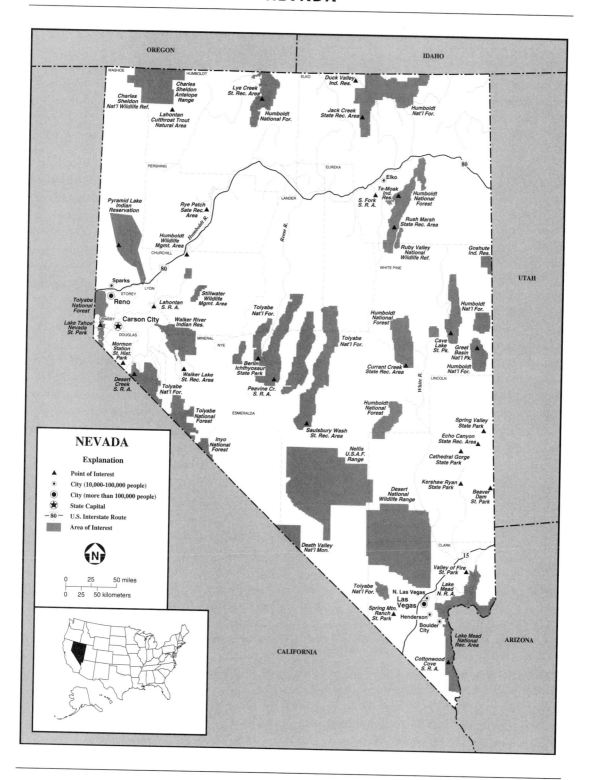

5 ENVIRONMENTAL PROTECTION

Preservation of the state's clean air, scarce water resources, and diminishing wildlife are the major environmental challenges facing Nevada. The Division of Wildlife sets quotas on the hunting of deer, antelope, bighorn sheep, and other game animals. Nevada has 120 municipal landfills and 2 curbside recycling programs. In 1994, there was one hazardous waste site in the state.

6 POPULATION

Nevada ranked 39th in the US with a 1990 census population of 1,201,833. This made it the fastest-growing state for the 1980–90 decade, with an increase of 50.1%. The federal estimate for Nevada's population in 1995 was 1,477,000, but the state estimated the population at 1,582,280 in mid-1995. Growth, although not as rapid, is expected to continue from 1995–2000, with a population of 1,691,000 in the year 2000. With a population density of about 13.3 persons per square mile (5.1 persons square kilometer) in 1994, Nevada remains one of the nation's most sparsely populated states. Las Vegas, the largest city, had 295,516 residents in 1992. Reno had a 1992 population of 139,884.

7 ETHNIC GROUPS

Some 79,000 black Americans made up about 6.6% of Nevada's population in 1990, and about 38,000 Asian/Pacific Islanders accounted for 3.2%. The Native American population was about 20,000 in 1990. About 124,000 Nevadans were of Hispanic origin, including 72,281 of Mexican ancestry.

8 LANGUAGES

Midland and Northern English dialects are intermixed in Nevada. In 1990, 964,298, Nevadans—86.8% of the resident population—spoke only English at home, and 85,474 spoke Spanish.

9 RELIGIONS

In 1991, Nevada had about 152,000 Roman Catholics. Other Christian denominations in 1990 included 89,033 members of the Church of Jesus Christ of Latter-day Saints (Mormons); 27,889 Southern Baptists; 6,219 Lutherans of the Missouri Synod; and 8,529 Methodists. In 1991, there were an estimated 20,500 Jews living in Nevada.

10 TRANSPORTATION

As of 1992, Nevada had 1,200 rail miles (1,931 kilometers) of railroads. The total number of Amtrak riders in 1991/92 was 163,362. In 1993 there were 45,778 miles (73,657 kilometers) of public roads and streets and 937,227 registered vehicles. The leading commercial air terminal is McCarran International Airport at Las Vegas, which handled 22.5 million arriving and departing passengers in 1993.

11 HISTORY

In modern times, four principal Native American groups have inhabited Nevada: Southern Paiute, Northern Paiute, Shoshoni, and Washo. Probably the first white explorer to enter the state was the Spanish priest Francisco Garces, in 1776.

Nevada's first permanent white settlement, Mormon Station (later Genoa), was founded in 1851 in what is now western Nevada, a region that became part of Utah Territory the same year. (The southeastern tip of Nevada was assigned to the Territory of New Mexico.) Farming and ranching communities were established in the northwest.

A separate Nevada Territory was established on 2 March 1861. Only three years later, on 31 October 1864, Nevada achieved statehood. Nevada's development during the rest of the century was determined by the discovery of the Comstock Lode, an immense concentration of silver and gold which attracted thousands of fortune seekers and established the region as a thriving mining center. The lode's rich ores were exhausted in the late 1870s, and Nevada slipped into a 20-year depression.

Nevada's economy revived following new discoveries of silver at Tonopah in 1902 and gold at Goldfield in 1904. A second great mining boom followed, bolstered and extended by major copper discoveries in eastern Nevada. Progressive politics in this pre-World War I period added recall, referendum, and initiative amendments to the state constitution and brought about the adoption of women's suffrage (1914).

1920s–1990s

The 1920s was a time of economic decline. Mining fell off, and not even the celebrated divorce trade, centered in Reno, was able to compensate. During the 1930s, the hard

Photo credit: Nevada Commission on Tourism.

View of the silver-mining town of Tonopah. Nevada leads the nation in the production of silver.

times of the depression were alleviated by federal public-works projects, most notably the construction of the Hoover (Boulder) Dam, and by state laws that aided the divorce business and legalizing gambling.

Gambling grew rapidly after World War II, becoming by the mid-1950s not only the mainstay of Nevada tourism but also the state's leading industry. Revelations during the 1950s and 1960s that organized crime had infiltrated the casino industry led to a state and federal crackdown and the imposition of new state controls.

From 1960s through the 1990s, Nevada was the fastest-growing of the 50 states. Much of its growth was associated with expansion of the gambling industry—centered in the casinos of Las Vegas and Reno—and of the military. In the 1980s, Nevada began to try to reduce its dependence on gambling by diversifying its economy. In an attempt to attract new businesses, particularly in high-technology industries, the state has been promoting such features as its absence of state corporate or personal income taxes, inexpensive real estate, low wages, and its ready access by air or land to California.

12 STATE GOVERNMENT

The state legislature consists of a senate with 21 members, each elected to a four-year term; and a house of representatives with 42 members, each serving two years. Executive officials elected statewide include the governor and lieutenant governor (who run separately), secretary of state, attorney general, and treasurer. A two-thirds vote of the elected members of each house is required to override a governor's veto.

13 POLITICAL PARTIES

Since World War II neither the Democrats nor the Republicans have dominated state politics, which are basically conservative. As of January 1995 there were 268,948 registered Democrats, 259,944 registered Republicans, and 90,657 persons registered with other parties or with no affiliation. In 1992, after choosing Republicans in each of the previous eight presidential elections, Nevadans elected Democrat Bill Clinton with 37% of the vote, giving Republican George Bush 35%, and Independent Ross Perot 26%.

Nevada is represented in the US Congress by two Democratic senators—Richard Bryan and Harry Reid. Bryan was reelected in 1994. Nevada's US Representatives include two Republicans. Democrat Robert J. Miller was reelected to the governorship in 1994. There were 13 Republicans and 8 Democrats in the state senate, and 21 Democrats and 21 Republicans in the state house.

Nevada Presidential Vote by Major Political Parties, 1948–92

YEAR	NEVADA WINNER	DEMOCRAT	REPUBLICAN
1948	*Truman (D)	31,290	29,357
1952	*Eisenhower (R)	31,688	50,502
1956	*Eisenhower (R)	40,640	56,049
1960	*Kennedy (D)	54,880	52,387
1964	*Johnson (D)	79,339	56,094
1968	*Nixon (R)	60,598	73,188
1972	*Nixon (R)	66,016	115,750
1976	Ford (R)	92,479	101,273
1980	*Reagan (R)	66,666	155,017
1984	*Reagan (R)	91,655	188,770
1988	*Bush (R)	132,738	206,040
1992**	*Clinton (D)	189,148	175,828

* Won US presidential election.
** Independent candidate, Ross Perot, received 132,580 votes.

14 LOCAL GOVERNMENT

As of 1992, Nevada was subdivided into 16 counties, 1 independent municipality (Carson City), and 16 other municipalities constituting the 16 county seats.

15 JUDICIAL SYSTEM

Nevada's supreme court consists of a chief justice and four other justices. As of 1995 there were 39 district court judges organized into 9 judicial districts. Nevada's overall crime rate in 1994 was 6,677.4 per 100,000 persons.

16 MIGRATION

Between 1940 and 1980, Nevada gained a total of 507,000 residents through migration. There was an additional net gain from migration of 233,000 during the 1980s. In 1990, only about 21.8% of Nevadans had been born within the state, the lowest proportion among the 50 states.

17 ECONOMY

Nevada has a dry climate and a shortage of usable land for farming, but it has a wealth of mineral resources—gold, silver, copper, and other metals. Mining remains important, though it has been overshadowed since World War II by tourism and gambling, which generate more than 50% of the state's income. Legalized gambling alone produces nearly half of Nevada's tax revenues.

18 INCOME

In 1994, per capita (per person) income in Nevada averaged $23,817 (seventh among the states). Total personal income was $34.7 billion in 1994. Some 9.8% of all Nevadans were below the federal poverty level as of 1993.

19 INDUSTRY

Industry in Nevada is limited but diversified, producing communications equipment, pet food, chemicals, and sprinkler systems, among other products. The total value of shipments by manufacturers in 1992 was $3.29 billion.

Photo credit: Nevada Commission on Tourism.

Aerial view of Hoover Dam.

20 LABOR

Nevada's total civilian labor force in 1994 was 779,000, of whom about 6.2% were unemployed. Some 18.4% of all workers in Nevada were union members as of 1994.

21 AGRICULTURE

Agricultural income in 1994 totaled $299 million (47th in the US). Chief crops in 1994 included 670,000 bushels of wheat, 1.4 million tons of hay, and 276 million pounds of potatoes. Nevada's barley crop in 1994 was 340,000 bushels.

22 DOMESTICATED ANIMALS

In 1994 Nevada ranches and farms had 500,000 cattle, 23,000 milk cows, and

107,000 sheep. Cattle and dairy products accounted for 43.6% and 16.9% of agricultural receipts in 1994, respectively.

23 FISHING

There is no commercial fishing industry in Nevada. The Lahontan National Fish Hatchery distributed over half a million (50,985 pounds) cutthroat trout within the state in 1992.

24 FORESTRY

Nevada in 1990 had 8,938,000 acres (3,617,000 hectares) of forestland, of which 5,150,000 acres (2,084,000 hectares) were in the National Forest System.

25 MINING

With an estimated value of $2.8 billion, Nevada ranked second among the states in 1994 nonfuel mineral production. Nevada remained the leading state in the production of gold (214,614 kilograms); silver (861 metric tons); and barite (441,000 metric tons). Nevada was second in the production of diatomite and lithium.

26 ENERGY AND POWER

In 1993, 19.8 billion kilowatt hours of power were produced, a decrease from the 1992 amount of 21 billion. Hoover Dam, anchored in the bedrock of Black Canyon east of Las Vegas, was the state's largest hydroelectric installation. In 1994, total oil production was 1,752,640 barrels. In 1992 Nevada's per capita (per person) energy expenditures were $1,894.

27 COMMERCE

Wholesale sales in 1992 totaled about $7.8 billion. Retail sales in 1993 exceeded $12.4 billion, a 7.5 increase over 1992. Service establishment receipts in 1992 totaled $17.5 billion. Foreign exports totaled $507 million in goods in 1992.

28 PUBLIC FINANCE

As of 30 June 1994, the total general obligation state debt was $820,906 million, or $549.83 per capita (per person). Total revenues for 1993 were $1,992,947,000; expenditures were $2,122,041,000.

29 TAXATION

As of 1994, Nevada levied a 6.5% state sales and use tax, along with taxes on liquor, soft drinks, cigarettes, jet fuel, and slot machines. There is no personal or corporate income tax, and real estate transfer taxes ended in 1980. Nevadans paid $5 billion in taxes in 1992.

30 HEALTH

Heart disease, cancer, and cerebrovascular disease were the leading causes of death. In 1992, Nevada had the highest suicide rate among the states, at 24.6 per 100,000 population. In 1990, Nevada ranked highest among the states in smoking-attributable mortalities, at 24% of all deaths. In 1992, Nevada had the nation's highest rates for marriage (90.7 per 1,000 population) and for divorce (9.6 per 1,000 population).

In 1993 there were 21 community hospitals, with 3,700 beds. The average expense to a hospital in the state for care provided in

Great Basin National Park, Bristlecone.

1993 came to $900 per inpatient day. The average cost per stay was $6,796. The state had 2,045 nonfederal physicians and approximately 7,100 nurses in 1993. In 1993 over 18% of Nevadans did not have health insurance.

31 HOUSING

In 1993, there were an estimated 595,000 housing units. In 1990, the median cost for an owner with a mortgage was $833; renters paid a median cost of $509. The median value of a home in 1990 was $45,700. Between 1990 and 1992, 57,300 new housing units were completed in the Las Vegas area.

32 EDUCATION

By 1990, 82.2% of Nevadans 25 years and over had completed at least high school. In 1993, 235,000 pupils were enrolled in Nevada's public schools: 174,000 in elementary, and 61,000 in secondary. In 1993/94, 64,397 students were enrolled in institutions of higher learning, nearly all of them in the University of Nevada system.

33 ARTS

Major exhibits are mounted by the Las Vegas Arts League and the Sierra Arts Foundation in Reno. Reno also has a symphony orchestra and an opera association. The state of Nevada generated

$4,163,498 in federal and state funds to support arts programs from 1992 to 1995.

34 LIBRARIES AND MUSEUMS

Nevada's public library system in 1994 had a combined book stock of 3,085,376 volumes and a circulation of 7,151,445. There are some 28 museums and historic sites, including the Nevada State Museum in Carson City, the museum of the Nevada Historical Society in Reno, and the Nevada State Museum and Historical Society in Las Vegas.

35 COMMUNICATIONS

In March 1993, 94.9% of Nevada's occupied housing units had telephones. In 1995, broadcasting comprised 75 radio stations (27 AM, 48 FM) and 17 television stations. In 1993, two large cable television systems served the Las Vegas and Reno areas.

36 PRESS

In 1995, the state had three morning newspapers, four evening papers, and four Sunday papers. The leading newspaper was the *Las Vegas Review–Journal,* with an all-day circulation of 142,582 and a Sunday circulation of 213,424. The *Reno Gazette–Journal,* with a daily circulation of 67,852 and Sunday circulation of 86,282, is the most influential newspaper in the northern half of the state.

37 TOURISM, TRAVEL, AND RECREATION

Tourism remains Nevada's most important industry. In 1993, tourists spent over $12.5 billion in the state. Tourists flock to "Vegas" for gambling and for the top-flight entertainers who perform there. Other Nevada attractions are Pyramid Lake and Lake Tahoe. There are 23 state parks and recreation areas.

38 SPORTS

There are no major league professional sports teams in Nevada. Las Vegas and Reno have hosted many professional boxing title bouts. Golfing and rodeo are also popular. The basketball team at the University of Nevada-Las Vegas became a highly ranked team in the late 1980s and early 1990s.

39 FAMOUS NEVADANS

Probably the most significant state historical figure is George Wingfield (b.Arkansas, 1876–1959), a mining millionaire who exerted great influence over Nevada's economic and political life in the early 20th century. Among the nationally recognized personalities associated with Nevada is Howard R. Hughes (b.Texas, 1905–76), an aviation entrepreneur who became a casino and hotel owner and wealthy recluse in his later years. Leading creative or performing artists have included operatic singer Emma Nevada (Emma Wixom, 1859–1940); painter Robert Caples (1908–79); and writer Walter Van Tilburg Clark (b.Maine, 1909–71).

40 BIBLIOGRAPHY

Hulse, James W. *The Nevada Adventure: A History.* 5th ed. Reno: University of Nevada Press, 1981.

Laxalt, Robert. *Nevada: A Bicentennial History.* New York: Norton, 1977.

Toll, David W. *The Complete Nevada Traveler.* Virginia City, Nev.: Gold Hill, 1981.

NEW HAMPSHIRE

State of New Hampshire

ORIGIN OF STATE NAME: Named for the English county of Hampshire.

NICKNAME: The Granite State.

CAPITAL: Concord.

ENTERED UNION: 21 June 1788 (9th).

SONG: "Old New Hampshire."

MOTTO: Live Free or Die.

FLAG: The state seal, surrounded by laurel leaves with nine stars interspersed, is centered on a blue field.

OFFICIAL SEAL: In the center is a broadside view of the frigate *Raleigh*; in the left foreground is a granite boulder; in the background is a rising sun. A laurel wreath and the words "Seal of the State of New Hampshire 1776" surround the whole.

STATE EMBLEM: Within an elliptical panel appears a replica of the Old Man of the Mountain, with the state name above and motto below.

ANIMAL: White-tailed deer.

BIRD: Purple finch.

FLOWER: Purple lilac.

TREE: White birch.

INSECT: Ladybug.

TIME: 7 AM EST = noon GMT.

1 LOCATION AND SIZE

Situated in New England in the northeastern US, New Hampshire ranks 44th in size among the 50 states. The total area of New Hampshire is 9,279 square miles (24,033 square kilometers). The state has a maximum extension of 93 miles (150 kilometers) east-west and 180 miles (290 kilometers) north-south. The state's total boundary line is 555 miles (893 kilometers). The three southernmost Isles of Shoals lying in the Atlantic belong to New Hampshire.

2 TOPOGRAPHY

The major regions of New Hampshire are the coastal lowland in the southeast; the New England Uplands, covering most of the south and west; and the White Mountains (part of the Appalachian chain) in the north. The latter includes Mt. Washington, which at 6,288 feet (1,917 meters) is the highest peak in the northeastern US.

There are some 1,300 lakes and ponds. Principal rivers include the Connecticut (forming the border with Vermont), Merrimack, Piscataqua, and Saco. Near the coast are the nine rocky Isles of Shoals, three of which belong to New Hampshire.

3 CLIMATE

New Hampshire has wide variations in daily and seasonal temperatures. Summers are short and cool; winters, long and cold. Concord's temperature ranges from 21°F (–6°C) in January to 70°F (21°C) in July. The record low temperature, set in 1925, was –46°F (–43°C); the all-time high was 106°F (41°C), set in 1911. Annual precipitation at Concord averages 36 inches (91 centimeters); the average snowfall is more than 100 inches (254 centimeters) yearly in the mountains.

4 PLANTS AND ANIMALS

Well forested, New Hampshire supports an abundance of elm, maple, beech, oak, pine, and fir trees. Among wildflowers, three orchids are classified as threatened. Among native New Hampshire mammals are the muskrat, beaver, and porcupine. The Indiana bat, lynx, and bald eagle are among the species on the state's endangered species list.

5 ENVIRONMENTAL PROTECTION

The Department of Resources and Economic Development (DRED) oversees the state's forests, lands, and parks. The Department of Environmental Services (DES) protects the environmental quality of air, groundwater, the state's surface waters, and solid waste. In the 1990s, DES focused on such issues as ground-level ozone, landfill closures, and protection of lakes, rivers, and other wetlands. New Hampshire had 17 hazardous waste sites as of 1994.

6 POPULATION

New Hampshire ranked 40th among the 50 states in the 1990 census, with a population of 1,109,252. The estimated 1995

New Hampshire Population Profile

Estimated 1995 population:	1,132,000
Population change, 1980–90:	20.5%
Leading ancestry group:	English
Second leading group:	Irish
Foreign born population:	3.7%
Hispanic origin†:	1.0%
Population by race:	
White:	98.0%
Black:	1.0%
Native American:	0.2%
Asian/Pacific Islander:	0.8%
Other:	0.0%

Population by Age Group

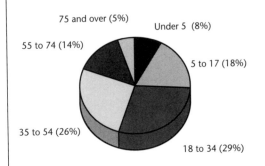

75 and over (5%)
Under 5 (8%)
55 to 74 (14%)
5 to 17 (18%)
35 to 54 (26%)
18 to 34 (29%)

Top Cities with Populations Over 25,000

City	Population	National rank	% change 1980–90
Manchester	97,307	210	9.5
Nashua	79,720	283	17.4
Concord	35,636	771	18.4
Rochester	26,318	1,045	23.5
Dover	24,836	1,066	11.9
Portsmouth	20,716	1,071	–1.3

Notes: †A person of Hispanic origin may be of any race. NA indicates that data are not available.
Sources: Economic and Statistics Administration, Bureau of the Census. *Statistical Abstract of the United States, 1994–95.* Washington, DC: Government Printing Office, 1995; Courtenay M. Slater and George E. Hall. *1995 County and City Extra: Annual Metro, City and County Data Book.* Lanham, MD: Bernan Press, 1995.

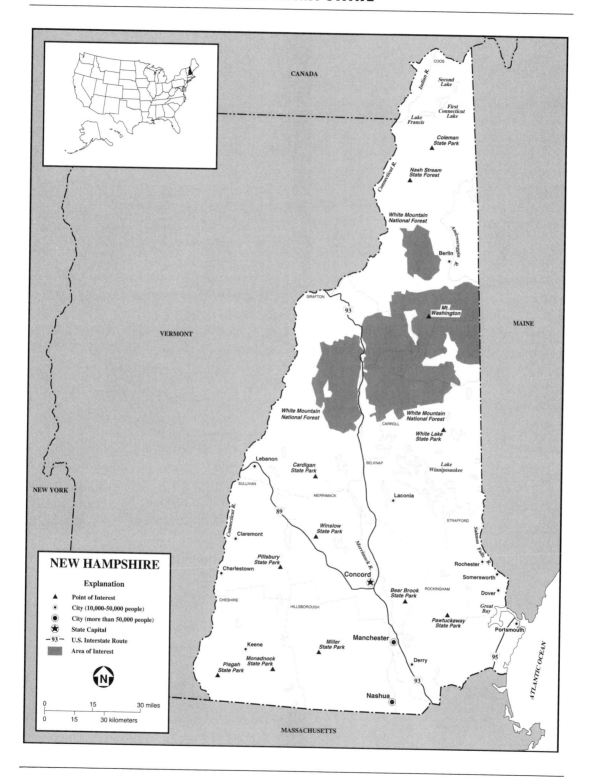

CANADA

COOS

Second
Lake

First
Connecticut
Lake

Indian R.

Lake
Francis

Coleman
State Park ▲

Connecticut R.

Nash Stream
State Forest ▲

White Mountain
National Forest

Androscoggin R.

Berlin •

GRAFTON

93

Mt.
Washington ▲

MAINE

VERMONT

White Mountain
National Forest

White Mountain
National Forest

CARROLL

White Lake
State Park ▲

Lebanon •

Cardigan
State Park ▲

BELKNAP

Lake
Winnipesaukee

SULLIVAN

MERRIMACK

Laconia •

NEW YORK

Connecticut R.

89

Winslow
State Park ▲

STRAFFORD

Salmon Falls R.

Claremont •

Pillsbury
State Park ▲

Merrimack R.

Rochester •

Somersworth •

Charlestown •

Concord ★

Bear Brook
State Park ▲

ROCKINGHAM

Dover •

CHESHIRE

HILLSBOROUGH

Pawtuckaway
State Park ▲

Great
Bay

Keene •

Miller
State Park ▲

Manchester ●

Portsmouth •

Pisgah
State Park ▲

Monadnock
State Park ▲

Derry •

95

93

ATLANTIC OCEAN

Nashua ●

MASSACHUSETTS

NEW HAMPSHIRE

Explanation

▲   Point of Interest
⊙   City (10,000-50,000 people)
◉   City (more than 50,000 people)
★   State Capital
—93—   U.S. Interstate Route
   Area of Interest

N

| 0 | 15 | 30 miles |
| 0 | 15 | 30 kilometers |

population was 1,132,000. Projections to 2000 foresee a population of 1,165,000, 5% more than in 1990. The population density in 1990 was 123.7 persons per square mile (47.5 persons per square kilometer). In 1990, about 49% of the population lived in rural areas and only 51% in cities and towns, well below the US average. Leading cities with their 1992 populations are Manchester, 97,307; Nashua, 79,720; and Concord, the capital, 35,639.

7 ETHNIC GROUPS

In 1990, a total of 265,668 New Hampshirites claimed English ancestry. Those claiming French ancestry numbered 205,455; and Irish, 232,409. There are also about 118,000 French Canadians. About 7,200 black Americans, 9,300 Asians and Pacific Islanders, and 2,100 Native Americans live in New Hampshire.

8 LANGUAGES

New Hampshire speech is essentially Northern. In 1990, 91.3% of all state residents aged five and above—a total of 935,825—spoke only English at home. Some 51,284 residents spoke French at home.

9 RELIGIONS

As of 1990, Protestant groups in New Hampshire had 134,632 known members. The leading denominations were United Church of Christ, 36,989; United Methodist, 19,328; and American Baptist, 18,663. There were 297,062 Roman Catholics and an estimated 6,680 Jews in 1990.

10 TRANSPORTATION

By 1992, the total rail mileage of railroad track in New Hampshire was only 472 miles (759 kilometers). In 1993, New Hampshire had a total of 14,938 miles (24,035 kilometers) of roads. There were 742,896 automobiles, 36,427 motorcycles, 1,725 buses, and 214,120 trucks registered in the state. The main airport is Grenier Field in Manchester.

11 HISTORY

When the first Europeans arrived in present-day New Hampshire, its Native American inhabitants, called Pennacook, were organized in a loose confederation centered along the Merrimack Valley. The coast of New England was explored by Dutch, English, and French navigators throughout the 16th century. The first English settlement was established along the Piscataqua River in 1623. From 1643 to 1680, New Hampshire was a province of Massachusetts, and the boundary between them was not settled until 1740. By 1760, the Pennacook had been forced out of the region.

By the first quarter of the 18th century, Portsmouth, the provincial capital, had become a thriving commercial port. Although nearly 18,500 New Hampshire men enlisted in the Revolutionary War, no battle was fought within its boundaries. New Hampshire was the first of the original 13 colonies to establish an independent government—on 5 January 1776, six months before the Declaration of Independence.

Photo credit: State of New Hampshire Tourism.

The New Hampshire State House in Concord.

During the 19th century, as overseas trade became less important to the New Hampshire economy, shoe and textile mills were built. These were established principally along the Merrimack River. So great was the demand for workers in these mills that immigrant labor was imported during the 1850s. A decade later, French Canadian workers began pouring south from Quebec. Although industry thrived, agriculture did not. New Hampshire hill farms could not compete against Midwestern farms. The population in farm towns dropped, and the people who remained began to cluster in small village centers.

Twentieth Century

World War I marked a turning point for New Hampshire industry. As wartime demand fell off, the state's old textile mills were unable to compete with newer cotton mills in the South, and New Hampshire's mill towns became as depressed as its farm towns. Only in the north, the center for logging and paper manufacturing, did state residents continue to enjoy moderate prosperity. The collapse of the state's railroad network spelled further trouble for the slumping economy. The growth of tourism aided the rural areas primarily, as old farms became spacious vacation homes for "summer people," who in some cases paid the bulk of local property taxes.

During the 1960s, New Hampshire's economic decline began to reverse, except in agriculture. In the 1970s and early 1980s, Boston's urban sprawl, interstate highway construction, and low New Hampshire taxes encouraged people and industry—notably high-technology businesses—to move into southern New Hampshire. The state's population almost doubled between 1960 and 1988, from 606,921 to 1.1 million. The rise in population strained government services, prompted an increase in local taxes, and provoked concern over the state's vanishing open spaces.

12 STATE GOVERNMENT

The General Court—the state legislature—consists of a 24-member senate and a 400-seat house of representatives (larger than that of any other state). The only executive elected statewide is the governor, who is assisted by a five-member executive council, which must approve all administrative and judicial appointments. A bill becomes law if signed by the governor, or if passed by the legislature and left unsigned by the governor for five days while the legislature is in session, or if a governor's veto is overridden by two-thirds of the legislators present in each house.

13 POLITICAL PARTIES

New Hampshire has almost always gone with the Republican presidential nominee in recent decades, but the Democratic and Republican parties have been much more evenly balanced in local and state elections. New Hampshire's presidential primary, traditionally the first state primary of the campaign season, places New Hampshirites in the political spotlight every four years. In the 1992 presidential election, New Hampshire voters defied their tradition and chose Democrat Bill Clinton over Republican incumbent George Bush by a scant 6,556 votes. Independent Ross Perot picked up 26% of the vote. As of 1994, both of New Hampshire's senators, Judd Gregg and Robert Smith, were Republicans. In the 1994 congressional elections, Republicans took both seats. The New Hampshire state senate in 1994 contained 13 Republicans and 11 Democrats. The state house had 257 Republicans and 138 Democrats.

New Hampshire Presidential Vote by Major Political Parties, 1948–92

YEAR	NEW HAMPSHIRE WINNER	DEMOCRAT	REPUBLICAN
1948	Dewey (R)	107,995	121,299
1952	*Eisenhower (R)	106,663	166,287
1956	*Eisenhower (R)	90,364	176,519
1960	Nixon (R)	137,772	157,989
1964	*Johnson (D)	182,065	104,029
1968	*Nixon (R)	130,589	154,903
1972	*Nixon (R)	116,435	213,724
1976	Ford (R)	147,635	185,935
1980	*Reagan (R)	108,864	221,705
1984	*Reagan (R)	120,347	267,050
1988	*Bush (R)	163,696	281,537
1992**	*Clinton (D)	209,040	202,484

* Won US presidential election.
** Independent candidate Ross Perot received 121,337 votes.

14 LOCAL GOVERNMENT

New Hampshire has ten counties, each governed by three commissioners. Other elected county officials include the sheriff, attorney, treasurer, and registrar of deeds.

As of 1992, New Hampshire also had 13 municipalities and 221 townships. The municipalities have elected mayors and councils. The basic unit of town government is the traditional town meeting.

15 JUDICIAL SYSTEM

The state's highest court, the supreme court, consists of a chief justice and four associate justices. The main trial court is the superior court. New Hampshire's total crime rate in 1994 was 2,741 per 100,000 persons.

16 MIGRATION

New Hampshire's population growth since 1960 has been fueled by migrants from other states. The net gain from migration was 74,000 from 1985 to 1990, but there was a loss of about 10,000 from 1990 to 1994. As of 1990, about 44.1% of the state's residents had been born in New Hampshire.

17 ECONOMY

New Hampshire is one of the most industrialized states in the US, ranking well above the national median in the proportion of the labor force that is employed in manufacturing. Between 1977 and 1982, manufacturing employment rose 13%, to 107,500, as many high-technology firms moved into the southern portion of the state. Since World War II, tourism has been one of the state's fastest-growing sources of income.

18 INCOME

In 1994, total personal income amounted to $26.9 billion. New Hampshire's per capita (per person) income in 1994 was $23,680, eighth in the US. Some 9.9% of state residents were below the federal poverty level in 1993.

19 INDUSTRY

The value of shipments by manufacturers in 1991 was over $9.7 million. In 1992, employment in industrial and commercial machinery and computer equipment accounted for 31% of all durable-goods manufacturing employment. Prominent manufacturing firms include Digital Equipment (computers) and Lockheed Sanders (aviation products).

20 LABOR

New Hampshire's estimated civilian labor force totaled 628,000 in 1994. There was an unemployment rate of 4.6%. Some 10.7% of all workers in the state were labor union members as of 1994.

21 AGRICULTURE

Only Rhode Island and Alaska generate less income from farming than New Hampshire. Farm income in 1994 was $151 million. In that year there were about 2,400 farms occupying about 470,000 acres (190,200 hectares). In 1994, leading crops and their output were hay, 163,000 tons; and commercial apples, 40 million pounds.

22 DOMESTICATED ANIMALS

Dairy and poultry products are the mainstays of New Hampshire's agriculture. In 1994, the state had 19,000 milk cows. Dairy products made up 28.3% of agricultural receipts in 1994.

23 FISHING

New Hampshire's commercial catch in 1992 consisted of 10,328,000 pounds, much of it cod and lobster, worth $11,503,000.

24 FORESTRY

New Hampshire had 5,740,000 acres (2,323,000 hectares) of forestland in 1990. Forests cover 87% of New Hampshire, and the forest products industry employs 16,000 workers.

25 MINING

The value of nonfuel mineral production in New Hampshire in 1994 was estimated to be $40 million. In 1992, 6.8 million short tons of construction sand and gravel were mined, worth $23.9 million. Sand and gravel are mined in every county, and dimension granite is quarried in Hillsborough, Merrimack, and Coos counties.

Photo credit: Candace Cochrane, State of New Hampshire Tourism.

Maple sugaring is a popular activity as the sap begins to run.

26 ENERGY AND POWER

In 1991, about 25% of the state's electricity came from coal-fired plants, another 13% from oil-fired plants, and only 9% from hydroelectric facilities. Power production totaled 14.6 billion kilowatt hours in 1993. In 1990, the controversial nuclear power plant at Seabrook began operating. This is the state's only nuclear plant. Nuclear power supplied 53% of New Hampshire's electricity in 1991. Energy expenditures were $1,796 per capita (per person) in 1992.

27 COMMERCE

New Hampshire's wholesale sales totaled $8.2 billion for 1992; retail sales were $12.6 billion for 1993; and service establishment receipts were $5.4 billion for 1992. Foreign exports of goods totaled $917 million in 1992 (39th in the US).

28 PUBLIC FINANCE

As of 1991/92, the combined debt of state and local governments was $5.37 billion, or about $4,838 per capita (per person). The expenditures for 1994/95 were $2,423 million; total revenues were $2,607 million.

29 TAXATION

New Hampshire has no general income or sales tax but does levy 5% taxes on interest and dividends, 7.5% on net corporate income, and 8% on rooms and meals. Levies on property, gasoline, alcoholic beverages, tobacco products, and many other items are also imposed. State tax revenues were only $565.27 per capita (per person) in 1992, ranking New Hampshire last among the 50 states.

30 HEALTH

In 1993 there were 28 community hospitals, with 3,400 beds. The average hospital expense for an inpatient day in 1993 was $976, or $6,964 for an average cost per stay. New Hampshire had 2,400 active, nonfederal physicians in 1993 and 10,800 nurses. Some 12.5% of state residents did not have health insurance in 1993.

31 HOUSING

In 1993, housing units for year-round use were estimated at 516,000. Almost 4,200 new housing units worth $381.4 million were built in 1993. .

32 EDUCATION

New Hampshire residents have a long-standing commitment to education. More than 82% of all adult state residents were high school graduates in 1993. In fall 1993, enrollment in public schools and approved public academies totaled 185,360. Expenditures on education averaged $5,635 per pupil (19th in the nation) in 1993. Private elementary and secondary schools had an enrollment of 18,651 in fall 1993. The best-known institution of higher education is Dartmouth College, at Hanover (1993/94 enrollment, 4,290). The University of New Hampshire, at Durham, had a 1993/94 undergraduate enrollment of 10,331.

33 ARTS

Hopkins Center at Dartmouth College features musical events throughout the year, while the Monadnock Music Concerts are held in several towns during the summer. The New Hampshire Music Festival takes place at Meredith. Theater by the Sea at Portsmouth presents classical and modern plays, and there is a year-round student theater at Dartmouth.

Principal galleries include the Currier Gallery of Art in Manchester, the Dartmouth College Museum and Galleries at Hanover, and the Lamont Gallery at Phillips Exeter Academy in Exeter.

34 LIBRARIES AND MUSEUMS

The leading academic collection is Dartmouth College's Baker Memorial Library in Hanover (1,940,586 volumes). Among the more than 71 museums and historic sites are the Museum of New Hampshire History and the New Hampshire Historical Society Library in Concord, and the Franklin Pierce Homestead in Hillsboro.

35 COMMUNICATIONS

In March 1993, 97.2% of New Hampshire's occupied housing units—about 419,000—had telephones. In 1993, the state had 66 radio stations (26 AM, 40 FM) and 4 commercial television stations. State residents also receive broadcasts from neighboring Massachusetts, Vermont, and Maine. A total of five major cable systems in 1993 served the state.

36 PRESS

In 1994, New Hampshire had nine daily newspapers and four Sunday papers. The best-known newspaper in the state is the *Manchester Union–Leader* (71,609 daily and 102,584 Sunday), published by conservative William Loeb until his death in 1981.

37 TOURISM, TRAVEL, AND RECREATION

Tourism ranks second only to manufacturing in the economy of New Hampshire. Tourists spent an estimated $3.3 billion in New Hampshire during 1992. Skiing, camping, hiking, and boating are the main outdoor attractions. Other attractions include Strawbery Banke, a restored village in Portsmouth; Daniel Webster's birthplace near Franklin; and the natural "Old Man of the Mountain" granite head profile in the Franconia subrange of the White Mountains, on which the state's official emblem is modeled.

38 SPORTS

There are no major league professional sports teams in New Hampshire. Major national and international skiing events are frequently held in the state. Dartmouth College competes in the Ivy League, and the University of New Hampshire belongs to the Yankee Conference.

39 FAMOUS NEW HAMPSHIRITES

Born in Hillsboro, Franklin Pierce (1804–69) was the only US chief executive to come from New Hampshire, serving from 1853 to 1857 as the nation's 14th president. Henry Wilson (Jeremiah Jones Colbath, 1812–75), US vice-president from 1873 to 1875, was a native of Farmington.

US Supreme Court chief justices Salmon P. Chase (1808–73) and Harlan Fiske Stone (1872–1946) were New Hampshirites. US cabinet members from New Hampshire included Henry Dearborn (1751–1829), secretary of war; and Daniel Webster (1782–1852), secretary of state.

Other figures of note are educator Eleazar Wheelock (b.Connecticut, 1711–79), the founder of Dartmouth College; the founder of Christian Science, Mary Baker Eddy (1821–1910); George Whipple (1878–1976), winner of the 1934 Nobel Prize for physiology/medicine; and labor organizer and US Communist Party leader Elizabeth Gurley Flynn (1890–1964).

Horace Greeley (1811–72), Charles Dana (1819–97), Alice Brown (1857–1948), and J(erome) D(avid) Salinger (b.New York, 1919) are among the prose writers and editors who have lived in New Hampshire. Poets have included Edward Arlington Robinson (b.Maine, 1869–1935) and Robert Frost (b.California, 1874–1963), one of whose poetry volumes is entitled *New Hampshire* (1923). More recent celebrities include astronaut Alan B. Shepard, Jr. (b.1923).

40 BIBLIOGRAPHY

Smith, Clyde H. *New Hampshire: A Scenic Discovery*. Dublin, N.H.: Yankee Books, 1985.

Stacker, Ann P., and Nancy C. Hefferman. *Short History of New Hampshire*. Grantham, N.H.: Thompson and Rutter, 1985.

Taylor, William L., ed. *Readings in New Hampshire and New England History*. New York: Irvington, 1981.

NEW JERSEY

State of New Jersey

ORIGIN OF STATE NAME: Named for the British Channel Island of Jersey.

NICKNAME: The Garden State.

CAPITAL: Trenton.

ENTERED UNION: 18 December 1787 (3d).

MOTTO: Liberty and Prosperity.

COLORS: Buff and Jersey blue.

COAT OF ARMS: In the center is a shield with three plows, symbolic of agriculture. A helmet above indicates sovereignty, and a horse's head atop the helmet signifies speed and prosperity. The state motto and the date "1776" are displayed on a banner below.

FLAG: The coat of arms on a buff field.

OFFICIAL SEAL: The coat of arms surrounded by the words "The Great Seal of the State of New Jersey."

ANIMAL: Horse.

BIRD: Eastern goldfinch.

FLOWER: Violet.

TREE: Red oak.

INSECT: Honeybee.

TIME: 7 AM EST = noon GMT.

1 LOCATION AND SIZE

Situated in the northeastern US, New Jersey is the smallest of the Middle Atlantic states and ranks 46th among the 50 states. The total area of New Jersey is 7,787 square miles (20,168 square kilometers). New Jersey extends 166 miles (267 kilometers) north-south; the extreme width east-west is 57 miles (92 kilometers). New Jersey's total boundary length is 480 miles (773 kilometers). Numerous barrier islands lie off the Atlantic coast.

2 TOPOGRAPHY

Although small, New Jersey has considerable physical variety. In the extreme northwest corner of the state are the Appalachian Valley and the Kittatinny Ridge and Valley, containing High Point, the state's highest point, at 1,803 feet (550 meters) above sea level. To the east and south is the highlands region, including the Ramapo Mountains. East of the highlands is a flat area broken by the high ridges of the Watchungs and Sourlands and—most spectacularly—by the Palisades, rising some 500 feet (150 meters) above the Hudson River. The Atlantic Coastal Plain claims the remaining two-thirds of the state. Its most notable feature is the Pine Barrens, 760 square miles (1,968 square kilometers) of pitch pines and white oaks.

Sandy Hook, a peninsula more than 5 miles (8 kilometers) long, extends northward into the Atlantic from Monmouth County. Major rivers include the Delaware, forming the border with Pennsylvania, and the Passaic, Hackensack, and Raritan. The largest natural lake is Lake Hopatcong, about 8 miles (13 kilometers) long.

3 CLIMATE

Most of New Jersey has a moderate climate with cold winters and warm, humid summers. In Atlantic City, the mean temperature ranges from 32°F (0°C) in January to 74°F (23°C) in July. Precipitation is plentiful, averaging 46 inches (117 centimeters) annually. Snowfall totals about 16 inches (41 centimeters). Statewide, the record high temperature is 110°F (43°C), set in 1936; the record low, –34°F (–37°C), was set in 1904.

4 PLANTS AND ANIMALS

Birch, beech, and elm all grow in the state, along with 20 varieties of oak. Common shrubs include the spicebush and mountain laurel. Common wildflowers include meadow rue, butterflyweed, and black-eyed Susan.

Among mammals native to New Jersey are the white-tailed deer, black bear, and raccoon. The herring gull and sandpiper are common shore birds, while the robin, cardinal, and Baltimore oriole are frequently sighted inland. Anglers prize the northern pike and various species of bass, trout, and perch. On the endangered list are six types of whale, four varieties of sea turtle, and the Pine Barrens treefrog.

New Jersey Population Profile

Estimated 1995 population:	7,931,000
Population change, 1980–90:	5.0%
Leading ancestry group:	Italian
Second leading group:	Irish
Foreign born population:	12.5%
Hispanic origin†:	9.6%
Population by race:	
White:	79.3%
Black:	13.4%
Native American:	0.2%
Asian/Pacific Islander:	3.5%
Other:	3.6%

Population by Age Group

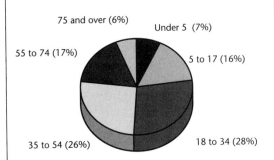

75 and over (6%)
Under 5 (7%)
55 to 74 (17%)
5 to 17 (16%)
18 to 34 (28%)
35 to 54 (26%)

Top Cities with Populations Over 25,000

City	Population	National rank	% change 1980–90
Newark	267,849	61	–16.4
Jersey City	228,575	71	2.2
Paterson	139,358	131	2.1
Elizabeth	107,915	179	3.6
Trenton	87,807	239	–3.7
Camden	86,926	243	3.0
Clifton	72,519	317	–3.6
East Orange	72,250	322	–5.3
Bayonne	61,804	389	–5.5
Union City	57,256	428	4.4

Notes: †A person of Hispanic origin may be of any race. NA indicates that data are not available.
Sources: Economic and Statistics Administration, Bureau of the Census. *Statistical Abstract of the United States, 1994–95.* Washington, DC: Government Printing Office, 1995; Courtenay M. Slater and George E. Hall. *1995 County and City Extra: Annual Metro, City and County Data Book.* Lanham, MD: Bernan Press, 1995.

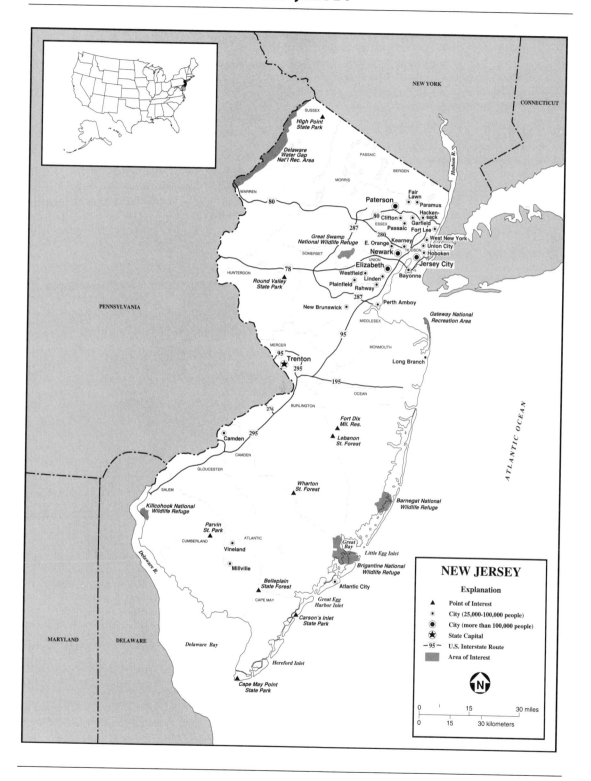

NEW YORK

CONNECTICUT

SUSSEX

High Point
State Park

Delaware
Water Gap
Nat'l Rec. Area

PASSAIC

BERGEN

MORRIS

Hudson R.

WARREN

80

Fair
Lawn

Paterson

Paramus

Hacken-
sack

80 Clifton

Garfield

287

Passaic

Fort Lee

ESSEX

280

West New York

Great Swamp
National Wildlife Refuge

Kearney

Union City

E. Orange

Newark

Hoboken

SOMERSET

HUDSON

Jersey City

UNION

Elizabeth

78

Westfield

Bayonne

HUNTERDON

Round Valley
State Park

Linden

Plainfield

Rahway

287

New Brunswick

Perth Amboy

Gateway National
Recreation Area

MIDDLESEX

95

MERCER

MONMOUTH

95

Trenton

Long Branch

295

195

OCEAN

ATLANTIC OCEAN

BURLINGTON

276

Fort Dix
Mil. Res.

295

Lebanon
St. Forest

Camden

CAMDEN

GLOUCESTER

Wharton
St. Forest

SALEM

Killcohook National
Wildlife Refuge

Barnegat National
Wildlife Refuge

Parvin
St. Park

CUMBERLAND

ATLANTIC

Great
Bay

Vineland

Little Egg Inlet

Brigantine National
Wildlife Refuge

Millville

Delaware R.

Belleplain
State Forest

CAPE MAY

Atlantic City

Great Egg
Harbor Inlet

NEW JERSEY

Explanation

▲ Point of Interest

◉ City (25,000-100,000 people)

◉ City (more than 100,000 people)

★ State Capital

— 95 — U.S. Interstate Route

▢ Area of Interest

Carson's Inlet
State Park

MARYLAND

DELAWARE

Delaware Bay

Hereford Inlet

Cape May Point
State Park

0   15   30 miles

0   15   30 kilometers

5 ENVIRONMENTAL PROTECTION

Laws and policies regulating the management and protection of New Jersey's environment and natural resources are administered by the Department of Environmental Protection (DEP). New Jersey has one of the most comprehensive air pollution control programs in the US, maintaining a network of 105 air pollution monitoring stations, as well as 60 stations that monitor just for particulates and 10 that monitor for radiation.

Water-quality degradation has been halted and the quality of streams has been stabilized or improved. However, some rivers in highly urbanized areas are still severely polluted. Approximately 1,500 treatment facilities discharge waste water into New Jersey's surface and ground waters. In 1991 there were about 50 landfills. In the same year, New Jersey had 26 curbside recycling programs. As of 1994, the state had 108 hazardous waste sites, the most of any state.

New Jersey's toxic waste cleanup program is among the most serious in the US. In 1993, 109 hazardous waste sites—more than in any other state—were listed as national priorities for cleanup with federal Superfund financing. A tax based on the transfer of hazardous substances and petroleum products is used for the cleanup of spills. New Jersey was the first state to begin a statewide search for sites contaminated by dioxin, a toxic by-product in the manufacture of herbicides.

Since 1961, the state has bought more than 240,000 acres (97,000 hectares) under a "Green Acres" program for conservation and recreation.

6 POPULATION

New Jersey ranked ninth among the 50 states in the 1990 census, with a total population of 7,730,188. The estimated population in 1995 was 7,931,000. With an average density of 1,042 persons per square mile (400 persons per square kilometer), New Jersey is the most densely populated state. It is projected that the state will record a 3.5% increase in population between 1995 and the year 2000.

The state's entire population is classified as living in metropolitan areas, a distinction claimed by no other state. Newark, the state's largest city, had an estimated 267,849 inhabitants in 1992. Populations of other New Jersey cities in 1992 were Jersey City, 228,575; Paterson, 139,358; Elizabeth, 107,915; and Trenton, 87,807.

7 ETHNIC GROUPS

New Jersey is one of the most ethnically diverse states. As of 1990, 966,610 New Jerseyites were of foreign birth. The leading countries of origin were Italy, 7.3%; Cuba, 6.5%; India, 5.4%; and Germany, 4.4%. The foreign-born continue to come, including many from Colombia, Poland, the Philippines, and the Dominican Republic.

Black people constitute the state's largest (13.4%) ethnic minority with 1,037,000 as of 1990. There were 740,000 state residents of Hispanic origin in 1990 divided into distinct ethnic communities: the Puerto Rican population numbered 219,942; there were 72,373 Cubans; and smaller Spanish-speaking groups included Colombians and Dominicans. The number of Asians living in New Jersey in 1990 was 273,000. The largest group of Asians is from India (54,039 in 1990). There were 51,821 Filipinos; 47,068 Chinese; 38,087 Koreans; and 19,948 Japanese. Native Americans numbered 15,000 in 1990.

8 LANGUAGES

English in New Jersey is rather evenly divided north and south between Northern and Midland dialects. Special characteristics of New York metropolitan-area speech occur in the northeast portion. In 1990, 5,794,548 New Jerseyites—80.5% of the resident population—spoke only English at home. Other languages spoken at home, with number of speakers, were Spanish, 621,416; Italian, 154,160; Polish, 69,145; German, 56,877; Portuguese, 55,285; and Chinese, 47,334. Place-names borrowed from the native Leni-Lanape tribe include Passaic, Totowa, and Piscataway.

9 RELIGIONS

Roman Catholics constitute New Jersey's single largest religious group, with a population of 3,189,315 in 1990. Passaic is the headquarters of the Byzantine-Ruthenian Rite in the Byzantine Catholic Church. The Jewish population was estimated at 429,885 in 1990. The largest Protestant denomination in 1990 was United Methodist, with 166,502 members, followed by the Presbyterian Church, with 138,763; Episcopal, 105,607; Evangelical Lutheran Church in America, 86,825; American Baptist Convention, 82,795; and Reformed Church in America, 41,392.

10 TRANSPORTATION

Ever since the first traders sought the fastest way to get from New York to Philadelphia, transportation has been of central importance to New Jersey and has greatly shaped its growth. Industry grew around the rail lines, and the railroads became a vital link in the shipment of products from New York and northern New Jersey. In 1992, there were 1,194 route miles (1,921 kilometers) of track in the state. About 79% of the total was Class I track operated by Conrail. About 40 Amtrak trains served 1,570,929 riders in 1991/92. However, the bulk of interstate passenger traffic consists of commuters to New York and Philadelphia on trains operated by regional transit authorities.

In 1993 there were 35,097 miles (56,471 kilometers) of roads in the state. Altogether, state-administered toll roads received over $530.5 million from motorists (second only to New York) in 1993, mostly from the New Jersey Turnpike and the Garden State Parkway. New Jersey highways are congested. On average, 4,734 vehicles used each mile of the state's highways every day in 1992, compared to a US average of 1,568. Many bridges and tunnels link New Jersey with New York State, Pennsylvania, and Delaware.

At the gateway to New York Harbor, ports at Elizabeth and Newark have overtaken New York City ports in cargo volume, and contribute greatly to the local economy. Rebuilt during the 1960s and 1970s, Newark International Airport has become the state's busiest by far. It handled 9,737,488 passengers (eighth highest

Courtesy New Jersey Division of Travel and Tourism.

Ford Mansion in Morristown, George Washington's headquarters in the winter of 1779–80.

in the nation) and 161,155 tons of freight in 1991. Statewide in 1991 there were 110 airports and 209 heliports.

11 HISTORY

The first known inhabitants of what is now New Jersey were the Leni-Lenape (meaning "Original People"). Members of the Algonkian language group, the Leni-Lenape were a peace-loving agricultural people who believed in monogamy, educated their children in the simple skills needed for wilderness survival, and maintained the tradition that a pot of food must always be warm on the fire to welcome all strangers.

The first European explorer to reach New Jersey was Giovanni da Verrazano, who sailed into what is now Newark Bay in 1524. Henry Hudson, an English captain sailing under a Dutch flag, landed at Sandy Hook Bay in 1609, establishing a Dutch claim to the New World. In 1660, Hollanders founded New Jersey's first town, called Bergen (now part of Jersey City). Native American lands were gained through a series of treaties. Ravaged by the introduction of guns, alcohol, and smallpox, only a few hundred of the "Original People" remained a century later.

England assumed control of the region in 1664. Eventually, the land passed into the hands of governing groups in two provinces called East Jersey and West Jersey.

East Jersey was settled mainly by Puritans from Long Island and New England; West Jersey was settled by Quakers from England. The split cost the colony dearly in 1702, when Queen Anne united East and West Jersey but placed them under New York rule. The colony did not get its own "home rule" until 1738.

Statehood

During the American Revolution, the colony was about equally divided between Revolutionists and Loyalists. However, in June 1776, the colony sent five delegates to the Continental Congress, all of whom voted for the Declaration of Independence. Two days before the Declaration was proclaimed, New Jersey adopted its first state constitution. George Washington and his battered troops made their winter headquarters in the state three times during the first four years of the war, and five major battles were fought in New Jersey. At the end of the war, Princeton became the temporary capital of the US until 1783.

With many of its pathway towns ravaged by the war, the state stagnated until railroads and canals brought new life in the 1830s and set it on a course of urbanization and industrialization. The coal brought in on railroad cars freed industry from waterpower; factories sprang up wherever the rails went. The Hudson County waterfront, eastern terminus for most of the nation's railway systems, became the most important railroad area in the US.

The Civil War split New Jersey bitterly. As late as the summer of 1863, after the Battle of Gettysburg, many state "peace Democrats" were urging the North to make peace with the Confederacy. However, the state sent its full quota of troops into service throughout the conflict. Most importantly, New Jersey factories poured forth streams of munitions and other equipment for the Union army. At war's end, political leaders stubbornly opposed the 13th, 14th, and 15th Amendments to the US Constitution, and blacks were not permitted to vote in the state until 1870.

Industry

During the last decades of the 19th century, New Jersey developed a reputation for factories capable of making the components necessary for thousands of manufacturing enterprises. In 1873, Isaac M. Singer opened a huge sewing machine plant at Elizabeth that employed 3,000 persons. Twentieth-century wars stimulated New Jersey's industries further.

During World War I, giant shipyards at Newark, Kearny, and Camden made New Jersey the nation's leading shipbuilding state. The Middlesex County area refined 75% of the nation's copper, and nearly 75% of US shells were loaded in the state. World War II revived the shipbuilding and munitions industries. Paterson became the nation's foremost airplane engine manufacturing center. Training and mobilization centers at Fort Dix and Camp Kilmer moved millions of soldiers into the front lines.

Urbanization

The US Census Bureau termed New Jersey officially "urban" in 1880, when the state population rose above one million for the first time. New Jersey has experienced many of the problems of urbanization. Its cities have declined; traffic congestion from commuters streaming into urban areas to work is intense. The suburbs now know the problems of urban growth: increased needs for schools, police and fire protection, sewers, and road maintenance, along with rising taxes.

The state has not surrendered to its problems, however. Voters since 1950 have passed a wide variety of multimillion dollar bond issues to establish or rebuild state colleges. Rutgers, the state university, has been rapidly expanded. Funds have been allocated for the purchase and development of new park and forest lands. Large bond issues have financed the construction of highways, reservoirs, and rapid transit systems.

In the 1970s and early 1980s, New Jersey experienced a recession. The unemployment rate climbed to almost 10%, and over 270,000 people left the state. The state's cities were hit particularly hard, suffering both from the loss of manufacturing jobs and from a flight of retailing to suburban malls. While the state lost over 200,000 manufacturing jobs, it gained 670,000 jobs in service industries, and the economy recovered in the 1980s. The rise in employment centered on such industries as services, transportation, and construction.

Politics

Since the end of World War II, New Jersey has had no predictable political pattern. It gave huge presidential majorities to Republican Dwight D. Eisenhower and Democrat Lyndon B. Johnson, and narrowly supported Democrat John F. Kennedy. The state favored Republican Gerald Ford over Democrat Jimmy Carter by a small margin, and gave two big majorities to Republican Ronald Reagan. In 1978 Democrat Bill Bradley, former Princeton University and New York Knickerbockers basketball star, was elected to the US Senate.

Republican Governor Thomas Kean, who served from 1983–89, helped to improve the public image of New Jersey, long perceived as dominated by smoke-belching factories and troubled cities. Kean was succeeded by Democrat Jim Florio, whose tax increases, which took effect just at the time that the New Jersey economy had begun to waver, angered voters. In 1993, Florio lost his bid for reelection to Republican Christine Todd Whitman, who promised to lower income taxes by 30%.

12 STATE GOVERNMENT

The state legislature consists of a 40-member senate and an 80-member general assembly. New Jersey is one of the few states in which the governor is the only elected administrative official. Given broad powers by the state constitution, the governor appoints the heads, or commissioners, of the 20 major state departments with the advice and consent of the senate.

A bill may be introduced in either house of the legislature. Once passed, it goes to the governor, who may sign it, return it to the legislature with recommendations for change, or veto it in its entirety. A two-thirds majority in each house is needed to override a veto.

13 POLITICAL PARTIES

Sweeping reforms—including a corrupt-practices act, a primary election law, and increased support for public education—were implemented during the two years (1911–13) that Woodrow Wilson, a Democrat, served as New Jersey's governor. Between 1913 and 1985, Democrats held the statehouse almost two-thirds of the time.

As of 1994 there were 1,175,041 registered Democrats, comprising 29% of the total number of registered voters; 817,837 Republicans, or 20%; and 2,067,459 independents, or 51%. In 1995, the state senate contained 24 Republicans and 16 Democrats, while the General Assembly consisted of 52 Republicans and 28 Democrats. In the 1992 presidential voting, Democrat Bill Clinton defeated incumbent George Bush, picking up 43% of the vote to Bush's 41%. Independent Ross Perot earned 16%. In 1993, New Jersey elected its first woman as governor, Republican Christine Todd Whitman. In 1992, the Democrats had a 7-6 majority among New Jersey's 13 US representatives. However, after the 1994 elections, the Republicans took the majority with eight seats to five for the Democrats.

New Jersey Presidential Vote by Political Parties, 1948–92

YEAR	NEW JERSEY WINNER	DEMOCRAT	REPUBLICAN	PROGRESSIVE	SOCIALIST	PROHIBITION	SOCIALIST LABOR
1948	Dewey (R)	895,455	981,124	42,683	10,521	10,593	3,354
1952	*Eisenhower (R)	1,015,902	1,373,613	5,589	8,593	—	5,815
				CONSTITUTION			
1956	*Eisenhower (R)	850,337	1,606,942	5,317	—	9,147	6,736
				CONSERVATIVE			
1960	*Kennedy (D)	1,385,415	1,363,324	8,708	—	—	4,262
1964	*Johnson (D)	1,867,671	963,843	—	—	—	7,075
				AMERICAN IND.	PEACE & FREEDOM		
1968	*Nixon (R)	1,264,206	1,325,467	262,187	8,084	—	6,784
					People's	American	
1972	*Nixon (R)	1,102,211	1,845,502	—	5,355	34,378	4,544
					US Labor	Libertarian	
1976	Ford (R)	1,444,653	1,509,688	7,716	1,650	9,449	3,686
1980	*Reagan (R)	1,147,364	1,546,557	8,203	—	20,652	2,198
					WORKERS WORLD		
1984	*Reagan (R)	1,261,323	1,933,630	—	8,404	6,416	—
				NEW ALLIANCE	PEACE & FREEDOM		CONSUMER
1988	* Bush (R)	1,320,352	1,743,192	5,139	9,953	8,421	3,454
					IND. (Perot)		IND. (Bradford)
1992	* Clinton (D)	1,436,206	1,356,865	3,513	521,829	6,822	4,749

* Won US presidential election.

14 LOCAL GOVERNMENT

As of 1992, New Jersey had 21 counties, 320 municipal governments, 247 townships, and 486 special districts. Counties are divided into six classes by population and location. These classes determine the number of members on the main county governing body (the board of freeholders) which administers county and state programs. County officers include the clerk, sheriff, and prosecutor.

Cities, boroughs, and towns may employ the mayor-council system, council-manager system, commission system, or other forms of their own devising. Cities, too, are classed by population and location into four categories. The budgets of all local units are supervised by the New Jersey Department of Community Affairs, which also offers municipal aid programs. By state law, all local budgets must be balanced.

15 JUDICIAL SYSTEM

The supreme court, the state's highest, consists of six associate justices and a chief justice, who is also the administrative head of the state court system. As the court of highest authority, the supreme court hears appeals on constitutional questions and of certain cases from the superior court, which comprises three divisions: chancery, law, and appellate. The chancery division has original jurisdiction over general equity cases, most probate cases, and divorce actions. All other original cases are tried within the law division. The appeals division hears appeals from the chancery and law divisions, from lower courts, and from most state administrative agencies.

A state tax court, empowered to review local property tax assessments, equalization tables, and state tax determinations, has been in operation since 1979. Municipal court judges hear minor criminal matters, motor vehicle cases, and violations of municipal ordinances. In 1994, New Jersey had a total crime rate of 4,660.9 per 100,000 persons. Prisoners under jurisdiction of state and federal correctional authorities in New Jersey numbered 23,831 in 1993.

16 MIGRATION

Newark's black population grew by 130,000 between 1950 and 1970. Black as well as Hispanic newcomers settled in major cities just as whites were departing for the suburbs. New Jersey's suburbs were also attractive to residents of New York City, Philadelphia, and other neighboring areas, who began moving to the state in massive numbers just after World War II. Nearly all of these suburbanites were white.

From 1940 to 1970, New Jersey gained a net total of 1,360,000 residents. Between 1970 and 1990, however, the state lost about 250,000 residents through migration. While the black, Hispanic, and Asian populations were still rising, whites were departing from New Jersey in increasing numbers.

17 ECONOMY

Petroleum refining, chemicals and pharmaceuticals, food processing, apparel, fabricated metals, electric and electronic equipment, and other machinery are all important. But the state is more noteworthy for the diversity of its manufacturers than for any dominant company or product. The service sector of the economy, led by wholesale and retail trade, continued to grow rapidly during the early 1980s. The heaviest concentrations of jobs are in and near metropolitan New York and Philadelphia. Fresh market vegetables are the leading source of farm income.

18 INCOME

Total personal income amounted to $219.3 billion in 1994, when New Jersey's per capita (per person) income of $27,742 ranked second among the 50 states. Some 10.9% of the state's residents were below the federal poverty level in 1993.

19 INDUSTRY

As of 1993, the chemical industry led all areas of the economy in manufacturing employment, with 21%. By value of shipments in 1991, the leading industrial categories were chemical and allied products (28.7%) and food products (11.3%). As of mid-1991, New Jersey's pharmaceutical production led the nation, and chemicals ranked sixth.

The following table shows the value of shipments by manufacturers for selected industries in 1991 (in million dollars):

Chemicals	$ 24,635.7
Food	9,700.6
Printing & Publishing	6,523.1
Instruments	5,301.5
Petroleum products	5,126.4
Industrial machinery	4,769.5
Fabricated metals	4,468.0
Electronic equipment	4,363.4
Rubber & misc. plastics	3,500.8
Paper products	3,198.3
Transportation equipment	2,493.4

Nearly every major US corporation has facilities in the state.

20 LABOR

The civilian labor force was estimated at 3,991,000 in 1994. There was an overall unemployment rate of 6.8%. Several migrant work camps are located near south Jersey tomato farms and fruit orchards, but the number of farm workers coming into the state is declining with the increased use of mechanical harvesters. As of 1994, 23.1% of all workers in the state belonged to labor unions. There were 14 national unions operating in the state in 1993.

21 AGRICULTURE

Although New Jersey is a leading producer of fresh market fruits and vegetables, its total farm income was only $768.4 million in 1994, 39th among the 50 states. New Jersey ranked second in the US in the production of cultivated blueberries and fourth in peaches. There were some 880,000 acres (356,000 hectares) in 8,900 farms in 1994.

Leading crops for 1994 (in millions of pounds) were sweet corn, 765; tomatoes, 653; and lettuce, 468. Fruit crops in 1994 (in pounds) included apples, 80,000,000; and peaches, 75,000,000.

22 DOMESTICATED ANIMALS

With cash receipts estimated at $182.5 million in 1994, New Jersey does not rank as a major livestock-producing state. At the close of 1994 there were 65,000 cattle, 24,000 hogs, and 16,900 sheep on New Jersey farms. Dairy products accounted for 6% of agricultural receipts in 1994; chicken eggs, 3.4%.

Atlantic City.

23 FISHING

New Jersey had a commercial fish catch of 204.3 million pounds (seventh in the US) in 1992, worth $97.5 million. Cape May-Wildwood was the 11th-largest fishing port in the US, bringing in 93.9 million pounds of fish, worth $34.9 million. Clams accounted for about 38% of the value of the state's total catch in 1991, with scallops, swordfish, tuna, squid, lobster, and flounder accounting for most of the rest.

24 FORESTRY

About 42% of New Jersey's land area, or 2,007,000 acres (822,870 hectares), was forested in 1992. The timber industry has not been economically significant since the late 17th century, when the state's lumber was used to make ships in southern New Jersey ports. As of 1992, the Bureau of Parks maintained 272,000 acres (110,000 hectares) of state land. The bureau operates 40 state parks, 12 natural areas, and a recreation area.

25 MINING

The value of nonfuel mineral production in New Jersey in 1994 was estimated to be $274 million. In 1992, 12 million short tons of construction sand and gravel were produced, for a total value of $56.9 million. Other mineral resources mined or recovered included crushed stone (16.4 million short tons, worth $120.8 million); industrial sand (1.7 million short tons, worth $25.5 million); as well as common and fire clays, peat, titanium, and zircon concentrates. New Jersey continued to be the only state that produced greensand, which is processed and sold mainly as a filtration medium to remove soluble iron and manganese from well water.

26 ENERGY AND POWER

Although it contains some of the largest oil refineries in the US, New Jersey produces little of its own energy, importing much of its electric power and virtually all of its fossil fuels. In 1991 there were 31 electric generating plants in New Jersey. Power production amounted to 34.3 billion kilowatt hours in 1993. Per capita (per person) energy consumption in 1992 was 307 million Btu. Nuclear generating stations accounted for 70% of the electric power used in the state in 1991, up from only 16.5% in 1983. The state had four nuclear power plants as of 1993. Energy expenditures were $2,066 per capita (per person) in 1992.

27 COMMERCE

With one of the nation's busiest ports and many regional distribution centers, New Jersey is an important commercial state. Wholesale sales for 1992 totaled $176 billion; retail sales for 1993 were $67.3 billion; and service establishment receipts for 1992 were $55.8 billion. In 1990, New Jersey exported nearly $10 billion of its own manufactures to foreign countries.

28 PUBLIC FINANCE

The public debt of state government as of 1993 was $3.6 billion. The recommended revenues for 1994/95 were $5,738,000,000; expenditures were $15,283,157,000.

29 TAXATION

New Jersey has levied a personal income tax since 1976. Other taxes include a 6% sales and use tax, corporation taxes, and taxes on motor fuels, cigarettes, inheritances, alcoholic beverages, realty transfers, insurance premiums, savings institutions, public utilities, and railroads.

Commuters from New York State pay a tax of 2–15% on income earned in New Jersey, in order to defray costs of subsidizing transportation between the two states. The major local tax is the property tax. In 1990, New Jersey paid $21 billion in federal income taxes. The $2,730 in total federal taxes per capita (per person) was the second highest among the 50 states.

30 HEALTH

The leading causes of death in the state are heart disease and cancer, for both of which New Jersey ranks above the national average. In 1990, New Jersey ranked higher than any other state in the proportion of breast cancer deaths per 100,000 women, at 32.9.

As of 1993, 97 community hospitals had 31,100 beds. The average expense of hospital care in 1993 was $829 per inpatient day. The average cost per stay was $6,540. There were 20,700 active nonfederal physicians in 1993 and 64,500 nurses. Some 13.7% of state residents did not have health insurance in 1993.

31 HOUSING

Poor housing was at least one of the causes of the Newark riots in 1967, and the state then established the Department

Ellis Island, now a museum, served as the entrance to America for millions of foreign immigrants. Although considered by most as a New York landmark, the island is physically closer to New Jersey and can be reached from New Jersey's Liberty State Park. Jurisdiction over the island has been a point of contention between the two states, with New York presently having jurisdiction above the waterline and New Jersey, below the waterline.

of Community Affairs to coordinate existing housing aid programs and establish new ones. As of 1993, the state had an estimated 3,123,000 year-round housing units. The median monthly cost to the owner of a mortgaged home in 1990 was $1,105 (higher than any other state); the median cost to a renter was $592.

32 EDUCATION

In 1990, the state was above the US norm in the proportion of persons over age 25 who were high school graduates (77%). In 1992, there were 2,292 public schools, of which 1,914 were elementary and 378 were secondary. There also were 83 schools for the disabled. The total public school enrollment in 1993 was 1,147,000. Total expenditures for education in 1993/94 were $5 billion. The state ranked second nationwide in expenditures per pupil in 1993, with an average spending of $9,491.

Rutgers, the state university—encompassing the separate colleges of Rutgers, Douglass, Livingston, and Cook, among others—enrolled over 33,000 in 1992. Altogether, over 334,000 students were enrolled in 1992 in the state's 37 four-year colleges and 25 two-year community colleges. The major private university in the state and one of the nation's leading institutions is Princeton University, founded in 1746, with an enrollment of 4,500 undergraduate students in 1990/91. Other major private universities are Seton Hall, Stevens Institute of Technology, and Fairleigh Dickinson.

33 ARTS

Around the turn of the century, Fort Lee was the motion-picture capital of the world, due partly to the fact that the first motion-picture system was developed by Thomas Edison at Menlo Park in the late 1880s. Most of the best-known "silents"—including the first, *The Great Train Robbery,* and episodes of *The Perils of Pauline*—were shot there.

The New Jersey Orchestra Association, established in 1966, supports orchestras throughout the state. The state's leading orchestra is the New Jersey Symphony, which makes its home in Newark's Symphony Hall. There are other symphony orchestras in Plainfield and Trenton. The New Jersey State Opera performs in Newark's Symphony Hall. Noteworthy dance companies include the Garden State Ballet, New Jersey Ballet, and Princeton Regional Ballet.

The jazz clubs of northern New Jersey and the seaside rock clubs in Asbury Park have helped launch the careers of many local performers. Famous stars perform in the casinos and hotels of Atlantic City. The state of New Jersey generated $93,491,415 in federal and state funds to support its arts programs from 1987 to 1991.

34 LIBRARIES AND MUSEUMS

Statewide, 311 public libraries in 1991 housed more than 27.5 million volumes and recorded a circulation of 39.3 million. The Newark Public Library was the largest municipal system with 1,219,951 volumes and 11 branches. Princeton University's library is the largest in the state, with 4,427,435 volumes in 1991. It is distinguished by special collections on African-American studies, art and archaeology, economics, and international affairs, among many others. Rutgers University ranked second with 3,800,000 volumes.

New Jersey has more than 145 museums, historic sites, botanical gardens and arboretums. Among the most noteworthy museums are the New Jersey Historical Society in Newark and Princeton University's Art Museum and Museum of Natural History. Also of interest are Grover Cleveland's birthplace in Caldwell; the Campbell Museum in Camden (featuring the soup company's collection of bowls and utensils); and one of the most popular attractions, the Edison National Historic Site, formerly the home and workshop of Thomas Edison, in West Orange.

35 COMMUNICATIONS

In March 1993, 94.1% of the state's 2,879,000 occupied housing units had telephones. Because the state lacks a major television broadcasting outlet, New Jerseyites receive more news about events in New York City and Philadelphia than in their own towns and cities. In 1993, there were 113 radio stations (37 AM, 76 FM) and 14 television stations, none of which matched the audience size and influence of

Photo credit: Atlantic City Convention & Visitors Authority.

Sandcastles on the beach in Atlantic City.

the stations across the Hudson and Delaware rivers. The state government operates five television stations under the Public Broadcasting Authority. In 1993, cable television service was provided by 25 large systems.

36 PRESS

Although several present-day newspapers, most notably the Newark *Star–Ledger*, have amassed considerable circulation, none have been able to muster statewide influence or match the quality or prestige of the nearby *New York Times* or *Philadelphia Inquirer*, both of which are read widely in the state, along with other New York City and Philadelphia papers. Leading New Jersey dailies with their 1994 daily circulations are the *Newark Star–Ledger* (485,362); the *Hackensack Record* (172,667); and the *Atlantic City Press* (78,442).

Numerous scholarly and historical books have been published by the university presses of Princeton and Rutgers. Prentice-Hall's publishing offices are in Englewood Cliffs, and those of Silver Burdett, a textbook publisher, are in Morristown. Periodicals published in New Jersey include *Home, New Jersey Monthly, Personal Computing,* and *Tiger Beat.*

37 TOURISM, TRAVEL, AND RECREATION

Tourism is a leading industry in New Jersey, accounting for more than $11 billion in income in 1993. The Jersey shore has been a popular attraction since 1801, when Cape May began advertising itself as a summer resort.

Of all the shore resorts, the largest has long been Atlantic City, which by the 1890s was the nation's most popular resort city. By the early 1970s, however, the city's only claims to fame were the Miss America pageant and the game of Monopoly, whose standard version uses its street names. In an effort to restore Atlantic City to its former luster and revive its economy, New Jersey voters approved a constitutional amendment in 1976 to allow casinos in the resort. Some 33 million people now visit Atlantic City annually.

State attractions include 10 ski areas in northwestern New Jersey, canoeing and camping at the Delaware Water Gap National Recreation Area, 31 public golf courses, and 30 amusement parks. State parks, forests, historic sites, and other areas attracted almost 11 million visitors in 1991. New Jersey's inland lakes, trout streams, and saltwater fishing facilities are popular with anglers.

38 SPORTS

New Jersey is historically significant in the births of two major national sports. Princeton and Rutgers played what is claimed to be the first intercollegiate football game on 6 November 1869 at New Brunswick. The first game of what we know today as baseball was also played in New Jersey at the Elysion Field in Hoboken between the Knickerbockers and the New York Nine on 19 June 1846.

New Jersey did not have a major league professional team until 1976, when the New York Giants of the National Football League moved across the Hudson River into the newly completed Giants Stadium in the Meadowlands Sports Complex at East Rutherford. The NFL's New York Jets began playing their home games at the Meadowlands in 1984. As New York teams who no longer play in their home state, the Giants and the Jets are scorned by some New York sports purists. When the Giants won the Super Bowl in 1987, New York's then mayor, Ed Koch, refused them the tickertape parade traditionally given to local sports champions. The Brendon Byrne Arena is the home of the New Jersey Nets of the National Basketball Association and the New Jersey Devils of the National Hockey League.

39 FAMOUS NEW JERSEYITES

While only one native New Jerseyite, (Stephen) Grover Cleveland (1837–1908), has been elected president of the US, the state can also properly claim (Thomas) Woodrow Wilson (b.Virginia, 1856–1924), who spent most of his adult life there. Elected governor of New Jersey in 1910, Wilson pushed through a series of sweeping reforms before entering the White House in 1913. Wilson's two presidential terms were marked by his controversial decision to declare war on Germany and his unsuccessful crusade for US membership in the League of Nations after World War I.

Two vice-presidents hail from New Jersey: Aaron Burr (1756–1836) and Garret A. Hobart (1844–99). Burr, born in

Newark and educated at what is now Princeton University, is best remembered for killing Alexander Hamilton in a duel at Weehawken in 1804.

Important historical figures include Molly Pitcher (Mary Ludwig Hays McCauley, 1754?–1832), a heroine of the American Revolution, and Zebulon Pike (1779–1813), the noted explorer. One of the world's most prolific inventors, Thomas Alva Edison (b.Ohio, 1847–1931) patented over 1,000 devices from workshops at Menlo Park and West Orange. Theoretical physicist Albert Einstein (b.Germany, 1879–1955), winner of a Nobel Prize in 1921, spent his last decades in Princeton. Norman Schwarzkopf (b. 1934), commander of US forces in Desert Storm (Gulf War), was born 22 August 1934, in Trenton, New Jersey.

The state's traditions in the arts began in colonial times. Patience Lovell Wright (1725–86) of Bordentown was America's first recognized sculptor. Authors after the Revolution included James Fenimore Cooper (1789–1851), one of the nation's first novelists; Stephen Crane (1871–1900), famed for *The Red Badge of Courage* (1895).

Quite a number of prominent 20th-century writers were born in or associated with New Jersey including Norman Mailer (b.1923); John McPhee (b.1931); Philip Roth (b.1933); Imamu Amiri Baraka (LeRoi Jones, b.1934); and Peter Benchley (b.New York, 1940).

Popular singers include Francis Albert "Frank" Sinatra (b.1915); Sarah Vaughan (b.1924); Dionne Warwick (b.1941); Paul Simon (b.1942); and Bruce Springsteen (b.1949). Jazz musician William "Count" Basie (1904–84) was born in Red Bank.

Other celebrities native to New Jersey are actors Jack Nicholson (b.1937); Michael Douglas (b.1944); Meryl Streep (b.1948); and John Travolta (b.1954). Comedians Lou Costello (1906–59), Jerry Lewis (b.1926), and Clerow "Flip" Wilson (b.1933) were also born in the state.

40 BIBLIOGRAPHY

Cohen, David. *The Folklore and Folklife of New Jersey.* New Brunswick, NJ.: Rutgers University Press, 1983.

Cunningham, John T. *This Is New Jersey.* New Brunswick, N.J.: Rutgers University Press, 1983.

McPhee, John. *The Pine Barrens.* New York: Farrar, Straus & Giroux, 1981.

NEW MEXICO

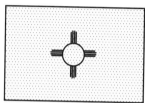

State of New Mexico

ORIGIN OF STATE NAME: Spanish explorers in 1540 called the area "the new Mexico."
NICKNAME: Land of Enchantment.
CAPITAL: Santa Fe.
ENTERED UNION: 6 January 1912 (47th).
SONGS: "O Fair New Mexico;" "Así es Nuevo México."
MOTTO: *Crescit eundo* (It grows as it goes).
FLAG: The sun symbol of the Zia Indians appears in red on a yellow field.
OFFICIAL SEAL: An American bald eagle with extended wings grasps three arrows in its talons and shields a smaller eagle grasping a snake in its beak and a cactus in its talons (the emblem of Mexico, and thus symbolic of the change in sovereignty over the state). Below the scene is the state motto. The words "Great Seal of the State of New Mexico 1912" surround the whole.
ANIMAL: Black bear.
BIRD: Roadrunner (chaparral bird).
FISH: Cutthroat trout.
FLOWER: Yucca.
TREE: Piñon.
FOSSIL: *Coelophysis* dinosaur.
GEM: Turquoise.
VEGETABLES: Frijol; chile.
TIME: 5 AM MST = noon GMT.

1 LOCATION AND SIZE

New Mexico is located in the southwestern US. Smaller only than Montana of the eight Rocky Mountain states, it ranks fifth in size among the 50 states, with an area of 121,593 square miles (314,926 square kilometers). New Mexico extends about 352 miles (566 kilometers) east-west and 391 miles (629 kilometers) north-south. Its total boundary length is 1,434 miles (2,308 kilometers).

2 TOPOGRAPHY

The Continental Divide extends from north to south through central New Mexico. The north–central part of the state lies within the Southern Rocky Mountains, the northwest forms part of the Colorado Plateau, and the eastern two-fifths of the state falls on the western fringes of the Great Plains. Major mountain ranges include the Southern Rockies. The highest point in the state is Wheeler Peak, at 13,161 feet (4,011 meters). Major rivers include the Rio Grande, San Juan, Pecos, and Gila. The largest bodies of inland water are the Elephant Butte and Conchas reservoirs. The Carlsbad Caverns, famed for their stalactite and stalagmite formations, are the largest known underground labyrinth in the world.

3 CLIMATE

New Mexico has a wide range of temperatures. Average January temperatures vary from about 35°F (2°C) in the north to about 55°F (13°C) in the southern and central regions. July temperatures range from about 78°F (26°C) at high elevations to around 92°F (33°C) at lower elevations. The record high temperature for the state is 116°F (47°C), set in 1934. The record low, –50°F (–46°C), was set on 1 February 1951 at Gavilan. Average annual precipitation ranges from under 10 inches (25 centimeters) to over 20 inches (50 centimeters) at high elevations.

4 PLANTS AND ANIMALS

New Mexico is divided into six life zones, with vegetation varying from desert shrubs and grasses to ponderosa pine and oak woodlands, and from mixed conifer and aspen forests to tundra wildflowers. The yucca is the state flower. Native animals range from pronghorn antelope in the lower Sonoran zone to elk and wild turkey in the transition zone. They vary from black bear and hairy woodpecker in the Canadian zone to bighorn sheep and ermine in the arctic-alpine zone. The river otter, gray wolf, and Gila monster are among species on the endangered list.

New Mexico Population Profile

Estimated 1995 population:	1,639,000
Population change, 1980–90:	16.3%
Leading ancestry group:	German
Second leading group:	Mexican
Foreign born population:	5.3%
Hispanic origin†:	38.2%
Population by race:	
White:	75.6%
Black:	2.0%
Native American:	8.9%
Asian/Pacific Islander:	0.9%
Other:	12.6%

Population by Age Group

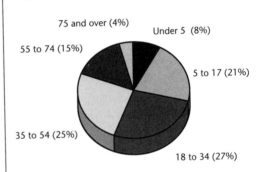

75 and over (4%)
Under 5 (8%)
55 to 74 (15%)
5 to 17 (21%)
35 to 54 (25%)
18 to 34 (27%)

Top Cities with Populations Over 25,000

City	Population	National rank	% change 1980–90
Albuquerque	398,492	36	16.0
Las Cruces	66,466	361	37.9
Santa Fe	59,004	414	14.1
Roswell	45,533	581	12.5
Rio Rancho	36,370	761	NA
Farmington	36,204	763	8.9
Clovis	33,405	836	–0.8
Hobbs	29,364	949	–0.1
Alamogordo	27,559	1,007	14.9

Notes: †A person of Hispanic origin may be of any race. NA indicates that data are not available.
Sources: Economic and Statistics Administration, Bureau of the Census. *Statistical Abstract of the United States, 1994–95.* Washington, DC: Government Printing Office, 1995; Courtenay M. Slater and George E. Hall. *1995 County and City Extra: Annual Metro, City and County Data Book.* Lanham, MD: Bernan Press, 1995.

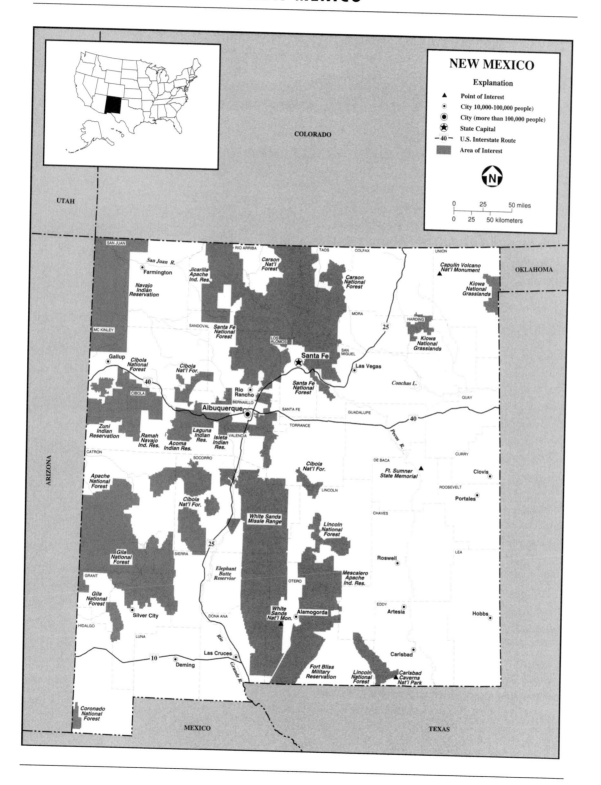

NEW MEXICO
Explanation
▲ Point of Interest
◉ City 10,000-100,000 people)
● City (more than 100,000 people)
★ State Capital
—40— U.S. Interstate Route
Area of Interest

0   25   50 miles
0   25   50 kilometers

COLORADO

UTAH

OKLAHOMA

ARIZONA

SAN JUAN

San Juan R.
Farmington

Navajo
Indian
Reservation

Jicarilla
Apache
Ind. Res.

RIO ARRIBA

Carson
Nat'l
Forest

TAOS   COLFAX

UNION

Capulin Volcano
Nat'l Monument ▲

Kiowa
National
Grasslands

Carson
National
Forest

MORA

25

HARDING

Kiowa
National
Grasslands

MC KINLEY

Gallup

Cibola
National
Forest

SANDOVAL

Santa Fe
National
Forest

LOS
ALAMOS

SAN
MIGUEL

Santa Fe ★ Santa Fe

Las Vegas

Conchas L.

QUAY

Cibola
Nat'l For.

CIBOLA

40

Rio
Rancho

BERNALILLO

Albuquerque ●

SANTA FE

Santa Fe
National
Forest

GUADALUPE

40

Pecos R.

Zuni
Indian
Reservation

Ramah
Navajo
Ind. Res.

Laguna
Indian
Res.

Acoma
Indian Res.

Isleta
Indian
Res.

VALENCIA

TORRANCE

CATRON

SOCORRO

Cibola
Nat'l For.

DE BACA

Ft. Sumner
State Memorial ▲

CURRY

Clovis

Apache
National
Forest

Cibola
Nat'l For.

LINCOLN

ROOSEVELT

Portales

CHAVES

White Sands
Missle Range

Lincoln
National
Forest

25

SIERRA

GRANT

Gila
National
Forest

Elephant
Butte
Resorvior

OTERO

Mescalero
Apache
Ind. Res.

Roswell

LEA

Gila
National
Forest

Silver City

HIDALGO

LUNA

DONA ANA

White
Sands
Nat'l Mon.

Alamogorda

EDDY

Artesia

Hobbs

10

Deming

Rio

Las Cruces

Carlsbad

Grande R.

Fort Bliss
Military
Reservation

Lincoln
National
Forest

Carlsbad
Caverns
Nat'l Park ▲

Coronado
National
Forest

MEXICO

TEXAS

5 ENVIRONMENTAL PROTECTION

The New Mexico Environment Department (NMED) is the state's leading environmental agency. As of 1992, New Mexico had 153 municipal landfills and 3 local curbside recycling programs. The state had 11 hazardous waste sites as of 1994.

6 POPULATION

In 1990, New Mexico had a census population of 1,515,069, 37th in the US. The state had a population density of 12.5 persons per square mile (4.8 persons per square kilometer). The estimated population for 1995 was 1,639,000. In 1990, 481,000 people, about one-third of New Mexico's population, lived in the Albuquerque metropolitan area. Albuquerque itself had 398,492 residents in 1992, and Las Cruces had 66,466. Santa Fe, the third-largest city and the state capital, had 59,004 inhabitants.

7 ETHNIC GROUPS

There were about 134,850 Native Americans in the state in 1990, 8.9% of the total population. There are 2 Apache reservations and 19 Pueblo villages, and 3 Navajo reservations that include 50 local Navajo chapters. The Hispanic population accounts for another 38.2% of New Mexicans. About 14,000 Asians and Pacific Islanders and 30,000 black Americans live in the state.

8 LANGUAGES

New Mexico English is a mixture of dominant Midland, with Northern, Southern, and South Midland features in some areas. In 1990, 896,049 New Mexicans—64.5% of the resident population—spoke only English at home. Other languages spoken at home, and number of speakers, include Spanish (388,186) and various Native American languages (79,087).

9 RELIGIONS

The state's Roman Catholic churches had 467,356 members in 1990. Major Protestant denominations in 1990 included 158,873 Southern Baptists and 54,664 United Methodists. The Jewish population was estimated at 6,075 in 1990. Other religions present in the state include Pentecostals and shamanists.

10 TRANSPORTATION

New Mexico had 2,006 rail miles (3,228 kilometers) of track in 1992. Amtrak provided passenger service to 88,826 people in 1991/92. In 1993, New Mexico had 60,812 miles (97,847 kilometers) of public roads and streets, including 998 miles (1,606 kilometers) of interstate highway. In that year, 1,451,897 road vehicles were registered in the state, of which 855,920 were automobiles, 561,321 trucks, 31,244 motorcycles, and 3,412 buses. Albuquerque has the state's main airport.

11 HISTORY

There were Native Americans living in present-day New Mexico when the first Europeans arrived. These included the Pueblo people, living initially along the upper Rio Grande; the Navajo, farmers and sheepherders; and the Apache, a more nomadic and warlike group who would

Photo credit: Ron Behrmann.

Dancers at the Pueblo Indian Cultural Center.

later pose a threat to all newcomers who arrived during the Spanish, Mexican, and American periods.

Francisco Vásquez de Coronado led the earliest major European expedition to New Mexico, beginning in 1540, 80 years before the Pilgrims landed at Plymouth Rock. In 1599, Don Juan de Oñate established the settlement of San Gabriel. In 1610, the Spanish moved their center of activity to Santa Fe, dominating New Mexico for more than two centuries. In 1821, Mexico gained its independence from Spain, and New Mexico came under Mexican rule until the Mexican-American War, 25 years later. The area officially

became a part of the US with the Treaty of Guadalupe-Hidalgo in 1848.

New Mexico became a US territory as part of the Compromise of 1850. An increasing number of people traveling on the Santa Fe Trail—in use since the early 1820s to carry goods between Independence, Missouri, and Santa Fe—were Americans seeking a new home in the Southwest. Native New Mexicans resisted, sometimes violently, the efforts of new non-Hispanic residents to take over lands assigned to them during the earlier Spanish and Mexican periods. The so-called Lincoln County War of 1878–81, a range war pitting cattle ranchers against merchants and involving, among others, William H.

Bonney (Billy the Kid), helped give the territory the image of a lawless region unfit for statehood.

Statehood

Despite the turmoil, New Mexico began to make substantial economic progress. In 1879, the Atchison, Topeka & Santa Fe Railroad entered the territory. By the end of the 19th century, disputes with the area's Native Americans had finally been resolved. New Mexico finally became a state on 6 January 1912, under President William H. Taft.

The decade of the 1920s was characterized by the discovery and development of new resources, including potash salts and petroleum reserves. A period of prosperity ended with the onset of the Great Depression, but World War II revived the economy. Scientists working at Los Alamos ushered in the Atomic Age with the explosion of the first atomic bomb at White Sands Proving Ground in June 1945.

The remarkable growth of the so-called Sunbelt during the postwar era has been most noticeable in New Mexico. Newcomers from many parts of the country have moved to the state, a population shift with profound social, cultural, and political consequences. Spanish-speaking New Mexicans, once an overwhelming majority, are now a minority. Nevertheless, they have been able to maintain their political influence. In 1982, former state attorney general Toney Anaya, a Democrat, became the only Hispanic state governor in the US.

12 STATE GOVERNMENT

The legislature consists of a 42-member senate and a 70-member house of representatives. Senators serve four-year terms, and house members serve two-year terms. The executive branch consists of ten elected officials, including the governor,

New Mexico Presidential Vote by Political Parties, 1948–92

YEAR	NEW MEXICO WINNER	DEMOCRAT	REPUBLICAN	PROGRESSIVE
1948	*Truman (D)	105,210	79,896	1,037
1952	*Eisenhower (R)	105,349	131,477	225
				CONSTITUTION
1956	*Eisenhower (R)	106,098	146,788	364
1960	*Kennedy (D)	156,027	153,733	570
1964	*Johnson (D)	194,017	132,838	1,217
				AMERICAN IND.
1968	*Nixon (R)	130,081	169,692	25,737
				AMERICAN
1972	*Nixon (R)	141,084	235,606	8,767
				SOC. WORKERS
1976	Ford (R)	201,148	211,419	2,462
				LIBERTARIAN
1980	*Reagan (R)	167,826	250,779	4,365
1984	*Reagan (R)	201,769	307,101	4,459
1988	*Bush (R)	244,497	270,341	3,268
1992**	*Clinton (D)	261,617	212,824	1,615

* Won US presidential election.
** Independent candidate Ross Perot received 91,895 votes.

lieutenant governor, secretary of state, auditor, and treasurer.

13 POLITICAL PARTIES

Democrats hold a large lead in voter registration. There were 412,023 registered Democrats and only 239,736 registered Republicans in 1994. Nevertheless, New Mexico has been a "swing state" in US presidential elections since it entered the Union. In 1992, Democratic nominee Bill Clinton captured 46% of the vote; Republican and incumbent George Bush received 37%; and Independent Ross Perot collected 16%. New Mexico's senators in 1994 were Democrat Jeff Bingamen and Republican Peter Domenici. New Mexico's U.S. Representatives consist of two Republicans and one Democrat. As of 1995, there were 26 Democrats, 15 Republicans, and 1 Independent in the state senate, and 47 Democrats and 23 Republicans in the state house.

14 LOCAL GOVERNMENT

There are 33 counties in New Mexico. Each is governed by commissioners elected for two-year terms. Municipalities are incorporated as cities, towns, or villages. Among the Native Americans, the Pueblo elect governors from each of 19 pueblos, and they form an unofficial coalition called the All-Indian Pueblo Council. Each Apache tribe elects its own president. The Navajo elect a chairperson, vice-chairperson, and council members for each chapter. The Navajo nation as a whole elects its president and vice-president.

15 JUDICIAL SYSTEM

The judicial branch consists of a supreme court, an appeals court, district courts, probate courts, magistrate courts, and other inferior courts as created by law. The state's 33 counties are divided into 13 judicial districts, served by 61 district judges. District courts have unlimited general jurisdiction and are commonly referred to as trial courts. They also serve as courts of review for decisions of lower courts and administrative agencies. In 1994, New Mexico had a total crime rate of 6,187.8 per 100,000 persons.

16 MIGRATION

In the 1980s, New Mexico had a net gain from migration of 63,000 residents, accounting for 28% of the state's population increase during those years. The proportion of native-born state residents was 51.7% in 1990.

17 ECONOMY

New Mexico was primarily an agricultural state until the 1940s, when military activities assumed major economic importance. Currently, major industries include primary metals (mining), petroleum, and food. Tourism also continues to flourish.

18 INCOME

Total personal income was $28.2 billion in 1994. Per capita (per person) income was $17,025 (48th among the 50 states). Some 17.4% of the population lived below the federal poverty level in 1993.

Photo credit: Ron Behrmann.

The plaza in Old Town, Albuquerque.

19 INDUSTRY

The value of shipments by manufacturers in New Mexico exceeded $8 billion in 1991. Manufacturing's share of total income and employment were far below the national average. Manufacturing has been heavily reliant on federal defense expenditures, which have been falling in recent years. Several companies that are not defense-related were expanding in 1992, including Intel and Philips Semiconductors, both in the field of computer chips.

20 LABOR

In 1994, the total civilian labor force of New Mexico was estimated at 770,000. Of that total, 6.3% were unemployed.

Services ranked as the largest employer in 1992, with 26.7% of the labor force. In 1994, 9.3% of all workers in the state belonged to labor unions.

21 AGRICULTURE

The first farmers of New Mexico were the Pueblo Indians, who raised corn, beans, and squash. In 1994, New Mexico's total farm marketings were $1.5 billion (34th in the US). Leading cash crops included hay and peppers. In 1994, hay production was 1,499,000 tons, and wheat production was 5,520,000 bushels.

22 DOMESTICATED ANIMALS

Meat animals, especially cattle, represent the bulk of New Mexico's agricultural income. At the end of 1994 there were 1,500,000 head of cattle, 315,000 sheep, and 25,000 hogs on New Mexico farms. Cattle marketings made up 43.4% of agricultural receipts in 1994; dairy products, 25.8%.

23 FISHING

There is no commercial fishing in New Mexico. In 1991, according to the US Fish and Wildlife Service, six hatchery facilities produced nine million fish to stock rivers for recreational fishing.

24 FORESTRY

Although lumbering ranks low as a source of state income, the forests of New Mexico are of crucial importance because of the role they play in water conservation and recreation. In 1993, 20% of New Mexico's land area—15.2 million acres (6.2 million hectares)—was forestland.

25 MINING

In 1994, nonfuel mineral production was valued at $914 million. In 1991, copper and potash again led other mineral commodities, with respective values of $609.4 million and $255 million. New Mexico leads the country in perlite and potash production.

26 ENERGY AND POWER

New Mexico is a major producer of oil and natural gas, and has significant reserves of low-sulfur bituminous coal. In 1992, the state consumed, per capita (per person), 369.4 million Btu of energy. Chief sources were petroleum, natural gas, and coal. In 1993, 68 million barrels of crude petroleum were produced. Natural gas

marketed production in 1993 totaled 1.4 trillion cubic feet.

The state generated 28.4 billion kilowatt hours of electric power in 1993, almost 90% of which was coal-fired. The state has no nuclear power plants. Energy expenditures per capita (per person) were $1,899 in 1992.

27 COMMERCE

New Mexico's wholesale sales totaled $6.3 billion for 1992; retail sales were $12.3 billion for 1993; and service establishment receipts were $6.9 billion for 1992. New Mexico's foreign exports totaled $356 million in 1992, 47th in the US.

28 PUBLIC FINANCE

The estimated general revenues for 1992/ 93 were $2,267.5 million; estimated expenditures were $2,168.2 million. New Mexico had a total outstanding debt of $1.6 billion in 1993, with a per capita (per person) debt of $989.

29 TAXATION

The state of New Mexico levies a gross receipts tax, various excise taxes, personal and corporate income taxes, property taxes, and mineral severance taxes. In 1990, New Mexicans' federal income tax bill amounted to $1.9 billion.

30 HEALTH

Deaths from heart disease and cancer are far below the national average. There were 37 community hospitals in 1993, with 4,100 beds. The state had 3,100 active nonfederal physicians in 1993 and 9,400 nurses. The average hospital cost per

Photo credit: Corel Corporation.

Adobe buildings. Adobe is a mixture of clay and straw that is shaped into bricks and then dried in the sun.

inpatient day was $1,046 in 1993, and the average cost per stay was $5,600. Some 22% of state residents did not have health insurance in 1993.

31 HOUSING

In 1993, New Mexico had an estimated 653,000 housing units. The median value of all owner-occupied housing in 1990 was $70,100. More than 8,800 new housing units valued at $775.1 million were authorized in 1993. In 1990, the median monthly cost for an owner with a mortgage in New Mexico was $651, and $163 for an owner without a mortgage. The median monthly rent was $372.

32 EDUCATION

Of 928,000 New Mexicans 25 years old and older in 1990, 77.0% had completed high school, and 20.9% had completed college. The public school system had 325,300 students in 1995. Expenditures on education averaged $4,643 per pupil (38th in the nation) in 1993. New Mexico had 20 institutions of higher education in 1995, plus 5 Native American institutions. The leading public institutions are the University of New Mexico in Albuquerque, and New Mexico State University in Las Cruces.

33 ARTS

New Mexico is a state rich in Native American, Spanish, Mexican, and contemporary art. Major exhibits can be seen at the University of New Mexico Art Museum in Albuquerque, and the Art Museum of the Harwood Foundation in Taos. Taos itself is an artists' colony of renown. The Santa Fe Opera is one of the nation's most distinguished regional opera companies. The state of New Mexico generated $19,110,760 in federal and state funds for the arts from 1987 to 1991.

34 LIBRARIES AND MUSEUMS

Public libraries in New Mexico had a combined total of 3,820,964 volumes and a circulation of 7,374,684 volumes in 1993/94. The largest municipal library is the Albuquerque Public Library. The largest university library is that of the University of New Mexico, with 1,473,265 volumes.

New Mexico has 96 museums. Noteworthy museums include the Maxwell Museum of Anthropology at Albuquerque and the Museum of International Folk Art in Santa Fe. Historic sites include the Palace of the Governors (1610), the oldest US capitol and probably the nation's oldest public building, in Santa Fe; and the Aztec Ruins National Monument, near Aztec.

35 COMMUNICATIONS

In March 1993, 89.1% of the state's 578,000 occupied housing units had telephones. In 1993 there were 62 AM radio stations and 81 FM stations. There were 17 commercial and 5 educational television stations in 1993, as well as 3 large cable systems.

36 PRESS

In 1994 there were 20 daily newspapers (including 5 morning and 14 evening) in the state. The leading dailies include the *Albuquerque Journal,* with a morning circulation in 1994 of 123,481 (162,394 on Sundays); and the *Santa Fe New Mexican,* with a morning circulation of 22,278 (24,819 on Sundays).

37 TOURISM, TRAVEL, AND RECREATION

The development of New Mexico's recreational resources has made tourism a leading economic activity. Hunting, fishing, camping, boating, and skiing are among the many outdoor attractions. The state has a national park—Carlsbad Caverns—and ten national monuments, including Aztec Ruins, Chaco Canyon, and Gila Cliff Dwellings. The state's tourism budget was close to $5.8 million for 1991/92.

38 SPORTS

New Mexico has no major league professional sports teams, though Albuquerque does have a minor league baseball team in the Class AAA Pacific Coast League. Thoroughbred and quarter-horse racing is an important spectator sport. The Lobos of the University of New Mexico compete in the Western Athletic Conference, while the Aggies of New Mexico State belong to the Pacific Coast Conference.

39 FAMOUS NEW MEXICANS

Among the earliest Europeans to explore New Mexico were Francisco Vásquez de Coronado (b.Spain, 1510–54) and Juan de Oñate (b.Mexico, 1549?–1624?), the founder of New Mexico. Army scout and trapper Christopher Houston "Kit" Carson (b.Kentucky, 1809–68) made his home in Taos. Among the more notorious of the frontier figures in New Mexico was Billy the Kid (William H. Bonney, b.New York, 1859–81).

New Mexico has attracted many artists and writers. Painters Bert G. Phillips (b.New York, 1868–1956) and Ernest Leonard Blumenschein (b.Ohio 1874–1960) started the famous Taos art colony in 1898. The most famous person to take up residence there was English novelist D. H. Lawrence (1885–1930). New Mexico's best-known artist is Georgia O'Keeffe (b.Wisconsin, 1887–1986). Entertainers born in the state include John Denver (b.1943) and Demi Moore (b.1962).

Other prominent persons who have made New Mexico their home include Pulitzer Prize-winning editorial cartoonist Bill Mauldin (b.1921); novelist N. Scott Momaday (b.Oklahoma, 1934); and golfer Nancy Lopez-Melton (b.California, 1957). Auto racers Bobby Unser (b.1924) and Al Unser (b.1939) are from Albuquerque.

40 BIBLIOGRAPHY

Reeve, Frank, and Alice Cleaveland. *New Mexico: Land of Many Cultures*. Rev. ed. Boulder, Colo., Pruett, 1980.

Simmons, Marc. *New Mexico: A Bicentennial History*. New York: Norton, 1977.

NEW YORK

State of New York

ORIGIN OF STATE NAME: Named for the Duke of York (later King James II) in 1664.

NICKNAME: The Empire State.

CAPITAL: Albany.

ENTERED UNION: 26 July 1788 (11th).

SONG: "I Love New York."

MOTTO: *Excelsior* (Ever upward).

COAT OF ARMS: Liberty and Justice stand on either side of a shield showing a mountain sunrise. Above the shield is an eagle on a globe. In the foreground are a three-masted ship and a Hudson River sloop, both representing commerce. Liberty's left foot has kicked aside a royal crown. Beneath the shield is the state motto.

FLAG: Dark blue with the coat of arms in the center.

OFFICIAL SEAL: The coat of arms surrounded by the words "The Great Seal of the State of New York."

ANIMAL: Beaver.

BIRD: Bluebird.

FISH: Brook or speckled trout.

FLOWER: Rose.

TREE: Sugar maple.

FRUIT: Apple.

FOSSIL: Prehistoric crab (Eurypterus remipes).

GEM: Garnet.

TIME: 7 AM EST = noon GMT.

1 LOCATION AND SIZE

Located in the northeastern US, New York State is the largest of the three Middle Atlantic states and ranks 30th in size among the 50 states. The total area of New York is 49,108 square miles (127,190 square kilometers). New York's width is about 320 miles (515 kilometers) east-west, not including Long Island, which extends an additional 118 miles (190 kilometers) southwest-northeast. The state's maximum north-south extension is about 310 miles (499 kilometers). Two large islands lie off the state's southeast corner: Long Island and Staten Island (a borough of New York City). Including these two islands, the total boundary length of New York State is 1,430 miles (2,301 kilometers).

2 TOPOGRAPHY

Two upland regions—the Adirondack Mountains and the Appalachian Highlands—dominate the topography of New

51

York State. The Adirondacks cover most of the northeast and occupy about one-fourth of the state's total area. The Appalachian Highlands, including the Catskill Mountains and Kittatinny Mountain Ridge, extend across the southern half of the state, from the Hudson River Valley to the basin of Lake Erie.

Between these two upland regions, and also along the state's northern and eastern borders, lies a network of lowlands. These include the Great Lakes Plain; the Hudson, Mohawk, Lake Champlain, and St. Lawrence valleys; and the coastal areas of New York City and Long Island. The state's highest peak, Mt. Marcy, 5,344 feet (1,629 meters), is found in the Adirondacks, along with many scenic lakes, including Lake Placid, Saranac Lake, and Lake George.

Three lakes—Erie, Ontario, and Champlain—form part of the state's borders. New York contains some 8,000 lakes. New York's longest river is the Hudson; the Mohawk River flows into it north of Albany. Other rivers include the Genesee, Oswego, St. Lawrence, Delaware, and Niagara. Niagara Falls, New York's most spectacular natural feature, is both a leading tourist attraction and a major source of hydroelectric power.

3 CLIMATE

Although New York lies entirely within the humid continental zone, there is much variation from region to region. The three main climatic regions are the southeastern lowlands, which have the warmest temperatures and the longest season between frosts; the uplands of the Catskills and

New York Population Profile

Estimated 1995 population:	18,178,000
Population change, 1980–90:	2.5%
Leading ancestry group:	German
Second leading group:	Italian
Foreign born population:	15.9%
Hispanic origin†:	12.3%
Population by race:	
White:	74.4%
Black:	15.9%
Native American:	0.3%
Asian/Pacific Islander:	3.9%
Other:	5.5%

Population by Age Group

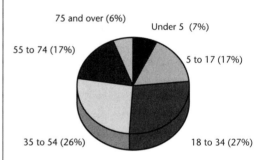

75 and over (6%)
Under 5 (7%)
55 to 74 (17%)
5 to 17 (17%)
35 to 54 (26%)
18 to 34 (27%)

Top Cities with Populations Over 25,000

City	Population	National rank	% change 1980–90
New York	7,311,966	1	3.5
Buffalo	323,284	50	−8.3
Rochester	234,163	69	−4.2
Yonkers	186,063	92	−3.7
Syracuse	162,835	109	−3.7
Albany	99,708	201	−0.6
New Rochelle	67,578	350	−5.0
Mount Vernon	67,050	357	0.7
Utica	66,849	359	−9.2
Schenectady	65,395	366	−3.5

Notes: †A person of Hispanic origin may be of any race. NA indicates that data are not available.
Sources: Economic and Statistics Administration, Bureau of the Census. *Statistical Abstract of the United States, 1994–95.* Washington, DC: Government Printing Office, 1995; Courtenay M. Slater and George E. Hall. *1995 County and City Extra: Annual Metro, City and County Data Book.* Lanham, MD: Bernan Press, 1995.

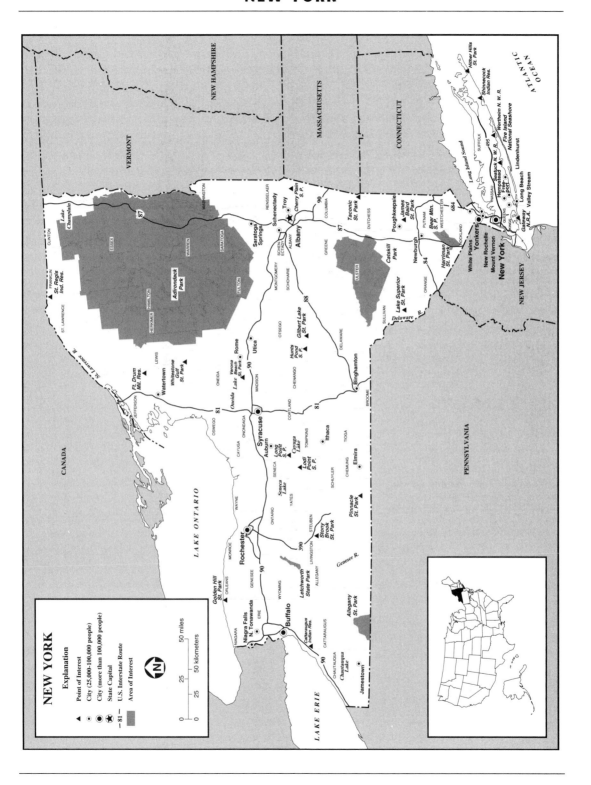

NEW YORK

Explanation

▲ Point of Interest
● City (25,000-100,000 people)
◉ City (more than 100,000 people)
★ State Capital
–81– U.S. Interstate Route
Area of Interest

0   25   50 miles
0   25   50 kilometers

Adirondacks, where winters are cold and summer cool; and the snow belt along the Great Lakes Plain, one of the snowiest areas of the US.

The record low temperature for the state is −52°F (−47°C), recorded at Stillwater Reservoir in the Adirondacks on 9 February 1934 and at Old Forge on 18 February 1979. The record high is 108°F (42°C), registered at Troy on 22 July 1926.

Annual precipitation ranges from over 50 inches (127 centimeters) in the higher elevations to about 30 inches (76 centimeters) in the areas near Lake Ontario and Lake Champlain, and in the lower half of the Genesee River Valley. New York City has an annual mean snowfall of 29 inches (74 centimeters), while Syracuse receives 110 inches (279 centimeters).

4 PLANTS AND ANIMALS

New York has some 150 species of trees. These include laurel magnolia, sweet gum, and hop trees near the Atlantic shore; oak, hickory, and chestnut in the Hudson and Mohawk valleys and the Great Lakes Plain; and birch, beech, and commercially valuable maple on the Appalachian Plateau and in the foothills of the Adirondack Mountains. The bulk of the Adirondacks and Catskills is covered with balsam fir, mountain ash, and white pine, as well as maple and other species. Spruce, balsam fir, and mountain ash rise to the timberline. Apple trees and other fruit-bearing species are important in western New York and the Hudson Valley.

Common meadow flowers include several types of rose (the state flower), along with Queen Anne's lace, goldenrod, and black-eyed Susan. Indian pipe, bunchberry, and goldthread flourish in the forests, while cattails grow along the Hudson and rushes cover the Finger Lakes shallows. Among protected plants are bayberry, lotus, and all native orchids.

Mammals found in abundance include woodchuck, squirrel, muskrat, and raccoon. The deer population was estimated in 1983 at 500,000, making them a pest causing millions of dollars annually in crop damage. More than 260 bird species have been observed. The most common year-round residents are the crow, hawk, and several types of woodpecker. Summer visitors include the bluebird (the state bird).

Water snakes and grass snakes are common. Freshwater fish include species of perch, bass, and trout (the state fish). Of insect varieties, the gypsy moth has been singled out as an enemy in periodic state-run pest-control programs. In 1992, endangered species included the Indiana bat, gray wolf, and shortnose sturgeon.

5 ENVIRONMENT PROTECTION

All state environmental programs are run by the Department of Environmental Conservation (DEC), established in 1970. Because of budget cuts by New York City, the state took over the operation of the city's air-monitoring network in 1978. The chief problem areas are Buffalo, where levels of particles (especially from the use of coke in steelmaking) are high, and New York City, where little progress has been made in cutting carbon monoxide emissions from motor vehicles. Despite

Photo credit: Susan D. Rock.

View of New York City from the Empire State Building.

air-quality efforts, acid rain has been blamed for killing fish and trees in the Adirondacks, Catskills, and other areas.

Before the 1960s, the condition of New York's waters was a national scandal. Raw sewage, arsenic, cyanide, and heavy metals were regularly dumped into the state's lakes and rivers, and fish were rapidly dying off. Environmental legislation in the 1960s and 1970s and a state fishery program have helped reverse the damage. The state has also taken action against corporate polluters, including a $7-million settlement with General Electric over that company's discharge of toxic polychlorinated biphenyls (PCBs) into the Hudson.

In addition, the state and federal governments spent perhaps $45 million between 1978 and 1982 on the cleanup of the Love Canal area of Niagara Falls, which was contaminated by the improper disposal of toxic wastes. Remaining problems include continued dumping of sewage and industrial wastes into New York Bay and Long Island Sound, industrial dumping in the Hudson Valley, nuclear waste problems in Cattaraugus County, and contamination of fish in Lake Erie.

By 1994, the state had 85 hazardous waste sites. New York ranks fourth in the number of hazardous waste sites in the country. A 1982 law requires a deposit on beer and soft-drink containers sold in the state, to encourage return and recycling of bottles and cans. State parks and recreational areas total 258,000 acres (104,000 hectares).

6 POPULATION

New York is no longer the most populous state, having lost that position to California in the 1970 census. However, New York City remains the most populous US city, as it has been at least since 1790. The 1990 census figures showed a population in New York State of 17,990,455. The estimated 1995 population was 18,178,000. New York's population is expected to increase from 1995–2000 to 18,237,000.

In 1990, 91.1% of New York's population lived in metropolitan areas (seventh highest in the nation). In 1990, the state's population density was 381 persons per square mile (146 persons per square kilometer). First in the state, as well as the nation, in population was New York City, with 7,311,966 residents in 1992. Other leading cities, with their 1992 populations were Buffalo, 323,284; Rochester, 234,163; Yonkers, 186,063; and Syracuse, 162,835. Albany, the state capital, had a population of 99,708. Because of industrial decline, all these cities have lost population since the 1970s.

7 ETHNIC GROUPS

During the 19th and 20th centuries, New York has been the principal gateway for European immigrants. The ethnic diversity of the state is reflected in such Manhattan neighborhoods as Harlem, Chinatown, Little Italy, and "Spanish,"

Photo credit: Larry White.

Children cooling off in the Washington Square Park Fountain.

or East, Harlem, with its large Puerto Rican concentration. Outside New York City there are also important ethnic communities in the Buffalo metropolitan area, with its large populations of Polish and Italian origin. As of 1990, among persons who reported at least one specific ancestry group, 2,898,888 named German; 2,837,904 Italian; 2,800,128 Irish; 1,566,019 English; 1,181,077 Polish; and 596,875 Russian. These figures do not distinguish the large numbers of European Jewish immigrants who identify themselves as Jews rather than by their country of origin.

New York has the largest black and Puerto Rican population of all the states. After World War I, blacks moving into New York City displaced the Jews, Italians, Germans, and Irish then living in Harlem, which went on to become the cultural capital of black America. The black population of New York State was 2,859,000 as of 1990—15.9% of the state's population, and first among the states in the number of blacks. With 2,101,000, New York City had more black people than any other US city.

The Hispanic population as of 1990 was 2,214,000, of whom 1,786,000 (81%) were in New York City. Puerto Ricans numbered 762,429 (34% of Hispanics in the state). Cubans, Dominicans, Colombians, Central Americans, and Mexicans are also present in growing numbers, including a large but undetermined number of illegal immigrants.

The Asian and Pacific Islander population was 694,000 in 1990, second only to California. Among state residents were 236,876 Chinese; 80,430 Asian Indians; 93,145 Koreans; 64,202 Filipinos; 39,859 Japanese; and 12,116 Vietnamese. According to the US Bureau of the Census, New York had 62,651 Native Americans in 1990.

8 LANGUAGES

Although the speech of metropolitan New York has its own characteristics, in the state as a whole the Northern dialect predominates. Regional variations distinguish the speech of such areas as the Hudson Valley, the eastern part of the state, and the Niagara peninsula. In the New York City area, many speakers pronounce *bird* almost as if it were /boyd/ and do not sound the /r/ after a vowel. New Yorkers stand *on line* (instead of *in line*) while waiting to buy a huge sandwich they call a *hero,* and may even pronounce *Long Island* with an inserted /g/ as /long giland/.

From the high proportion of New York Yiddish speakers (nearly 40% of all those in the US in 1990) have come such terms as *schlock, schmaltz,* and *chutzpah.* Place-names such as Manhattan, Adirondack, and Chautauqua were borrowed from the Iroquois.

Serious communication problems have arisen in New York City, especially in the schools, because of the major influx since World War II of Spanish speakers from the Caribbean region, and, more recently, of Asians. These are in addition to the ever-present large numbers of speakers of other languages. As a result, schools in some areas have emphasized teaching English as a second language.

According to the 1990 census, 76.7% of all New Yorkers five years of age or older spoke only English at home. The following table shows other major languages spoken at home by New York State residents:

Language	Speakers	Language	Speakers
Spanish	1,848,825	Korean	80,394
Italian	400,218	Russian	78,310
Chinese	247,334	Tagalog	46,276
French	236,099	Arabic	44,060
German	128,525	Other Slavic	34,931
Polish	120,923	Portuguese	33,089
Yiddish	117,323	South Slavic	26,377
Greek	87,608	Hungarian	23,394

9 RELIGIONS

As of 1990, New York had 7,280,488 Roman Catholic church members. The Jewish population of New York State was estimated at 1,843,240 in 1990. Membership of leading Protestant denominations in 1990 included United Methodist, 466,586; Episcopal, 231,690; Presbyterian, 199,519; Evangelical Lutheran Church in America, 187,551; Lutheran Church-Missouri Synod, 90,837; Reformed Church in America, 79,865; and United Church of Christ, 73,353.

Because of diversified immigration, New York City has small percentages but significant numbers of Buddhists, Muslims, Hindus, and Orthodox Christians. There is also a wide variety of religious-nationalist sects and cults, including the Nation of Islam (Black Muslims) and the Hare Krishna group.

10 TRANSPORTATION

New York City is a major transit point for both domestic and international passenger and freight traffic. In 1992, New York ranked 13th among the states in total rail mileage, with 4,012 miles (6,455 kilometers) of railroad track. In 1991, there were 3 Class I lines, 6 regional, 21 local, and 8 switching and terminal railroads. Much of New York's rail network is operated by ConrailAmtrak, which owns and operates lines along the eastern corridor from Boston through New York City to Washington, D.C. In 1991/92, the total number of riders was 7,465,206.

The Long Island Railroad, an important commuter carrier, is run by the Metropolitan Transportation Authority (MTA), which also operates the New York City subways. The only other mass-transit rail line in the state is Buffalo's 6.4- mile (10.3-kilometer) light rail system, of which 5.2 miles (8.4 kilometers) is underground. Among cities served by municipal, county, or metropolitan-area bus systems are Albany, Binghamton, Buffalo, Elmira, and Syracuse.

New York City is connected with the rest of the state by an extensive network of good roads, although road and rail transport within the metropolitan region is sagging with age. In 1993, 10,162,501 motor vehicles were registered in New York State, including 8,746,964 automobiles, 40,809 buses, and 1,374,728 trucks. At the beginning of 1994, the state had 111,882 miles (180,018 kilometers) of roads and highways.

Of the total mileage, 1,500 miles (2,414 kilometers) consisted of interstate highway. In 1992, local, state, and federal authorities spent over $2.4 billion on highway maintenance. The major toll road, and the nation's longest toll superhighway, is the Thomas E. Dewey Thruway, operated by the New York State Thruway Authority, which extends 559 miles (900 kilometers) from just outside New York City to Buffalo and the Pennsylvania border in southwestern New York. Although New York was second to California in the total number of traffic injuries (291,264), it ranked first in the number of nonfatal pedestrian injuries (21,082) in 1993.

By 1872, New York's canal system was carrying over six million tons of cargo a year. But an absolute decline in freight tonnage began after 1890 (the relative decline had begun 40 years earlier, with the rise of the railroads). By the mid-1980s, the canals carried less than 10% of the tonnage for 1880.

Buffalo, on Lake Erie, is the most important inland port. In 1991, it handled 1,895,302 tons of cargo, representing a 53% drop in traffic from 1983–91, evidence of Buffalo's decline as an industrial center. Albany, the major port on the Hudson, handled 5,966,982 tons of cargo, and Port Jefferson, on Long Island Sound, handled 2,231,990 tons in 1991.

It would be hard to exaggerate the historic and economic importance of New York Harbor—a haven for explorers, point of entry for millions of refugees and immigrants, and the nation's greatest seaport until recent years, when it was passed by New Orleans and Houston in terms of cargo tonnage. In 1991, it handled 126,860,940 tons of cargo, valued at over $49.5 billion. The port ranked first nationally in the value of exports handled.

At the beginning of 1992, New York State had 512 airfields, including 364 airports, 123 heliports, and 25 seaplane bases. By far the busiest airports in the state are John F. Kennedy International and La Guardia, both in New York City. In 1991, Kennedy handled 8,245,014 passengers, 67,537 aircraft departures, and 236,013 tons of freight. La Guardia handled 9,194,825 passengers, 120,412 departures, and 22,190 tons of freight. The Greater Buffalo International Airport is the largest in the state outside New York City.

11 HISTORY

In 1570, after European explorers had discovered New York but before the establishment of any permanent European settlements, the main Iroquois tribes—the Onondaga, Oneida, Seneca, Cayuga, and Mohawk—established the League of the Five Nations. For the next 200 years, members of the League generally kept peace among themselves but made war on other tribes, using not only traditional weapons but also the guns they were able to get from the French, Dutch, and English. In 1715, a sixth nation joined the League—the Tuscarora, who had fled the British in North Carolina. For much of the 18th century, the Iroquois skillfully balanced competing French and British interests.

The first European known to have entered New York Harbor was the Florentine navigator Giovanni da Verrazano, on 17 April 1524. The Frenchman Samuel de Champlain began exploring the St. Lawrence River in 1603. Six years later, the English mariner Henry Hudson, in the service of the Dutch East India Company, entered New York Bay and sailed up the river that would later bear his name. The first permanent Dutch settlement was established in 1624, and New Amsterdam was founded in 1626, when Peter Minuit bought Manhattan (from the Indian word *manahatin,* "hill island") from the Indians for goods worth—as tradition has it—about $24.

Though small and weak, the Dutch colony—named New Netherland—was an annoyance to the English, interfering with their trade monopoly and forming a political barrier between New England and two other English colonies, Maryland and Virginia. In 1664, King Charles II claimed "all the land from the west side of the Connecticutte River to the East Side of De La Ware Bay" for his brother, the Duke of York and Albany (the future King James II), and the English took control after a peaceful surrender by the Dutch. Thus New Netherland became New York. It remained an English colony for the next 112 years, except for a period in 1673 when Dutch rule was briefly restored.

British Control

The first decades under the English were stormy. Leadership of the colony changed hands several times, reflecting political instability in England itself, as James became king and was then deposed in the Glorious Revolution of 1688. The succeeding decades were marked by conflict between the English and French and by the rising power of the provincial assembly in relations with the British crown. In 1756, the English determined to drive the French out of the region once and for all, defeating them decisively in 1760. The Treaty of Paris (1763), ending the French and Indian War, ceded almost all territory east of the Mississippi to England.

The signing of the Treaty of Paris was followed by English attempts to tighten control over the colonies, in New York as elsewhere. In 1774, after Paul Revere brought news of the Boston Tea Party to New York City, British tea was also dumped into that city's harbor. Nearly one-third of all battles during the Revolutionary War took place on New York soil. The action there began when troops under Ethan Allen captured Fort Ticonderoga in May 1775. The following year, George Washington's forces were driven from Long Island and Manhattan by the British, and New York City remained in British hands for the rest of the war. British General John Burgoyne was defeated in October 1777 at Saratoga, in a battle that is often considered the turning point of the war. Washington marched into New York City on 25 November 1785, the day the British evacuated their forces.

Statehood

On 6 February 1778, New York had become the second state to ratify the Articles of Confederation. After much debate, in which the Federalist Alexander Hamilton played a leading role, the state ratified the US Constitution (with amendments) on 26 July 1788. New York City served as the seat of the US government from 11 January 1785 to 12 August 1790, and the first US president, George Washington, was inaugurated in the city on 30 April 1789.

The end of the War of 1812 signaled the opening of an era of major economic expansion for the state, which was receiving large numbers of migrants from New England. New York was the site of the early 19th century's most ambitious engineering project: construction of the Erie Canal. Ground was broken for the canal in 1817, and the first vessels passed through the completed canal in 1825. The textile industry had established itself by the mid-1820s, and the dairy industry was thriving.

Commercial progress during this period was matched by social and cultural advancement. New York City became a center of literary activity during the 1820s. Slavery was abolished as of 4 July 1827, and New Yorkers soon took the lead in the growing antislavery movement. The first women's rights convention in the US was held in Seneca Falls in 1848. Also during the 1840s, the state saw the first of several great waves of European immigration.

1860–1930

The majority of New Yorkers voted for Abraham Lincoln in the presidential election of 1860, and New Yorkers were among the readiest recruits to the Union side in the Civil War. Enthusiasm for the conflict waned during the next two years, leading to civil unrest when the military draft reached New York City on 11 July 1863. But New York was not a wartime battleground, and overall the war and Reconstruction were very good for business.

The decades after the Civil War ushered in an era of extraordinary commercial growth, accompanied, however, by political corruption. This was the Gilded Age, during which entrepreneurs became multimillionaires and New York was transformed from an agricultural state to an industrial giant. The key to this transformation was the development of the railroads. The boom period for railroad construction reached its high point after 1867, when "Commodore" Cornelius Vanderbilt took over the New York Central. During the century's last two decades, corporate names that today are household words began to emerge: Westinghouse

Electric in 1886; General Electric (as Edison Electric) in 1889; Eastman Kodak in 1892. In 1882, another native New Yorker, John D. Rockefeller, formed the Standard Oil Trust. Although the trust would eventually be broken up, the Rockefeller family would help shape New York politics for many decades to come.

The period immediately following the Civil War also marked a new high in political influence for the Tammany Society (or "Tammany Hall"), headed by Democrat William March "Boss" Tweed, who effectively dominated New York City by buying votes and bribing legislators from 1857 until his exposure by the press in 1871. However, New York also produced outstanding and upright political leaders—many of whom went on to national prominence—during the nation's second century. Grover Cleveland, though born in New Jersey, became mayor of Buffalo, then governor of New York, and finally the 22d US president in 1885.

Theodore Roosevelt was governor of New York, then became US vice-president, and finally president of the US in 1901. In 1910, Charles Evans Hughes resigned the governorship to become an associate justice of the US Supreme Court. He also served as secretary of state, and in 1930 was appointed chief justice of the US. Alfred E. Smith was four times elected governor and in 1928 became the first Roman Catholic candidate to be nominated by a major party for the presidency of the US. That year saw the election of Franklin D. Roosevelt (FDR) as governor of New York.

1930s–1990s

The 1930s, a period of depression, ushered in a new wave of progressive government. From 1933 until 1945, FDR was in the White House. Roosevelt's successor as governor was Herbert H. Lehman, whose Little New Deal established the basic pattern of present state social welfare policies. The mayor of New York City at this time was the colorful and popular Fiorello H. La Guardia.

The decades since World War II have seen extraordinary expansion of New York social services, including construction of the state university system, but also a decline in the state's industry. The greatly increased scale of government in the 1970s brought on a financial crisis unheard of in its scope and implications. The city's short-term debt grew from nearly zero to about $6 billion between 1970 and 1975. Eventually a package totaling $4.5 billion in aid was needed to avoid bankruptcy.

From the late 1970s through the late 1980s, New York enjoyed an economic boom, especially in finance, insurance, real estate, and construction. Prosperity did not reach all sectors of the economy or the population, however. Manufacturing jobs declined by 30%. By 1984, 25% of the residents of New York City lived below the poverty level. The collapse of the stock market in October of 1987, in which the market plunged 36% in two months, signaled the end of the boom and the beginning of a recession.

Racial and ethnic tensions increased in the mid- and late 1980s. The most heavily publicized incidents involved the deaths of blacks at the hands of white attackers in the mostly white New York City neighborhoods of Howard Beach and Bensonhurst, and the accidental killing of a seven-year-old black boy by a Hasidic man in Crown Heights. Rumors that the Hasidim in the car that struck the boy and his cousin had received medical treatment before the black children were interpreted as evidence of preferential treatment of whites by police and other authorities.

12 STATE GOVERNMENT

The legislature consists of a 61-member senate and 150-member assembly. Senators and assembly members serve two-year terms and are elected in even-numbered years. Either senators or assembly members may introduce or amend a bill. To pass, a bill requires a majority vote in both houses. A two-thirds majority is required to override the governor's veto. The state's only elected executives are the governor, lieutenant governor, comptroller, and attorney general. Each serves a four-year term. The governor appoints the heads of 15 of the 20 major executive departments, 13 of them with the advice and consent of the senate.

A bill becomes law when passed by both houses of the legislature and signed by the governor. While the legislature is in session, a bill may also become law if the governor fails to act on it within ten days of its receipt. The governor may veto a bill or, if the legislature has adjourned, may kill a bill simply by taking no action on it for 30 days.

13 POLITICAL PARTIES

In 1994, the state had 4,256,952 registered Democrats, or 47% of all registered voters; 2,776,954 registered Republicans, or 31%; and 1,999,188 independents, or 22%. The Democratic power base was— and has remained—the big cities, especially New York City. The Republican Party's support comes from the state's rural counties, the smaller cities and towns, and the New York City suburbs (although not so much as in earlier decades). Minor parties have sometimes meant the difference between victory and defeat for major party candidates in state and national elections. James Buckley, of

New York's Conservative Party, was elected to the US Senate in 1970.

In the November 1980 presidential elections, Republican nominee Ronald Reagan (with Conservative Party backing) won the state's 41 electoral votes. Reagan carried the state again in 1984, despite the presence on the Democratic ticket of US Representative Geraldine Ferraro of Queens as the running mate of Walter Mondale. New Yorkers chose Democratic nominees Michael Dukakis and Bill Clinton in 1988 and 1992, respectively. Clinton captured 50% of the vote in 1992 while the incumbent, Republican George Bush, won 34% of the vote. Independent Ross Perot picked up 16%.

New York Presidential Vote by Political Parties, 1948–92

YEAR	NEW YORK WINNER	DEMOCRAT	LIBERAL[1]	REPUBLICAN	PROGRESSIVE[2]	SOCIALIST	SOCIALIST WORKERS
1948	Dewey (R)	2,557,642	222,562	2,841,163	509,559	40,879	2,675
1952	*Eisenhower (R)	2,687,890	416,711	3,952,815	64,211	2,664	2,212
1956	*Eisenhower (R)	2,458,212	292,557	4,340,340	—	—	—
1960	*Kennedy (D)	3,423,909	406,176	3,446,419	—		14,319
						SOC. LABOR	
1964	*Johnson (D)	4,570,670	342,432	2,243,559		6,118	3,228
					AMERICAN IND.[3]		
1968	Humphrey (D)	3,066,848	311,622	3,007,932	358,864	8,432	11,851
					CONSERVATIVE[4]		
1972	*Nixon (R)	2,767,956	183,128	3,824,642	368,136	4,530	7,797
						LIBERTARIAN	
1976	*Carter (D)	3,244,165	145,393	2,825,913	2724,878	12,197	6,996
							RIGHT TO LIFE
1980	*Reagan (R)	2,728,372	467,801	2,637,700	256,131	52,648	24,159
1984	*Reagan (R)	3,001,285	118,324	3,376,519	288,244	11,949	—
							NEW ALLIANCE
1988	Dukakis (D)	3,255,487	92,395	2,838,414	243,457	12,109	15,845
1992[5]	*Clinton (D)	3,346,894	97,556	2,041,690	177,000	13,451	15,472

* Won US presidential election.
[1] Supported Democratic candidate except in 1980, when John Anderson ran on the Liberal line.
[2] Ran in the state as the American Labor Party.
[3] Appeared on the state ballot as the Courage Party.
[4] Supported Republican candidate.
[5] Independent candidate Ross Perot received 1,090,721 votes.

Democrat Mario M. Cuomo was defeated in his run for a fourth term as governor in November 1994 by Republican George Pataki. New York's senators were Alphonse D'Amato, a Republican serving his third term, and Democrat Daniel Moynihan who was also serving his third term. After the 1994 elections, New York's US Representatives included 16 Democrats and 13 Republicans. Republicans held 35 seats in the state senate while Democrats held 26. In the state assembly there were 100 Democrats and 50 Republicans. In November 1993, New York City Mayor David Dinkins, a Democrat and New York's first black mayor (in office since 1990), was defeated by a Republican, Rudolph Giuliani.

14 LOCAL GOVERNMENT

The state constitution, endorsing the principle of home rule, recognizes many different levels of local government. In 1982, New York had 62 counties, 620 municipal governments, 929 towns, and 714 school districts. With the exception of some counties within New York City, each county has a county attorney and a district attorney, a sheriff, a treasurer, and other officers.

Cities are contained within counties, with one outstanding exception: New York City is made up of five counties, one for each of its five boroughs. Traditionally, counties are run by an elected board of supervisors or county legislature; however, a growing number of counties have vested increased powers in a single elected county executive.

Towns are run by a town board. The most important board member is the town supervisor, who is the board's presiding officer and acts as town treasurer. A group of people within a town or towns may also incorporate themselves into a village, with their own elected mayor and elected board of trustees. Some villages have administrators or managers. The constitution grants the state legislature the power to decide which taxes the local governments may levy and how much debt they may incur.

New York City is governed by a mayor and city council, but much practical power resides in the Board of Estimate. On this board sit the city's three top elected officials—the mayor, comptroller, and City Council president. The board also includes the five borough presidents. New York City government is further complicated by the fact that certain essential services are provided not by the city itself but by independent "authorities."

15 JUDICIAL SYSTEM

New York's highest court is the court of appeals, in Albany, with appeals jurisdiction only, consisting of a chief judge and six associate judges. Below the court of appeals is the supreme court, which in 1994 consisted of 597 justices in 12 judicial districts. The supreme court of New York State does not sit as one body; instead, most supreme court justices are assigned original jurisdiction in civil and criminal matters, while 24 justices are assigned to one of the court's 4 appeals divisions.

The New York court of claims, which sits in Albany, consisted in 1992 of 18 judges appointed by the governor to nine-year terms, along with 46 judges sitting as acting Supreme Court justices in felony trials. This special trial court hears civil cases involving claims by or against the state.

Outside New York City, each county has its own county court to handle criminal cases, although some are delegated to be handled by lower courts. Many counties have a surrogate's court to handle such matters as wills and estate, and each county has its own family court. A county's district attorney has authority in criminal matters. Most cities (including New York City) have their own court systems. Village police justices and town justices of the peace handle minor violations and other routine matters.

FBI data for New York showed a crime rate of 5,070.6 per 100,000 population in 1994. In 1993, 64,569 inmates were in state and federal facilities.

16 MIGRATION

Since the early 1800s, New York has been the primary port of entry for Europeans coming to the US. The Statue of Liberty—dedicated in 1886 and beckoning "your tired, your poor, /Your huddled masses yearning to breathe free" to the shores of America—was often the immigrants' first glimpse of America. The first stop for some 20 million immigrants in the late 19th and early 20th centuries was Ellis Island (now a national park, administered by New Jersey).

The first great wave of European immigrants arrived in the 1840s, impelled by the potato famine in Ireland. They were followed by Germans and, later in the century, Eastern European Jews and Italians. Migration from the 1840s onward followed a recurring cycle: as one group dispersed from New York City throughout the state and the nation, it was replaced by a new wave of immigrants.

Yankees, arriving from New England between 1790 and 1840, made up the first great wave of domestic migration. There was a slow, steady migration of blacks from slave states to New York before the Civil War, but massive black migration to New York, and especially to New York City, began during World War I and continued well into the 1960s.

The third great wave of domestic migration came after World War II, from Puerto Rico. By 1960, the census showed well over 600,000 New Yorkers of Puerto Rican birth or parentage. As of 1990, Puerto Rican-born New Yorkers numbered 143,974. Many other Caribbean natives—especially Dominicans, Jamaicans, and Haitians—followed.

The fourth and most recent domestic migratory trend is unique in New York history—an outward migration from New York to other states since the 1960s, mostly by white residents and mostly from New York City. According to a private study, a net total of 700,000 whites left the state during 1975-80, while only 50,000 blacks left during the same period. White emigrants went to suburban areas of New Jersey and Connecticut, but many also went to two Sunbelt states, Florida and California.

Intrastate migration has followed the familiar pattern of rural to urban, and then urban to suburban. By 1990, 84% of all New Yorkers lived in urban areas, and the suburban population has grown steadily. The number of New Yorkers living in suburbs nearly doubled between 1950 (3,538,620, or 24% of all state residents) and 1980 (7,461,161, or 42%).

17 ECONOMY

No other state—and few countries—can match New York in the value of its banking, securities, and communications industries. By the mid-1980s, the state was a national power in printing and publishing, fashion and apparel, instruments, machinery, and electronic equipment.

New York State cannot be economically healthy if New York City does not remain so. However, the city's manufacturing industries and its skilled laborers have been emigrating to the suburbs and to other states since World War II. Between 1969 and 1976, the city lost 600,000 jobs. In 1975, short-term aid from Congress, the state government, and the labor union pension funds were needed to save the city from default.

The early 1980s saw New York's fortunes on the rise. A shift in dependence from manufacturing to services, and particularly to finance, helped the state and New York City weather the 1981–82 recession. In 1983, the state's three largest industrial and commercial employers (excluding public utilities) were all banks based in New York City. Financial services led the city's economic expansion, adding 100,000 jobs from 1980 to 1987.

The expanding economy moved New York from tenth place in per capita (per person) income in 1980 to fifth place in 1990, when the state's per capita income reached $21,073.

New York's economy not only grew during the 1980s but also underwent a restructuring. Manufacturing witnessed a decline in its share of total employment from 20% in 1980 to 14% in 1990. However, business-related, health care, education, and social services grew 52% during the decade. The surge in financial services employment ended with the crash of the stock market in October of 1987, in which stock prices dropped 36% in two months. The market crash prompted the layoff of 9,000 employees on Wall Street and a downsizing of the banking and securities industries.

18 INCOME

With an income per capita (per person) of $25,731 in 1994, New York ranked third among the 50 states. In 1993, 16.4% of the state's population had incomes below the poverty level. As of 1990, New York also had 74 residents whose assets each exceeded $260 million, more than any other state. Although personal per capita income in the area of New York City exceeds that of the state and much of the nation, in 1993 the cost of living in the New York City area was estimated at more than double that of the national average.

19 INDUSTRY

Until the 1970s, New York was the nation's foremost industrial state, ranking first in practically every general category. However, by 1982, it ranked third in value of shipments and new spending, and manufacturing jobs declined by 2% between 1982 and 1987. In 1992, New York ranked sixth in value of shipments, at $154.2 billion. Important industries are instruments and related products, industrial machinery and equipment, electronic and electric equipment, printing and publishing, and textiles.

The Buffalo region, with its excellent transport facilities and abundant power supply, is the main center for heavy industry in the state. Factories in the region manufacture iron and steel, aircraft, automobile parts and accessories, and machinery, as well as flour, animal feed, and various chemicals. However, the Buffalo area's biggest private industrial employer, Bethlehem Steel, closed its Lackawanna plant in 1983.

Light industry is distributed throughout the state. Rochester is especially well known for its photographic (Kodak) and optical equipment (Bausch & Lomb), and office machines (Xerox). The city is the world headquarters of the Eastman Kodak Company, a world leader in photography. The state's leadership in electronic equipment is in large part attributable to the International Business Machines Corporation (IBM), which ranked as the fourth-leading US industrial corporation in 1992. The presence of two large General Electric plants has long made Schenectady a leader in the manufacture of electric machinery.

New York City excels not only in the apparel and publishing trades but also in food processing, meat packing, chemicals, leather goods, metal products, and many other manufactures. In addition, the city serves as headquarters for many large industrial corporations whose manufacturing activities often take place entirely outside New York. Two of the largest US industrial corporations—Philip Morris and RJR Nabisco Holdings—had their headquarters in New York City in 1992.

20 LABOR

The civilian labor force totaled 8,571,000 in 1994, of whom 6.9% were unemployed. Some 28% of all workers in the state were union members in 1994, making it the most heavily unionized state.

21 AGRICULTURE

New York ranked 27th in farm income in 1994, with cash receipts from farming at $2,857,581,000. About 66% came from livestock products, mostly dairy goods. The state ranked second in the production of corn for silage and apples, third in grapes, and fourth in pears. New York is an important dairy state, but urbanization has reduced its overall agricultural output. In 1994, there were only 36,000 farms, and farm employment was only 2.2% of the state total.

The west-central part of the state is the most intensively farmed. Chautauqua County, in the extreme southwest, leads the state in grape production, while Wayne County, along Lake Ontario, leads in apples and cherries. The dairy industry is concentrated in the St. Lawrence Valley. Grain growing dominates the plains between Syracuse and Buffalo. Potatoes

© NYS Department of Economic Development. 1975

A farm near Ithaca, New York.

are grown mostly in Suffolk County, on eastern Long Island.

Production of leading field crops in 1994 (all figures in thousands) included hay, 3,961 tons; corn for grain, 68,440 bushels; corn for silage, 8,216 tons; oats, 7,040 bushels; and wheat, 6,095 bushels. Leading vegetable crops were cabbage, onions, sweet corn, and carrots. State vineyards produced 191,000 tons of grapes for wine and juice in 1994, while the apple crop totaled 1 billion pounds.

22 DOMESTICATED ANIMALS

New York is a leading dairy state. In 1994, New York was third in the US in milk and cheese production. Of the nearly

$1.9 billion earned for livestock and livestock products, 52.4% came from dairy products.

The St. Lawrence Valley is the state's leading cattle-raising region, followed by the Mohawk Valley and Wyoming County, in western New York. At the end of 1994, the state had 1,450,000 head of cattle, and 710,000 milk cows. Other livestock included 72,000 hogs, 72,000 sheep, and 5,200,000 chickens.

23 FISHING

Fishing, though an attraction for tourists and sport-fishers, plays only a minor role in the economic life of the state. In 1992, the commercial catch was 50,112,000 pounds. Important species for commercial use are menhaden and, among shellfish, clams and oysters. Montauk, on the eastern end of Long Island, was the state's leading fishing port in 1992, at 14,100,000 pounds. In recent decades, the Department of Environmental Conservation has taken an active role in restocking New York's inland waters.

24 FORESTRY

About 60% of New York's surface area is forestland. The most densely forested counties are Hamilton, Essex, and Warren in the Adirondacks, and Delaware, Greene, and Ulster in the Catskills. In 1994, the Division of Lands and Forests harvested timber from 15,736 acres (6,371 hectares) of state forestland, bringing in revenue of $3,885,340.

The state Department of Environmental Conservation manages about 3,000,000 acres (1,200,000 hectares) in the Catskills and Adirondacks as Forest Preserves, and an additional 800,000 acres in State Forests and Wildlife Management Areas (where timber harvesting is allowed as part of their management plans). The Saratoga Tree Nursery distributed 2,100,000 tree seedlings and 275,000 shrub seedlings in 1994.

25 MINING

The value of nonfuel mineral production in New York in 1994 was estimated to be $871 million. Leading mineral commodities in terms of value were crushed stone, salt, portland cement, construction sand and gravel, zinc, and wollastonite.

Other commodities produced included masonry cement, clays, garnet, gypsum, peat, industrial sand, dimension stone, talc, and byproduct lead and silver. The combined value of cement, abrasive garnet, crude gypsum, lead, industrial sand and gravel, silver, talc and pyrophyllite, wollastonite, zinc, and peat in 1992 was $248,899,000. Nationally, the state ranked 14th overall in the value of nonfuel minerals produced. New York was one of only two states where garnet was mined.

26 ENERGY AND POWER

About 20% of the state's annual electric power output comes from hydroelectric plants. Almost 20% comes from oil-fired units, 20% from coal-fired units, 16% from gas-fired units, and 23% from nuclear power plants. Electrical output totaled 106.3 billion kilowatt hours in 1993.

The largest nonfederal hydroelectric plant in the US is the Niagara Power Project, which had a capacity of 2,400,000 kilowatts at the end of 1991. Sales of public and private electric power totaled 129.4 billion kilowatt hours in 1991, of which 36% went to commercial users, 24% to industrial purchasers, 30% to residential users, and 10% for other purposes. Electric bills for New York City are the highest in the nation. Energy expenditures were $1,599 per capita (per person) in 1992.

Oil output in 1992 was 403,000 barrels—a tiny fraction of the national total. Because New York has a large number of motor vehicles and because more than half of all occupied housing units in the state are heated by oil, the state is a very large importer of petroleum products. The state's estimated natural gas reserves as of December 1991 were 331 billion cubic feet. Net gas marketed production in 1993 totaled 21 billion cubic feet. New York had six nuclear power plants as of 1993.

27 COMMERCE

New York had 1992 wholesale sales that totaled $287.7 billion; retail sales in 1993 were $127.5 billion; service establishment receipts in 1992 were $115.9 billion. The state's long border with Canada, its important ports on Lakes Erie and Ontario, and its vast harbor on New York Bay ensure it a major role in US foreign trade. Exports totaled $22.6 billion in 1992, fourth among the states.

28 PUBLIC FINANCE

New York State and New York City have the second- and third-largest budgets (behind California), respectively, of all states or municipalities in the US. The estimated state revenues for 1993 were $78,209,000,000; expenditures were $74,280,000,000.

As of 1993, the total state debt in New York was $59.5 billion, or $3,262 per capita (per person).

29 TAXATION

On a per capita (per person) basis, New York's state taxes are well above the national average, but far from the highest. State tax revenues rank second to Alaska's. Personal income tax is the state's largest source of revenue. The state imposes a corporate income tax and a 4% sales tax, but cities and towns may levy an additional tax. Other taxes include an estate tax, charges on motor fuel, cigarettes, alcoholic beverages, petroleum gross receipts, and motor vehicle and highway usage. State tax receipts in 1991 totaled $28.3 billion. New York ranked second to California in federal taxes paid in 1992. The state tax burden was $114.3 billion.

30 HEALTH

While New York has some of the finest hospital and medical education facilities in the US, it also has large numbers of the needy with serious health problems. The state ranks above the national average in deaths due to heart disease and cancer, but below the national average in deaths due to cerebrovascular diseases, suicide, and accidents.

Major public health problems in the 1980s included drug abuse, alcoholism, venereal disease, and acquired immune deficiency syndrome (AIDS). New York City was heavily hit by the outbreak of AIDS, first recognized in 1981. As of 1994, nearly 83,200 of all reported AIDS cases (19.5% of the US total) were in New York, more than in any other state.

The Division of Substance Abuse Services of the Department of Mental Hygiene funds and assists over 400 community-based programs. In 1993, New York State had 231 community hospitals, with 77,400 beds. Medical personnel licensed to practice in the state included 60,800 active nonfederal physicians (1993) and 159,300 nurses. The average hospital cost per inpatient day was $784 in 1993, and the average cost per stay was $7,716. Some 13.9%

of state residents did not have health insurance in 1993.

31 HOUSING

As of 1990, about 46% of New York's housing units were in New York City. A striking feature of housing in the state is the dominance of multi-unit dwellings. New York State had the lowest percentage of owner-occupied housing (47.9%) of all states in the US in 1990. From 1990 to 1992, 27,200 new housing units were completed in the New York City area, of which less than one-third were one-family houses. During the same period, however, nearly two-thirds of the new units completed in the greater New York City area (including suburban New Jersey and Connecticut) were one-family houses.

In 1990, the median monthly cost for an owner with a mortgage in the New York City area of New York was $1,147 and $400 for an owner without a mortgage. The median rent was $579 per month. Characteristic of housing in New York is a system of rent controls that began in 1943.

The state's tight housing market was not helped by a slump in housing construction from the mid-1970s to the mid-1980s. In New York City, more units were demolished than built every year from 1974 to 1981. In 1993, 28,604 new units valued at $3.6 billion were authorized. The overall decline in construction was coupled with a drastic drop in new public housing.

32 EDUCATION

The educational establishment of New York State is larger and better funded than that of most countries. During 1992, public school systems in the state received a total of $21 billion. New York also has one of the nation's largest public university systems and an extensive system of private schools and universities. The percentage of high school graduates—77.9% in 1990—among New Yorkers age 25 and older was slightly above the US average. The percentage of New York college graduates—23.7%—was above the US average.

In the fall of 1993, about 2,723,000 students were enrolled in public elementary and secondary schools in the state. Public schools in the state employed about 188,500 classroom teachers in the fall of 1994. New York State had 2,155 nonpublic elementary and secondary schools in the fall of 1992, with enrollment of 469,357. Expenditures on education averaged $8,794 per pupil (third in the nation) in 1993.

There were 250 institutions of higher learning in 1992/93. Enrollment in all institutions of higher learning totaled 997,000 in the fall of 1992. There are two massive public university systems: the State University of New York (SUNY) and the City University of New York (CUNY). In 1992, SUNY was the largest university system in the country, with a total enrollment of 396,006. CUNY's total degree-credit enrollment in the fall of 1992 was 192,964. Under an open-enrollment policy adopted in 1970, every New York City resident with a high school diploma is guaranteed the chance to earn a college degree within the CUNY system.

Columbia University, the oldest private university in the state, had 18,371 students in 1992/93; another 2,200 (all women) were enrolled in Barnard College. Other major private institutions are Cornell University in Ithaca, Fordham University in Manhattan, New York University in Manhattan, Syracuse University, and the University of Rochester. Among the state's many smaller but highly distinguished institutions are the Juilliard School of Music (New York City), the New School for Social Research (New York City), Sarah Lawrence College (Bronxville), Vassar College (Poughkeepsie), and Yeshiva University (New York City).

33 ARTS

New York City is the cultural capital of the state, and leads the nation in both the creative and the performing arts. The state's foremost arts center is Lincoln Center for the Performing Arts, in Manhattan, which includes Avery Fisher Hall, home of the New York Philharmonic, and the Metropolitan Opera House. The New York State Theater presents both the New York City Opera and the New York City Ballet. The best-known arts center outside New York City is the Saratoga Performing Arts Center at Saratoga Springs. Classical music, opera, and plays are also performed at the Chautauqua Festival. The state of New York generated $449,993,037 in federal and state funds to support arts programs from 1987 to 1991.

In addition to its many museums, New York City has more than 350 galleries devoted to the visual arts. The city's most famous artists' district is Greenwich Village. During the late 1940s and early 1950s, abstract painters—including Jackson Pollock, Mark Rothko, and Willem de Kooning—helped make the city a center of modern art.

The emergence of New York as the center of the US publishing and communications industries attracted writers from across the country and the world. The growth of the Broadway stage made New York City a vital forum for playwriting, songwriting, and theatrical production. There are more than 35 Broadway theaters—large theaters in midtown Manhattan that present full-scale, sometimes lavish productions with top-ranked performers.

New York's leading symphony orchestra is the New York Philharmonic, whose history dates back to 1842. Leading US and foreign orchestras and soloists appear at both Avery Fisher Hall and Carnegie Hall. Important orchestras outside New York City include the Buffalo Philharmonic, the Rochester Philharmonic, and the Eastman Philharmonia, the orchestra of the Eastman School of Music (University of Rochester).

New York City is one of the world centers of ballet. Of special renown is the New York City Ballet. Many other ballet companies, including the American Ballet Theatre and the Alvin Ailey American Dance Theatre, make regular appearances in New York. Rochester, Syracuse, Cooperstown,

The Metropolitan Museum in New York City.

Chautauqua, and Binghamton have opera companies, and Lake George has an opera festival. Jazz and popular artists perform at more than 60 night spots in New York City. The New York State Council on the Arts is the nation's leading state arts-funding institution.

34 LIBRARIES AND MUSEUMS

New York State has three of the world's largest libraries, and New York City has several of the world's most famous museums. In 1991, the New York State Library in Albany coordinated 23 public library systems covering every county in the state, with book holdings of 63,819,417 volumes and a combined circulation of 116,716,286 volumes.

Among the leading public library systems as of 1991 were the New York Public Library, the Brooklyn Public Library, the Suffolk Cooperative system, and the Buffalo and Erie County system. The New York Public Library (NYPL) is the most complete municipal library system in the world. The library's main building, at 5th Avenue and 42d Street, is one of the city's best-known landmarks. Two private university libraries—at Columbia University and Cornell University—rank among the world's major libraries.

There are about 595 museums in New York State. In addition, some 300 sites of historic importance are maintained by local historical societies. Of the major art

Photo credit: Larry White.

Exterior view of Radio City Music Hall.

The sciences are represented by the American Museum of Natural History, the Hayden Planetarium, and the New York Botanical Garden and New York Zoological Society Park (Bronx Zoo). The New York State Museum in Albany contains natural history collections and historical artifacts. Buffalo has several museums of note, including the Albright-Knox Art Gallery (for contemporary art), the Buffalo Museum of Science, and the Buffalo and Erie County Historical Society museum.

35 COMMUNICATIONS

As of March 1993, 93.7% of New York's 6,875,000 occupied housing units had telephones. New York State had 165 AM stations and 293 FM stations operating in 1993. New York City operates its own radio stations, WNYC-AM and -FM, devoted largely to classical music and educational programming. There were 56 television stations (including 14 noncommercial educational) in the state in 1993; of these, 9 were operating in New York City.

museums in New York City, the Metropolitan Museum of Art has more than one million art objects and paintings from practically every period and culture. The Cloisters, a branch of the Metropolitan Museum, is devoted entirely to medieval art and architecture. Other notable museums are the Frick collection and the Whitney Museum of American Art. Two famous modern collections belong to the Museum of Modern Art and the Solomon R. Guggenheim Museum, which was designed by Frank Lloyd Wright in a distinctive spiral pattern.

The city is the headquarters for most of the major US television networks, including the American Broadcasting Company (ABC), Columbia Broadcasting System (CBS), and National Broadcasting Company (NBC). The New York metropolitan area's public broadcasting affiliate, WNET, is a leading producer of programs for the network. As of 1993, 31 large cable television systems served the state.

36 PRESS

New York is the center of the US newspaper, magazine, and book-publishing industries. All of New York City's major newspapers have claims to fame. The *New York Times*, the nation's "newspaper of record," is highly influential in political and cultural circles and widely circulated to US libraries. The *New York Post*, founded in 1801, is the oldest US newspaper published continuously without changing its name. The *New York Daily News* has the largest daily and Sunday circulation of all general-interest newspapers in the US. The *Wall Street Journal*, published Monday through Friday, is a major nationwide news source, presenting mostly business news in four regional editions.

In 1994, New York had 21 morning newspapers, 52 evening papers, two all-day papers, and 33 Sunday editions. Leading papers in New York City, with their average daily circulations in 1994 include the *New York Times* (1,209,225); the *Wall Street Journal* (1,852,959, Eastern edition only); the *Daily News* (781,796); and the *New York Post* (644,738). Leading papers outside New York City include the *Buffalo News* (314,830); the *Albany Times-Union* (108,954); the *Syracuse Post-Standard* (88,392); and the *Syracuse Herald-Journal* (85,842).

Many leading US magazines are published in New York City, including the news magazines *Time* and *Newsweek*, and business journals *Fortune, Forbes,* and *Business Week. Reader's Digest* is published in Pleasantville. The *New Yorker* carries up-to-date listings of cultural events and exhibitions in New York City, and its journalism, criticism, fiction, and cartoons have long made it a literary standard-bearer for the entire nation. *New York* magazine was the model for a new type of state and local magazine. Another weekly, the *Village Voice* became the model for a host of alternative or "underground" newspapers.

New York City is also the center of the nation's book-publishing industry and home to such publishers as McGraw–Hill, Macmillan, Simon & Schuster, and Random House.

37 TOURISM, TRAVEL, AND RECREATION

New York State is a popular destination for both domestic and foreign travelers. Although New York City is the primary attraction, each of the major state regions has features of interest. Over seven million foreign tourists per year visit the state.

A typical visit to New York City might include a boat ride to the Statue of Liberty; visits to the World Trade Center, the Empire State Building, the United Nations headquarters, Rockefeller Center, and the New York Stock Exchange; walking tours of the Bronx Zoo, Chinatown, and the theater district; and a sampling of the city's many museums, restaurants, shops, and shows.

Second to New York City as a magnet for tourists comes Long Island, with its beaches, racetracks, and other recreational facilities. Attractions of the Hudson Valley include the US Military Academy (West Point), the Franklin D. Roosevelt home at

© NYS Department of Economic Development. 1970

Niagara Falls, one of New York's major tourist attractions.

Hyde Park, and Bear Mountain State Park. North of Hudson Valley is Albany, with its massive government center, often called the Empire State Plaza; Saratoga Springs, home of an arts center, racetrack, and spa; and the Adirondack region, with its forest preserve, summer and winter resorts, and abundant hunting and fishing.

Scenic sites in central New York include the resorts of the Catskills and the scenic marvels of the Finger Lakes region. Farther west lie the Genesee Valley and Letchworth State Park; and Buffalo and Niagara Falls. South of the Niagara Frontier is the Southwest Gateway, among whose dominant features are Chautauqua Lake and Allegany State Park, the state's largest.

38 SPORTS

New York has nine major league professional sports teams: the New York Yankees and the New York Mets of major league baseball; the New York Giants, the New York Jets, and the Buffalo Bills of the National Football League; the New York Knickerbockers (usually called the Knicks) of the National Basketball Association; and the New York Islanders, the New York Rangers, and the Buffalo Sabres of the National Hockey League.

Three New York teams moved to New Jersey during the 1970s and 1980s: the Nets in basketball and the Giants and Jets in football. The Giants and Jets remained, in name, New York teams (unlike the Nets who are now the New Jersey Nets), although the moves remain controversial.

Horse-racing is important to New York State, both as a sport attraction and because of the tax revenues that betting generates. The main thoroughbred race tracks are Aqueduct in Queens, Belmont in Nassau County, and the Saratoga Race Course. Belmont is the home of the Belmont Stakes, one of the three jewels in the Triple Crown of US racing. New York City hosts several major professional tennis tournaments every year, including the US open in Flushing and the WCT Invitational in Forest Hills.

In collegiate sports, basketball is perhaps most popular. Historically, the City College of New York produced many nationally ranked teams. The New York City marathon, which is held in October, has become one of the world's largest, most prestigious marathons in the world.

39 FAMOUS NEW YORKERS

New York State has been the home of five US presidents, eight US vice-presidents (three of whom also became president), many statesmen of national and international repute, and a large number of writers and entertainers. Martin Van Buren (1782–1862), the eighth US president, became governor of New York in 1828. He was elected to the vice-presidency as a Democrat under Andrew Jackson in 1832, and succeeded Jackson in the election of 1836. The 13th US president, Millard Fillmore (1800–74), was elected vice-president under Zachary Taylor in 1848. He became president in 1850 when Taylor died.

New York's other US presidents had more distinguished careers. Grover Cleveland (1837–1908) served as mayor of Buffalo and as governor of New York before his election to his first presidential term in 1884. He was again elected president in 1892. Theodore Roosevelt (1858–1919), a Republican, was elected governor in 1898. He won election as vice-president under William McKinley in 1900, and became the nation's 26th president after McKinley was murdered in 1901. Reelected in 1904, he was awarded the Nobel Peace Prize in 1906 for helping to settle a war between Russia and Japan.

Franklin Delano Roosevelt (FDR, 1882–1945), a fifth cousin of Theodore Roosevelt, was elected governor of New York in 1928 and served until 1932, when US voters chose him as their 32d president. Reelected in 1936, 1940, and 1944, FDR is the only president ever to have served more than two full terms in office. Roosevelt guided the US through the Great Depression and World War II, and his New Deal programs greatly enlarged the federal government's role in social welfare.

Two well-known US vice-presidents, though not born in New York, were New Yorkers by the time they became vice-president: Aaron Burr (1756–1836) and Nelson Aldrich Rockefeller (1908–79). Two native New Yorkers have become chief justices of the US: John Jay (1745–1829) and Charles Evans Hughes (1862–1948). Ruth Bader Ginsberg (b. 1933) was President Bill Clinton's first appointment to the Supreme Court.

Photo credit: Larry White.

Yankee Stadium.

Prominent US senators have included Robert F. Kennedy (1925–68), who, though born in Massachusetts, was elected to represent New York in 1964; Jacob K. Javits (1904–86), who served continuously in the Senate from 1957 through 1980; and Daniel Patrick Moynihan (b.1927), who has represented New York since 1977. Colin Powell (b. 1937), the first African-American to lead the US Armed Forces, attended the City University of New York. Alan Greenspan (b. 1926), a chairman of the Federal Reserve Bank, was born in New York City.

Governors who made important contributions to the history of the state include Alfred E. Smith (1873–1944); Herbert H. Lehman (1878–1963); W.

Averell Harriman (1891–1986), who also held many US diplomatic posts; and Thomas E. Dewey (1902–71). Mario M. Cuomo (b.1932) served three terms as governor from 1982–94. One of the best-known and best-loved mayors in New York City history was Fiorello H. La Guardia (1882–1947), a reformer who held the office from 1934 to 1945. Edward I. Koch (b.1924) was first elected to the mayoralty in 1977 and served until 1989, when he was succeeded by David Dinkins (b.1927), New York City's first black mayor.

Native New Yorkers have won Nobel prizes in every category. Winners of the Nobel Peace Prize besides Theodore Roosevelt were Elihu Root in 1912 and

Frank B. Kellogg in 1929. The lone winner of the Nobel Prize for literature was Eugene O'Neill (1888–1953) in 1936. The chemistry prize was awarded to William Howard Stein (1911–80) in 1972. Melvin Schwartz (b. New York City, 1932) was a co-recipient of the 1988 Nobel prize in physics. New Yorkers awarded the Nobel Prize for physiology/medicine include Rosalyn Sussman Yalow (b.1921) in 1977, and Hamilton O. Smith (b.1931) in 1978. The Nobel Prize for economic science was won by Milton Friedman (b.1912) in 1976.

New York is also the birthplace of national labor leader George Meany (1894–1980) and economist Walter Heller (1915–87). Other distinguished state residents were Mormon leader Brigham Young (b.Vermont, 1801–77), botanist Asa Gray (1810–88), inventor-entrepreneur George Westinghouse (1846–1914), and Jonas E. Salk (b.1914), developer of the poliomyelitis vaccine.

Writers born in New York include the storyteller and satirist Washington Irving (1783–1859); poets Walt Whitman (1819–92) and Ogden Nash (1902–71); and playwrights Eugene O'Neill (1888–1953), Arthur Miller (b.1915), and Neil Simon (b.1927). Two of America's greatest novelists were New Yorkers: Herman Melville (1819–91) and Henry James (1843–1916). Other novelists include James Fenimore Cooper (b.New Jersey, 1789–1851), Henry Miller (1891–1980), James Michener (b.1907), J(erome) D(avid) Salinger (b.1919), Joseph Heller (b.1923), and James Baldwin (1924–87). New York City has produced two famous journalist-commentators, Walter Lippmann (1889–1974) and William F. Buckley, Jr. (b.1925).

Broadway is the showcase of American drama and the birthplace of the American musical theater, whose pioneers include Jerome Kern (1885–1945), Oscar Hammerstein II (1895–1960), Richard Rodgers (1902–79), Alan Jay Lerner (1918–86), and Stephen Sondheim (b.1930). *Porgy and Bess,* by George Gershwin (1898–1937), raised the musical to its highest artistic form. Other important US composers who were New Yorkers include Irving Berlin (b.Russia, 1888–1989), Aaron Copland (1900–90), Elliott Carter (b.1908), and William Schuman (1910–92). New York was the adopted home of ballet director and choreographer George Balanchine (b.Russia, 1904–83). Leaders in the visual arts include the popular illustrator Norman Rockwell (1894–1978), Willem de Kooning (b.Netherlands, 1904), and the photographer Margaret Bourke-White (1906–71).

Many of America's best-loved entertainers come from the state. A small sampling would include comedians Groucho Marx (Julius Marx, 1890–1977), George Burns (b.1896), Lucille Ball (1911–89), and Danny Kaye (David Daniel Kominsky, 1913–87); comedian-film directors Mel Brooks (Melvin Kaminsky, b.1926) and Woody Allen (Allen Konigsberg, b.1935); and stage and screen stars Humphrey Bogart (1899–1957), James Cagney (b.1904-1986), Zero Mostel (Samuel Joel Mostel, 1915–77), and Lauren Bacall (Betty Joan Perske, b.1924).

Also prominent are pop, jazz, and folk singers Lena Horne (b.1917), Pete Seeger (b.1919), Sammy Davis, Jr. (1925–90), Harry Belafonte (b.1927), Joan Baez (b.1941), Barbra Streisand (b.1942), and Mariah Carey (b.1969). Opera stars include Robert Merrill (b.1919), Maria Callas (Maria Kalogeropoulos, 1923–77), and Beverly Sills (Belle Silverman, b.1929). Also noteworthy are film directors George Cukor (1899–1983) and Stanley Kubrick (b.1928).

Among many prominent sports figures born in New York are first-baseman Lou Gehrig (1903–41), football coach Vince Lombardi (1913–70), pitcher Sanford "Sandy" Koufax (b.1935), and basketball stars Kareem Abdul-Jabbar (Lew Alcindor, b.1947) and Julius Erving (b.1950). Orel Leonard Hershiser IV (b. 1958), who set the record for most consecutive scoreless innings pitched, was born in Buffalo, New York.

40 BIBLIOGRAPHY

Auletta, Ken. *The Streets Were Paved with Gold.* New York: Random House, 1980.

Bliven, Bruce. *New York.* New York: Norton, 1981.

Ellis, David M. *New York: State and City.* Ithaca: Cornell University Press, 1979.

Howe, Irving. *World of Our Fathers.* New York: Harcourt Brace Jovanovich, 1976.

NORTH CAROLINA

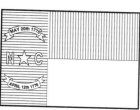

State of North Carolina

ORIGIN OF STATE NAME: Named in honor of King Charles I of England.
NICKNAME: The Tarheel State.
CAPITAL: Raleigh.
ENTERED UNION: 21 November 1789 (12th).
SONG: "The Old North State."
MOTTO: *Esse quam videri* (To be rather than to seem).
FLAG: Adjacent to the fly of two equally sized bars, red above and white below, is a blue union containing a white star in the center, flanked by the letters N and C in gold. Above and below the star are two gold scrolls, the upper one reading "May 20th 1775," the lower one "April 12th 1776."
OFFICIAL SEAL: Liberty, clasping a constitution and holding aloft on a pole a liberty cap, stands on the left, while Plenty sits besides a cornucopia on the right; behind them, mountains run to the sea, on which a three-masted ship appears. "May 20, 1775" appears above the figures; the words "The Great Seal of the State of North Carolina" and the state motto surround the whole.
MAMMAL: Gray squirrel.
BIRD: Cardinal.
FISH: Channel bass.
REPTILE: Eastern box turtle.
INSECT: Honeybee.
FLOWER: Dogwood.
TREE: Pine.
SHELL: Scotch bonnet.
PRECIOUS STONE: Emerald.
ROCK: Granite.
TIME: 7 AM EST = noon GMT.

1 LOCATION AND SIZE

Located in the southeastern US, North Carolina ranks 28th in size among the 50 states. The total area of North Carolina is 52,669 square miles (136,413 square kilometers). North Carolina extends 503 miles (810 kilometers) east-west; the state's maximum north-south extension is 187 miles (301 kilometers). The total boundary line of North Carolina is 1,270 miles (2,044 kilometers).

2 TOPOGRAPHY

North Carolina has three major topographic regions. The coastal plain is flat and often swampy near the ocean and more elevated further inland. Except for sand hills to the southwest, this region constitutes the state's principal farming country.

The Piedmont is a rolling plateau of red clay soil. The fall line, a sudden change in elevation, separates the piedmont from the coastal plain and produces numerous rapids in the rivers that flow between the regions. North Carolina's westernmost region contains the highest and most rugged portion of the Appalachian chain. The two major ranges are the Blue Ridge and Great Smoky Mountains. Mt. Mitchell, at 6,684 feet (2,037 meters), is the tallest peak east of the Mississippi River.

The Outer Banks, narrow islands of shifting sandbars, screen most of the coastal plain from the ocean. Cape Hatteras Lighthouse is the tallest in the US, rising 208 feet (63 meters). The shallow Pamlico and Albemarle sounds and broad salt marshes lying behind the Outer Banks serve as valuable habitats for marine life but as further hindrances to water transportation. No single river basin dominates North Carolina. Rivers include the Catawba, Yadkin, Cape Fear, Neuse, Roanoke, New, and French Broad. The largest artificial lakes are Lake Norman on the Catawba, Lake Gaston on the Roanoke, Jordan Lake on the Haw, and High Rock Lake on the Yadkin.

3 CLIMATE

North Carolina has a humid, subtropical climate. Winters are short and mild, while summers are usually very sultry. In most of the state, temperatures rarely go above 100°F (38°C) or fall below 10°F (–12°C), but differences in altitude and proximity to the ocean create significant local variations. Average January temperatures in North Carolina range from 36°F (21°C) to

North Carolina Population Profile

Estimated 1995 population:	7,150,000
Population change, 1980–90:	12.7%
Leading ancestry group:	African American
Second leading group:	German
Foreign born population:	1.7%
Hispanic origin†:	1.2%
Population by race:	
White:	75.6%
Black:	22.0%
Native American:	1.2%
Asian/Pacific Islander:	0.8%
Other:	0.4%

Population by Age Group

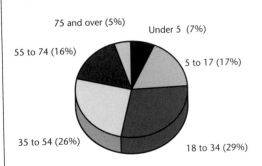

75 and over (5%)
Under 5 (7%)
55 to 74 (16%)
5 to 17 (17%)
35 to 54 (26%)
18 to 34 (29%)

Top Cities with Populations Over 25,000

City	Population	National rank	% change 1980–90
Charlotte	416,294	34	25.9
Raleigh	220,524	74	38.4
Greensboro	189,924	87	17.9
Winston–Salem	144,791	121	8.8
Durham	140,926	127	35.5
Fayetteville	76,651	298	27.2
High Point	70,752	334	9.7
Asheville	62,791	383	15.0
Wilmington	59,487	408	26.2
Gastonia	57,076	434	15.7

Notes: †A person of Hispanic origin may be of any race. NA indicates that data are not available.
Sources: Economic and Statistics Administration, Bureau of the Census. *Statistical Abstract of the United States, 1994–95.* Washington, DC: Government Printing Office, 1995; Courtenay M. Slater and George E. Hall. *1995 County and City Extra: Annual Metro, City and County Data Book.* Lanham, MD: Bernan Press, 1995.

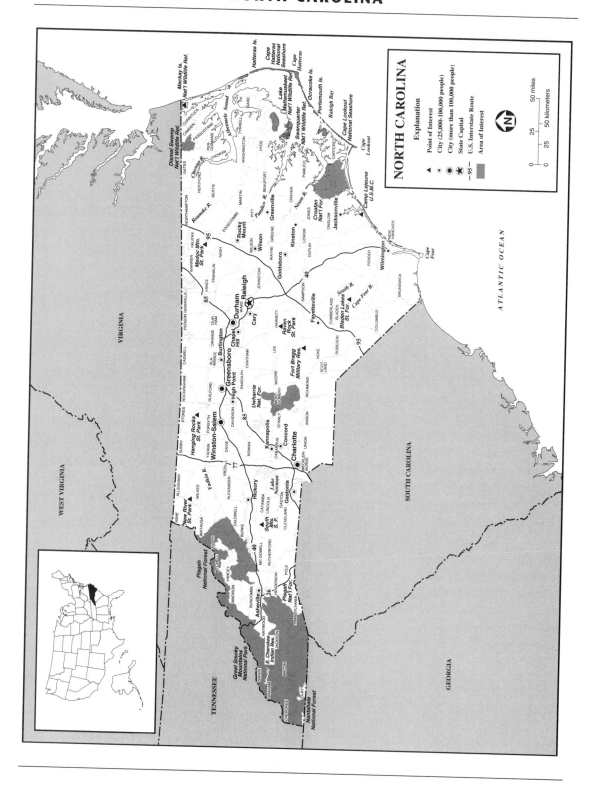

48°F (9°C). Average July temperatures range from 68°F (20°C) to 80°F (27°C). The coldest temperature ever recorded in North Carolina was –29°F (–34°C) in 1966; the hottest, 110°F (43°C), occurred in 1983.

In the southwestern section of the Blue Ridge, moist southerly winds rising over the mountains drop more than 80 inches (203 centimeters) of precipitation per year. The piedmont region gets between 44 and 48 inches (112 to 122 centimeters) of precipitation per year, while 44 to 56 inches (112 to 142 centimeters) annually fall on the coastal plain. During late summer and early autumn, the eastern region is vulnerable to high winds and flooding from hurricanes.

4 PLANTS AND ANIMALS

North Carolina has approximately 300 species and subspecies of trees and almost 3,000 varieties of flowering plants. Sea oats predominate on the dunes, and salt-meadow and cordgrass in the marshes. Blackwater swamps support dense areas of cypress and gum trees. Kudzu—a vine introduced from Japan in the 1930s to combat erosion—is a less attractive feature of the landscape. In the mountains, deciduous forests contain Carolina hemlock, sugar maple, yellow birch, and other species, including the common trees of the piedmont. Spruce and fir dominate the high mountain peaks.

The white-tailed deer is the principal big-game animal of North Carolina, and the black bear is a tourist attraction in the Great Smoky Mountains National Park. Beavers are the state's principal furbearers.

The largest native carnivore is the bobcat. North Carolina game birds include the mourning dove, wild turkey, and many varieties of duck and goose. Trout and smallmouth bass flourish in North Carolina's clear mountain streams, while catfish, pickerel, and perch thrive in fresh water elsewhere. The sounds and surf of the coast yield channel bass, striped bass, and bluefish to anglers.

Endangered species include the Florida manatee, bald eagle, and ivory woodpecker, and Atlantic ridley and hawksbill turtles.

5 ENVIRONMENTAL PROTECTION

North Carolina's citizens and officials worked actively (along with those in Tennessee) to establish the Great Smoky Mountains National Park during the 1920s, the same decade that saw the establishment of the first state agency for wildlife conservation. The Coastal Management Act of 1974 mandated comprehensive land-use planning for estuaries, wetlands, beaches, and adjacent areas of environmental concern.

Air quality in most of North Carolina's eight air-quality-control regions is good, although the industrialized areas of the piedmont and mountains experience pollution from engine exhausts and coal-fired electric generating plants. Water quality ranges from extraordinary purity in mountain trout streams to serious pollution in major rivers and coastal waters. Large areas of the coast are unsafe for commercial shellfishing. As of 1994, North Carolina had 23 hazardous waste sites.

6 POPULATION

North Carolina had 6,628,367 inhabitants in 1990 (10th in the US). The estimated population in 1995 was 7,150,000. North Carolina's estimated population density was 136 persons per square mile (52 persons per square kilometer) in 1990. Most North Carolinians live in and around a relatively large number of small and medium-sized cities and towns, many of which are concentrated in the Piedmont Crescent, between Charlotte, Greensboro, and Raleigh. Leading cities in 1992 were Charlotte, 416,294; Raleigh, 220,524; Greensboro, 189,924; Winston-Salem, 144,791; and Durham, 140,926.

7 ETHNIC GROUPS

By the first half of the 19th century, North Carolina's ethnic European population formed a relatively homogeneous body of native-born Protestants. In 1990, only 1.7% (115,077) of North Carolina residents were foreign-born, mostly from Germany, the United Kingdom, and Mexico.

According to the 1990 federal census there were some 80,000 Native Americans living in North Carolina, the 7th-largest number in any state, and the largest number in any state east of the Mississippi. The Lumbee of Robeson County and the surrounding area are the major tribe, with smaller groups including the Haliwa–Saponi, Meherrin, Waccamaw–Siouan, and Coharie. The only North Carolina tribe with a reservation are the Eastern Band of the Cherokee.

The 1,456,000 blacks in North Carolina comprised 22% of its total population in 1990, and 52,000 Asian/Pacific Islanders accounted for 0.8%. The overall proportion of blacks in North Carolina rose throughout the 19th century but fell steadily in the 20th, until about 1970, as hundreds of thousands migrated to northern and western states. Some of the earliest demonstrations of the civil rights movement, most notably a 1960 lunch counter sit-in at Greensboro, took place in the state.

8 LANGUAGES

Many regional language features are widespread, but others sharply distinguish the western half of the state from the eastern coastal plain. Terms common to South Midland and Southern speech occur throughout the state. In 1990, 5,931,435 North Carolinians—96.1% of the population—spoke only English at home. Other languages spoken at home, and the number of speakers, included Spanish, 105,963; French, 37,590; and German, 24,689.

9 RELIGIONS

The majority of North Carolinians are Protestant. The churches of the Southern Baptist Convention reported 1,446,228 members in 1990; the United Methodist Church claimed 605,362; the American Zion Church had 312,693; and the Presbyterian Church USA, 205,548. In 1990, the state had 149,483 Roman Catholics and an estimated 28,870 Jews.

10 TRANSPORTATION

As of 1992, North Carolina had 3,315 route miles (5,339 kilometers) of railroad track. Amtrak provides passenger service

Skyline of Charlotte.

to most large North Carolina cities; there were 360,460 North Carolina riders in 1991/92. In the 1920s, state roads came to rival the railroads as the principal means of transport. By 1993 there were 96,028 miles (154,509 kilometers) of public roads in the state; 3,840,995 automobiles were registered in 1993. Nearly all North Carolinians who commute to work travel by private automobile; intercity bus connections are poor, and commuter trains are nonexistent.

The Atlantic Intracoastal Waterway follows sounds, rivers, and canals down the entire length of eastern North Carolina, connecting the two state ports at Morehead City and Wilmington. Morehead City freight traffic in 1991 was 5,185,513 tons; Wilmington traffic was 6,913,989 tons. Regularly scheduled commercial airlines serving North Carolina cities in 1991 boarded over 13 million passengers; the airports at Charlotte, Raleigh–Durham, and Greensboro–High Point handled 96% of this traffic.

11 HISTORY

When Europeans arrived on the North Carolina coast, Native American tribes inhabiting the region included the Roanoke Hatteras and the Cherokee along the coast and Tuscarora farther inland. There also were Siouan, Iroquoian, and Algonquian groups there. Contact with Europeans brought disease, and magnified warfare and enslavement, which had long been practiced among the various tribes. By 1838, the federal government, responding in part to the demands of land-hungry whites, forcibly removed most of the Cherokee to Indian Territory (present-day Oklahoma) along what became known as the Trail of Tears.

European penetration began when Giovanni da Verrazano, a Florentine navigator in French service, discovered the North Carolina coast in 1524. The Spanish entered the region later in the century but made no permanent contribution to the colonization of North Carolina. Sixty years after Verrazano's voyage, an expedition was sent to gather information about the region. Sir Walter Raleigh later sponsored a colony on Roanoke Island, founded in 1587 under John White as governor. However, during a trip by White to gather supplies in England (with his return delayed due to the threat posed by the Spanish Armada), all the settlers disappeared. The fate of this "Lost Colony" has never been satisfactorily explained.

In 1629, Charles I granted the territory then called Carolana to his attorney general, Sir Robert Heath, who made no attempt to settle it. After Charles II became king in England in 1660, he thanked eight of his supporters through the Carolina Charter of 1663, which made them lords of the new province.

British Rule

The lords divided Carolina into three counties and appointed a governor for each one. From the beginning, relations between the settlers and their newly imposed government were stormy. In 1711, Cary's Rebellion was touched off by laws passed against the colony's Quakers. During the confusion, Tuscarora Indians launched a war against the settlers but were defeated by 1713.

South Carolina officially split off in 1712 and received a royal governor in 1721. In 1729, North Carolina became a royal colony. In the decades that followed, thousands of new settlers poured in; by 1775 the population had swelled to 345,000, making North Carolina the fourth most populous colony. Western settlers practiced self-sufficient farming, but eastern North Carolinians used slave labor to carve out rice and tobacco plantations. The eastern-dominated colonial assembly often rejected proposals beneficial to western interests while passing laws favorable to their own.

When England tightened its colonial administration, North Carolinians joined their fellow colonists in protests against the Stamp Act and similar measures. In April 1776, the North Carolina provincial congress resolved in favor of American independence, the first colonial representative body to do so. General Charles Cornwallis invaded the state from South Carolina in the fall of 1780. Pursuing the elusive American army under General Nathanael Greene, Cornwallis won a costly victory at Guilford Courthouse in March 1781 but finally succumbed to a trap set at Yorktown, Virginia, by an American army and a French fleet.

Statehood

North Carolina waited until November 1789 to ratify the US Constitution. The state did not share in the general prosperity of the early federal period. It had given up its lands beyond the Great Smokies, and thousands of North Carolinians migrated to the new western territories. Poor transportation facilities hampered efforts to expand commercial agriculture, and illiteracy remained widespread.

In 1835, as a result of reforms in the state constitution, the political climate changed. North Carolina initiated a program of state aid to railroads and other public works, and established the first state-supported system of common schools in the South. When South Carolina and six other states seceded and formed the Confederate States of America in 1861, North Carolina refused to join, trying instead to work for a peaceful settlement of the issues. However, after the outbreak of hostilities at Fort Sumter, South Carolina, public opinion swung to the Confederate side. North Carolina became the last state to withdraw from the Union, joining the Confederacy on 20 May 1861.

North Carolina provided more troops to the Confederacy than any other state, and its losses added up to more than one-fourth of the total for the entire South, but support for the war was mixed. North Carolina became a haven for deserters from the front lines in Virginia. At the war's end, General Joseph E. Johnston surrendered the last major Confederate army to General William T. Sherman at Bennett House (on the western edge of Durham) on 26 April 1865.

Post–Civil War Era

Reconstruction marked a bitter political and social struggle in North Carolina. United in the Conservative Party, most of the prewar slaveholding elite fought to preserve as much as possible of the former system, but a Republican coalition of blacks and nonslaveholding white Unionists instituted democratic reforms. Election of a Conservative governor in 1876 and the removal of federal troops in 1877 signaled the end of the Reconstruction era.

Once in power, the Conservatives—or Democrats, as they renamed themselves—enacted legislation to guarantee the power of landlords over tenants and sharecroppers. They cooperated with the consolidation of railroads under northern ownership, and they supported a massive drive to build cotton mills on the swiftly flowing streams of the piedmont. By 1880, industry had surpassed its prewar level.

As the Industrial Revolution gained ground in North Carolina, small farmers protested their steadily worsening condition. The Populist Party expressed their demands for reform, and for a brief period in the 1890s shared power with the Republican Party in the Fusion movement. In 1900, voters elected conservative Democrat Charles Brantley Aycock governor and approved a constitutional amendment that barred all illiterates from voting, except for those whose ancestors had voted before 1867.

In the decades after Aycock's election, an alliance of business interests and moderate-to-conservative Democrats dominated North Carolina politics. The industrial trio of textile, tobacco, and furniture manufacturers, joined by banks and insurance companies, controlled the state's economy. The Republican Party shriveled to small pockets of minor activity scattered around the state as blacks were forced out of the electorate. Political leaders emphasized fiscal responsibility, honest government, state assistance to aid economic growth, a tolerable level of social services, and a relative absence of racist extremism.

Post–World War II Era

In the years since World War II, North Carolina has taken its place in the booming Sunbelt economy. The development of Research Triangle Park—equidistant from the educational facilities of Duke University (Durham), North Carolina State University (Raleigh), and the University of North Carolina at Chapel Hill—has provided a home for dozens of scientific laboratories for government and business. Between 1987 and 1990, more manufacturing plants came to North Carolina than to any other state, and an increase in the state's per capita (per person) income moved it from 44th to 34th nationally.

Identification of the Democratic party in the early 1970s with liberal causes and with opposition to the Vietnam War helped the conservative wing of the Republican party gain popularity. In 1972, North Carolina elected its first Republican US senator (Jesse A. Helms)

and governor (James E. Holshouser, Jr.) since Fusion days, and Republican strength has continued to build.

In 1990, Harvey Gantt, the liberal black mayor of Charlotte, challenged Helms in his bid for re-election to a fourth term. Helms, a conservative member of the Senate, accused Gantt of supporting quotas which would give preference to minorities over more-qualified whites. Helms won by a margin of 8% of the vote.

12 STATE GOVERNMENT

Under the 1971 constitution, the general assembly consists of a 50-member senate and a 120-member house of representatives. All members of the general assembly serve two-year terms. The only state governor without a veto, North Carolina's chief executive has powers of appointment, supervision, and budgetary recommendation. The governor and lieutenant governor run separately. The voters also elect a secretary of state, treasurer, auditor, and other executives to four-year terms.

Bills become law when they have passed three readings in each house of the general assembly, and take effect 30 days after adjournment. Constitutional amendments may be proposed by a convention called by a two-thirds vote of both houses and a majority of the voters, or may be submitted directly to the voters by a three-fifths consent of each house. In either case, the proposed amendments must be ratified by a popular majority before becoming part of the constitution.

13 POLITICAL PARTIES

The Conservative Party, representing a coalition of pre-Civil War Democrats and former Whigs, became the Democratic Party after winning the governorship in 1876; from that time and for most of the 20th century, North Carolina was practically a one-party state.

Republican presidential candidates picked up strength in the 1950s and 1960s and have carried the state since Richard Nixon's election in 1968, except for 1976, when Jimmy Carter carried it, and 1992, when Democrat Bill Clinton and Republican George Bush each won 43% of the vote. In 1990, Jesse Helms was reelected to the Senate, defeating black mayor Harvey Gantt in a bitterly contested race. Lauch Faircloth, a Republican, captured the other Senate seat in 1992. James B. Hunt won reelection to the governorship in 1992. Following the November 1994 elections, 8 of North Carolina's 12 US Representatives were Republicans. In the state legislature, 39 of the state senators were Democrats and 11 were Republicans. There were 78 Democrats and 42 Republicans in the state assembly. In 1994, 2,313,520 voters (61%) were registered as Democrats; 1,217,114 (32%) as Republicans; and 2,86,746 as Independents.

14 LOCAL GOVERNMENT

As of 1992, North Carolina had 100 counties, 518 municipalities, and 335 special districts. Counties are the primary governmental units for most citizens. All counties are led by boards of commissioners; more than half the counties employ a county manager. Counties are subdivided into townships, but these do not exercise any independent government functions.

North Carolina Presidential Vote by Political Parties, 1948–92

YEAR	NORTH CAROLINA WINNER	DEMOCRAT	REPUBLICAN	STATES' RIGHTS DEMOCRAT	PROGRESSIVE
1948	*Truman (D)	459,070	258,572	69,652	3,915
1952	Stevenson (D)	652,803	558,107	—	—
1956	Stevenson (D)	590,530	575,069	—	—
1960	*Kennedy (D)	713,136	655,420	—	—
1964	*Johnson (D)	800,139	624,841	—	—
					AMERICAN IND.
1968	*Nixon (R)	464,113	627,192	—	496,188
					AMERICAN
1972	*Nixon (R)	438,705	1,054,889	—	25,018
				LIBERTARIAN	
1976	Carter (D)	927,365	741,960	2,219	5,607
1980	*Reagan (R)	875,635	915,018	9,677	—
1984	*Reagan (R)	824,287	1,346,481	3,794	—
					NEW ALLIANCE
1988	*Bush (R)	890,167	1,237,258	1,263	5,682
					IND. (Perot)
1992	Bush (R)	1,114,042	1,134,661	5,171	357,864

*Won US presidential election.

Photo credit: North Carolina Division of Travel and Tourism.

The state capitol building in Raleigh.

County and municipal governments share many functions, but the precise distribution of authority varies in each case. Most cities use the council-manager form of government, with council members elected from the city at large.

15 JUDICIAL SYSTEM

North Carolina's general court of justice is a unified judicial system that includes appeals courts (supreme court and court of appeals) and trial courts (superior court and district court). The state's highest court, the supreme court, consists of a chief justice and 6 associate justices. It hears cases from the court of appeals as well as certain cases from lower courts.

The court of appeals comprises 12 judges. Superior courts, in 44 districts, have original jurisdiction in most major civil and criminal cases. District courts try misdemeanors, civil cases involving less than $5,000, and all domestic cases. In 1994 North Carolina's overall crime rate per 100,000 persons was 5,625.2. North Carolina had 21,892 prisoners in state and federal institutions in 1993.

16 MIGRATION

The state suffered a net loss of population from migration in every decade from 1870 to 1970. Between 1940 and 1970, 539,000 more blacks left North Carolina than moved into the state; most of these emigrants sought homes in the North and

West. After 1970, however, black out-migration abruptly fell as economic conditions in eastern North Carolina improved. Net migration to North Carolina was estimated at 278,000 (sixth among the states) from 1970 to 1980, at 347,000 (fifth among the states) from 1985 to 1990, and at 208,000 (fifth among the states) from 1990 to 1994.

17 ECONOMY

North Carolina's economy was dominated by agriculture until the closing decades of the 19th century, with tobacco the major cash crop; today, tobacco is still the central factor in the economy of the coastal plain. The biggest employers in the state are the textile and furniture industries.

Since the 1950s, state government has made a vigorous effort to recruit outside investment and to improve the state's industrial mix. The greatest industrial growth, however, has come not from wholly new industries but from fields related to industries that were firmly established. Apparel manufacture spread across eastern North Carolina during the 1960s as an extension of the textile industry, and other new firms produce chemicals and machinery for the textile and furniture business.

The major test for North Carolina's continued economic growth will be whether the state can break out of the low-skill, low-wage trap. Despite recent improvements, North Carolina remains well below the national average in total personal income and value of goods produced.

18 INCOME

In 1994, North Carolina's per capita (per person) personal income averaged $19,576, 34th among the 50 states. Total personal income was $138.4 billion. Some 14.4% of North Carolina residents were below the poverty level in 1993.

19 INDUSTRY

North Carolina has had a predominantly industrial economy for most of the 20th century. Today, the state remains the nation's largest manufacturer of textiles, cigarettes, and furniture. The textile industry was the largest manufacturing sector in 1991, followed by tobacco manufacturers, chemicals and allied products, industrial machinery, food products, electronic and electrical equipment, furniture and fixtures, and rubber and plastics products.

The total value of shipments by manufacturers exceeded $118.2 billion in 1991, with the textile and apparel industries contributing 16% of this total. Gaston County near Charlotte contains the largest concentration of textile factories in the US.

20 LABOR

North Carolina's civilian labor force numbered 3,609,000 in 1994. The overall unemployment rate was 4.4%. North Carolina working conditions have brought the state considerable negative attention in recent years. The overall labor climate is anti-union, and only 5.2% of all workers belonged to a labor union in 1994.

The major symbol of resistance to unionization in recent decades has been J. P. Stevens & Company, a textile firm found guilty of illegal labor practices 21 times between 1966 and 1979, the highest conviction rate in US history. The Amalgamated Clothing and Textile Workers Union (AFL-CIO) won the right to represent employees at seven J. P. Stevens mills in Roanoke Rapids but waged a 17-year battle to use it; not until 1980 was a contract finally approved.

21 AGRICULTURE

Farm marketings in North Carolina totaled nearly $6.4 billion in 1994, eighth among the 50 states; farm industry income was $3 billion. North Carolina led the nation in the production of tobacco and sweet potatoes, ranked third in peanuts, fourth in blueberries, and was also a leading producer of corn, grapes, pecans, apples, tomatoes, and soybeans.

Farm life plays an important role in the culture of the state. The relatively large number of family farm owner-operators who depend on modest-scale tobacco farming to make their small acreages profitable is the basis for North Carolina's opposition to the US government's anti-smoking campaign and its fight to preserve tobacco price supports. In 1994, tobacco production was 597,525,000 pounds, 35.6% of US production, and worth over $942 million.

Production data for North Carolina's other principal crops were as follows: corn, 81,900,000 bushels; soybeans, 41,850,000 bushels; peanuts, 483,200,000 pounds; and sweet potatoes, 496 million pounds.

Photo credit: Robert Cavin, RCMS Photography.

Statue of General Greene in Greensboro.

22 DOMESTICATED ANIMALS

Livestock and poultry production, increasingly important contributors to North Carolina's farm economy, accounted for 52% of the state's agricultural income in 1994. North Carolina led the nation in turkeys raised and accounted for 9.3% of the nation's broiler receipts. As of the end of 1994, there were 1,130,000 cattle and 7,000,000 hogs on North Carolina farms and ranches. Dairy cows numbered 89,000 that year.

23 FISHING

North Carolina's fishing industry ranks second only to Virginia's among the South

Atlantic states, but its overall economic importance has declined. The 1992 catch was 154 million pounds, valued at $54.4 million. Flounder, menhaden, and sea trout are the most valuable finfish; shrimp, crabs, and clams are the most sought-after shellfish.

24 FORESTRY

As of 1990, forests covered 19,277,549 acres (7,801,624 hectares) in North Carolina, or about 62% of the state's land area. The largest tracts are found along the coast and in the Western Mountains, where most counties are more than 70% tree-covered. Today, the state produces mainly saw logs, pulpwood, and veneer logs.

25 MINING

The estimated 1994 value of minerals produced in North Carolina increased to $705 million. Crushed stone, valued at $264 million, was the state's leading mineral commodity. Production was estimated at 49 million short tons and accounted for over 46% of the total value of mineral production. Phosphate rock and lithium minerals were the next most valuable mineral commodities. In 1991, North Carolina continued to lead the nation in the production of lithium compounds.

26 ENERGY AND POWER

Except for a modest volume of hydroelectric power, the energy consumed in North Carolina comes from outside sources. The state used 1.96 quadrillion Btu of energy in 1991, of which 40% came from petroleum, 27% from coal, 9% from natural gas, 17% from nuclear power, 3% from hydropower, and the remainder imported from other states. In 1993, electric power production reached 88.8 billion kilowatt hours. No petroleum or natural gas has been found in North Carolina. The state has five nuclear power plants. In 1992, energy expenditures per capita (per person) were $1,913.

27 COMMERCE

North Carolina had 1992 wholesale sales of $76.4 billion; 1993 retail sales were $55.2 billion; and 1992 service establishment receipts were $24.6 billion. North Carolina exported over $10.4 billion worth of goods to foreign markets in 1992 (14th in the US).

28 PUBLIC FINANCE

North Carolina's total state indebtedness was $632.8 million as of 30 November 1993, or $91.81 per capita (per person). Revenues for 1993/94 were $16,714.8 million; expenditures were $16,714.8 million.

29 TAXATION

North Carolina anticipated more than $7.9 billion in tax revenues in 1991. More than 50% of anticipated state tax revenues in 1991 was expected to come from individual and corporate income tax. The state portion (4%) of the sales and use tax was projected to account for almost 30% of projected state tax revenues. Prescription drugs and certain other articles are exempt from sales tax, but food is not. The state also levies inheritance, estate, gift, insurance, beverage, and franchise taxes. North Carolina taxpayers contributed $10 billion to the federal treasury in 1990.

30 HEALTH

Health conditions and health care facilities in North Carolina vary widely from region to region. In the larger cities, quality health care is readily available. On the other hand, Tyrrell County, on the Albemarle Sound, had no physician in-patient care in 1991. A particularly serious public health problem in North Carolina is byssinosis, or brown lung disease. Caused by prolonged inhalation of cotton dust, byssinosis cripples the lungs of longtime textile workers, causing serious disability and even death.

The leading causes of death in North Carolina are similar to those in the rest of the US, although, as of 1992, North Carolinians died less frequently from heart disease and cancer than other Americans, and more frequently from cerebrovascular disease, accidents, and suicide.

The 117 community hospitals in North Carolina contained 22,700 beds in 1993. Average hospital expenses were $763 per inpatient day, and an average cost per stay was $5,571. The number of nonfederal physicians was 13,600 in 1993, and there were 47,600 nurses. About 14% of state residents did not have health insurance in 1993.

31 HOUSING

In 1993 there were an estimated 2,977,000 units of year-round housing in North Carolina. Almost 53,200 new housing units were authorized in 1993; their combined value was over $4.4 billion.

32 EDUCATION

North Carolina established the first state university in the US to open its doors to students. The proportion of high school graduates (age 25 and older) in 1990 was 71%, below the national average of 77.6%. Total enrollment in all public schools was 1,126,000 in 1993. Expenditures on education averaged $4,894 per pupil (34th in the nation) for 1993.

The University of North Carolina (UNC) system now embraces 16 campuses under a common board of governors; total enrollment stood at 150,818 in the fall of 1992. The three largest campuses are North Carolina State University at Raleigh (the first land-grant college for the study of agriculture and engineering), UNC-Chapel Hill, and East Carolina University at Greenville. There were 760,537 students enrolled in North Carolina's 42 community colleges and 16 technical institutes in 1991/92.

Duke University at Durham is North Carolina's premier private institution. There were 38 private four-year colleges and universities in 1992. Wake Forest University in Winston-Salem and Davidson College in Davidson are also noteworthy.

33 ARTS

North Carolina has been a pioneer in exploring new channels for state support of the arts. It was the first state to fund its own symphony, to endow its own art museum, to found a state school of the arts, to create a statewide arts council, and to establish a cabinet-level Department of Cultural Resources. The North Carolina

Symphony, at Raleigh, gives free concerts to about 250,000 public school children, and performs 120 evening concerts annually. Twelve North Carolina cities support amateur or semiprofessional symphonies and opera groups, while music festivals in Greensboro and Brevard reach large summer audiences.

The North Carolina Dance Theater is a professional company attached to the North Carolina School of the Arts in Winston-Salem. The American Dance Festival, one of the nation's oldest and most respected summer dance festivals, has made its permanent home at Duke University since 1978. Summer stock theater is a longstanding tradition in the mountains.

Traditional mountain string music inspired bluegrass, a forerunner of modern country and western music. Festivals, fiddlers' conventions, gospel concerts, and other public occasions keep this heritage alive and spread it to a new generation and a wider audience. The state of North Carolina generated $34,935,311 in federal and state funds to support its arts programs from 1987 to 1991.

34 LIBRARIES AND MUSEUMS

Public libraries are linked together through the State Library, ensuring that users in all parts of the state can have access to printed, filmed, and recorded materials. Total volumes in public libraries numbered 11,796,506 in 1991/92, when circulation reached 27,754,243. Major university research libraries are located at Chapel Hill, Raleigh, and Greensboro campuses of the University of

North Carolina and at Duke University in Durham.

North Carolina had 172 museums and historical sites in 1994. The North Carolina Museum of Art, in Raleigh, is one of only two state-supported art museums in the US (the other is in Virginia). The Museum of Natural Sciences in Raleigh is maintained by the state Department of Environment, Health, and Natural Resources; smaller science museums exist in Charlotte, Greensboro, and Durham.

35 COMMUNICATIONS

In March 1993, 93% of the state's 2,646,000 occupied housing units had telephones. There were 214 AM radio stations in North Carolina in 1992, and 153 FM stations. Commercial television stations numbered 34, and there were 11 noncommercial stations. As of 1993, cable television service was provided by 19 large systems.

36 PRESS

As of 1994, North Carolina had 11 morning newspapers, 31 evening dailies, and 33 Sunday papers. Daily circulation of the largest newspapers as of 1994 was: the *Charlotte Observer* (238,555); the *Raleigh News and Observer* (191,338); and the *Greensboro News and Record* (113,403). The *Charlotte Observer* won a 1981 Pulitzer Prize for its series on brown lung disease.

North Carolina has been the home of several nationally recognized "little reviews" of literature, poetry, and criticism, including *Southern Poetry Review.*

The bimonthly *Mother Earth News* is published in Hendersonville.

37 TOURISM, TRAVEL, AND RECREATION

Travelers spent $7.9 billion in North Carolina in 1993. Tourists are attracted by North Carolina's coastal beaches, by golf and tennis opportunities (including the world-famous golf courses at Pinehurst), and parks and scenery in the North Carolina mountains. Sites of special interest are the Revolutionary War battlegrounds at Guilford Courthouse and Moore's Creek Bridge; Bennett Place, in western Durham, where the last major Confederate army surrendered; Fort Raleigh, the site of the Lost Colony; and the Wright Brothers National Memorial at Kitty Hawk.

Cape Hatteras and Cape Lookout receive 1.5 million visitors annually. The Blue Ridge Parkway, a scenic motor route that winds over the crest of the Blue Ridge in Virginia, North Carolina, and Georgia, attract millions of visitors to North Carolina yearly. Another popular attraction, Great Smoky Mountains National Park, straddling the North Carolina-Tennessee border, annually attracts about 9 million visitors to North Carolina.

38 SPORTS

There are two major league professional sports teams in North Carolina. The Charlotte Hornets of the National Basketball Association, and the Carolina Panthers of the National Football League, one of two expansion teams beginning play in the 1995 season. Two other professional sports that feature prominently in the state are golf and stock-car racing. The Greater Greensboro Open and the Hall of Fame Classic at Pinehurst are major tournaments on the Professional Golfers' Association tour. The North Carolina Motor Speedway in Rockingham hosts the Carolina 500 annually, while the Charlotte Motor Speedway is the home of the World 600.

College basketball is the ruling passion of amateur sports fans in North Carolina. Organized in the Atlantic Coast Conference, the University of North Carolina at Chapel Hill, North Carolina State University, Wake Forest University, and Duke University consistently sponsor nationally competitive basketball teams.

39 FAMOUS NORTH CAROLINIANS

Three US presidents had North Carolina roots, but all three reached the White House from Tennessee. Andrew Jackson (1767–1845), the 7th president, studied law and was admitted to the bar in North Carolina before moving to frontier Tennessee in 1788. James K. Polk (1795–1849), the 11th president, was born in Mecklenburg County. Another native North Carolinian, Andrew Johnson (1808–75), was a tailor's apprentice in Raleigh before moving to Tennessee at the age of 18. Johnson served as Abraham Lincoln's vice-president for six weeks in 1865 before becoming the nation's 17th president when Lincoln was assassinated.

The infamous Edward Teach (or Thatch, b.England, ?–1718) made his headquarters at Bath and terrorized coastal waters as the pirate known as Blackbeard.

Among major politicians of the 20th century are Samuel J. Ervin, Jr. (1896–1985), US senator from 1954 to 1974 and chairman of the Senate Watergate investigation, and Jesse Helms (b.1921), senator since 1973. Civil rights leader Jesse Jackson (b.1941) began his career as a student activist in Greensboro. The most famous native North Carolinian living today is probably evangelist Billy Graham (b.1918).

The Wright brothers, Wilbur (b.Indiana, 1867–1912) and Orville (b.Ohio, 1871–1948), achieved the first successful powered airplane flight at Kitty Hawk, on the Outer Banks, on 17 December 1903. Kary Mullis (b.1944), 1993 winner of the Nobel prize for chemistry was born in Lenoir, North Carolina.

A number of North Carolinians have won fame as literary figures. They include William Sydney Porter (1862–1910), a short-story writer who used the pseudonym O. Henry; and novelists Thomas Wolfe (1900–38) and Reynolds Price (b.1933). Journalists Edward R. Murrow (1908–65), Tom Wicker (b.1926), and Charles Kuralt (b.1934) were all North Carolina natives.

Jazz artists Thelonious Monk (1918–82) and John Coltrane (1926–67) were born in the state, as were country singer Randy Travis (b.1963), folksinger Arthel "Doc" Watson (b.1923), bluegrass banjo artist Earl Scruggs (b.1924), and actor Andy Griffith (b.1926). North Carolina athletes include Michael Jordan (b.New York, 1963) who grew up in Wilmington and played college basketball at the University of North Carolina; he went on to fame as a National Basketball Association star.

40 BIBLIOGRAPHY

Chafe, William H. *Civilities and Civil Rights: Greensboro, North Carolina and the Black Struggle for Freedom.* New York: Oxford University Press, 1980.

Nathans, Sydney. *The Quest for Progress: The Way We Lived in North Carolina, 1870–1920.* Chapel Hill: University of North Carolina Press, 1983.

Powell, William S. *North Carolina: A Bicentennial History.* New York: Norton, 1977.

NORTH DAKOTA

State of North Dakota

ORIGIN OF STATE NAME: The state was formerly the northern section of Dakota Territory; *dakota* is a Siouan word meaning "allies."

NICKNAME: Peace Garden State. (Also: Flickertail State.)

CAPITAL: Bismarck.

ENTERED UNION: 2 November 1889 (39th).

SONG: "North Dakota Hymn."

MARCH: "Spirit of the Land."

MOTTO: Liberty and Union, Now and Forever, One and Inseparable.

FLAG: The flag consists of a blue field with yellow fringes; on each side is depicted an eagle with outstretched wings, holding in one talon a sheaf of arrows, in the other an olive branch, and in his beak a banner inscribed with the words *"E Pluribus Unum."* Below the eagle are the words "North Dakota"; above it are 13 stars surmounted by a sunburst.

OFFICIAL SEAL: In the center is an elm tree; beneath it are a sheaf of wheat, a plow, an anvil, and a bow and three arrows, and in the background a Native American chases a buffalo toward a setting sun. The depiction is surrounded by the state motto, and the words "Great Seal State of North Dakota October 1st 1889" encircle the whole.

BIRD: Western meadowlark.

FISH: Northern pike.

FLOWER: Wild prairie rose.

TREE: American elm.

GRASS: Western wheatgrass.

STONE: Teredo petrified wood.

BEVERAGE: Milk.

TIME 6 AM CST = noon GMT; 5 AM MST = noon GMT.

1 LOCATION AND SIZE

Located in western north-central US, North Dakota ranks 17th in size among the 50 states. Its total area is 70,703 square miles (183,121 square kilometers). Its maximum length east-west is about 360 miles (580 kilometers); its extreme width north-south is about 210 miles (340 kilometers).

The total boundary length is 1,312 miles (2,111 kilometers).

2 TOPOGRAPHY

Most of eastern North Dakota consists of the Drift Prairie. The Missouri Plateau occupies the western half of the state, and has the highest point in North Dakota—White Butte, 3,506 (1,069 meters). North

Dakota has two major rivers: the Red River and the Missouri River.

3 CLIMATE

North Dakota lies in the northwestern continental interior of the US. Summers are hot, winters very cold, and rainfall sparse to moderate. The average annual temperature ranges from 7°F (–14°C) in January to 69°F (21°C) in July. The record low temperature, –60°F (–51°C), was set in 1936; the record high, 121°F (49°C), in the same year. The average yearly precipitation is about 18 inches (46 centimeters).

4 PLANTS AND ANIMALS

Indian, blue, and buffalo grasses grow on the plains; the wild prairie rose is the state flower. American elm, green ash, and cottonwood grow as well, and cranberries, juneberries, and wild grapes are common. The white-tailed and mule deer and pronghorn antelope populations have been restored. North Dakota has the largest sharptailed grouse population in the US. The black-footed ferret and northern swift fox are listed as endangered.

5 ENVIRONMENTAL PROTECTION

North Dakota has little urban or industrial pollution. The state faces the challenge of using its coal resources without damaging the land through strip mining or polluting the air with coal-fired industrial plants. To conserve water and provide irrigation, nearly 700 dams have been built. The state has 97 municipal landfills and 5

North Dakota Population Profile

Estimated 1995 population:	637,000
Population change, 1980–90:	–2.1%
Leading ancestry group:	German
Second leading group:	Norwegian
Foreign born population:	1.5%
Hispanic origin†:	0.7%
Population by race:	
White:	94.6%
Black:	0.6%
Native American:	4.1%
Asian/Pacific Islander:	0.5%
Other:	0.2%

Population by Age Group

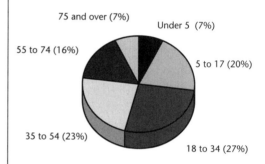

75 and over (7%)
Under 5 (7%)
55 to 74 (16%)
5 to 17 (20%)
35 to 54 (23%)
18 to 34 (27%)

Top Cities with Populations Over 25,000

City	Population	National rank	% change 1980–90
Fargo	77,052	294	20.7
Bismarck	51,319	507	10.7
Grand Forks	49,332	538	12.9
Minot	34,446	799	5.2

Notes: †A person of Hispanic origin may be of any race. NA indicates that data are not available.
Sources: Economic and Statistics Administration, Bureau of the Census. *Statistical Abstract of the United States, 1994–95.* Washington, DC: Government Printing Office, 1995; Courtenay M. Slater and George E. Hall. *1995 County and City Extra: Annual Metro, City and County Data Book.* Lanham, MD: Bernan Press, 1995.

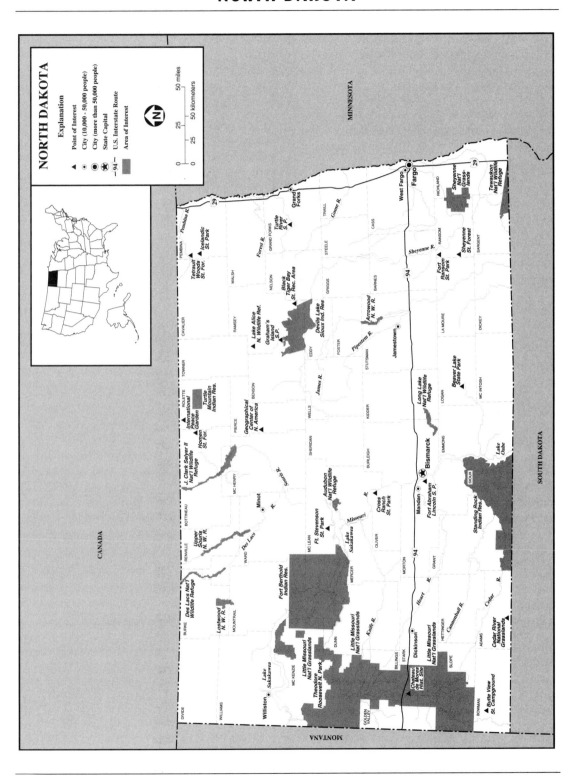

NORTH DAKOTA

Explanation

▲ Point of Interest
⊙ City (10,000 - 50,000 people)
◉ City (more than 50,000 people)
✸ State Capital
—94— U.S. Interstate Route
▨ Area of Interest

50 miles
50 kilometers
0 25 50
0 25

CANADA

MONTANA

SOUTH DAKOTA

MINNESOTA

Fargo
West Fargo
Grand Forks
Sheyenne Nat'l Grass-lands
Tewaukon Nat'l Wildlife Refuge
Turtle River S.P.
Icelandic St. Park
Tetrault Woods St. For.
Sheyenne St. Forest
Fort Ransom St. Park
Black Tiger Bay St. Rec. Area
Devils Lake Sioux Ind. Res.
Lake Alice N. Wildlife Ref.
Graham's Island S.P.
Arrowwood N. W. R.
Jamestown
Beaver Lake State Park
Turtle Mountain Indian Res.
International Peace Garden
Homen St. For.
Geographical Center of N. America
J. Clark Salyer II Nat'l Wildlife Refuge
Long Lake Nat'l Wildlife Refuge
Lake Oahe
Upper Souris N. W. R.
Des Lacs Nat'l Wildlife Refuge
Minot
Audubon Nat'l Wildlife Refuge
Ft. Stevenson St. Park
Lake Sakakawea
Cross Ranch St. Park
Bismarck
Mandan
Fort Abraham Lincoln S.P.
Standing Rock Indian Res.
Lostwood N. W. R.
Williston
Lake Sakakawea
Fort Berthold Indian Res.
Little Missouri Nat'l Grasslands
Theodore Roosevelt N. Park
Little Missouri Nat'l Grasslands
Dickinson
Chateau de Mores Hist. Site
Little Missouri Nat'l Grasslands
Cedar River National Grasslands
Butte View St. Campground

Pembina R.
Forest R.
Goose R.
Sheyenne R.
James R.
Pipestem R.
Souris R.
Des Lacs
Missouri R.
Knife R.
Heart R.
Cannonball R.
Cedar R.

PEMBINA
CAVALIER
TOWNER
ROLETTE
BOTTINEAU
RENVILLE
BURKE
DIVIDE
WILLIAMS
MCKENZIE
GOLDEN VALLEY
BILLINGS
SLOPE
BOWMAN
ADAMS
HETTINGER
STARK
DUNN
MERCER
OLIVER
MORTON
GRANT
SIOUX
EMMONS
MCLEAN
MCHENRY
MOUNTRAIL
WARD
PIERCE
BENSON
RAMSEY
WALSH
GRAND FORKS
NELSON
EDDY
FOSTER
WELLS
SHERIDAN
BURLEIGH
KIDDER
STUTSMAN
LOGAN
LA MOURE
MCINTOSH
DICKEY
STEELE
TRAILL
CASS
GRIGGS
BARNES
RANSOM
RICHLAND
SARGENT

29
29
94
94
94

101

curbside recycling programs. There were two hazardous waste sites as of 1994.

6 POPULATION

North Dakota ranked 47th in the US with a 1990 census population of 638,800. The estimated population for 1995 was 637,000. The population density in 1990 was 9.3 persons per square mile (3.5 persons per square kilometer). Leading cities as of 1992 were Fargo, 77,052; Bismarck, the capital, 51,319; and Grand Forks, 49,332.

7 ETHNIC GROUPS

As of 1990, about 94.6% of the state's population was white. The Native American population was 26,000, and there were some 4,000 Blacks, representing 0.6% of the population. Of European origin, the leading groups were Germans, who made up 50% of the total population, and Norwegians, who made up 29%.

8 LANGUAGES

A few Norwegian food terms like *lefse* and *lutefisk* have entered the Northern dialect that is characteristic of North Dakota, and some Midland terms have intruded. In 1990, 92.1% of the population five years old or older spoke only English at home; German, the next most frequently used language, was spoken by 24,453 residents.

9 RELIGIONS

As of 1990 there were an estimated 310,713 members of Protestant groups, representing nearly one-half of the state's total population. Leading denominations

Photo credit: Dawn Charging/North Dakota Tourism.

The spectacular rock formations of the Badlands, Theodore Roosevelt National Park.

were the Evangelical Lutheran Church in America with 179,711 members; Lutheran Church–Missouri Synod, 25,691; United Methodist Church, 23,850; and United Presbyterian Church, 11,960. As of 1990, the state had 173,432 Roman Catholics and an estimated 483 Jews.

10 TRANSPORTATION

In 1992, there were 3,880 rail miles (6,243 kilometers) of railroad track in North Dakota. Railroad lines transported over 66.8 million tons of freight by rail in 1991. The total number of North Dakota Amtrak riders was 78,391 in 1991/92.

Public roads, streets, and highways in North Dakota covered 86,727 miles (139,544 kilometers) in 1993. There were 661,831 registered motor vehicles and 437,942 licensed drivers. The state had 456 airports and 7 heliports in 1991, and there were 12,697 scheduled aircraft departures.

11 HISTORY

In the 17th century, present-day North Dakota was inhabited by the Yanktonai Sioux, in the southeastern quarter of the state; the Teton Sioux west of the Missouri River; and the Ojibwa, in the northeast. European penetration of the Dakotas began in 1738, when the Frenchman Pierre Gaultier de Varennes, Sieur de la Vérendrye, traded for furs in the Red River region. After the Lewis and Clark expedition (1804–06) explored the Missouri, the American Fur Company traded there, with buffalo hides the leading commodity.

In 1812, Scottish settlers from Canada moved up the Red River to Pembina. This first white farming settlement in North Dakota also attracted numerous *métis*, persons of mixed Native American and European ancestry. An extensive trade in furs and buffalo hides, which were transported first by heavy carts and later by steamboats, sprang up between Pembina, Fort Garry (Winnipeg, Canada), and St. Paul, Minnesota.

In 1861 North Dakota was organized as part of the Dakota Territory, including the present-day Dakotas, Montana, and Wyoming. The confinement of Native Americans to reservations and the arrival of the Northern Pacific Railroad at Fargo in 1872 led to the rise of homesteading, as settlers poured in. This short-lived "Great Dakota boom" ended in the mid-1880s with drought and depressed farm prices. As many of the original American and Canadian settlers left, they were replaced by Norwegians, Germans, and other Europeans. By 1910, North Dakota, which had entered the Union in 1889, was among the leading states in percentage of foreign-born residents.

Between 1898 and 1915, the "Second Boom" brought an upsurge in population and railroad construction. The 1920s, a period of bank failures, low farm prices, drought, and political disunity, saw the beginnings of an exodus from the state. Matters grew even worse during the depression of the 1930s. William Langer was elected governor by hard-pressed farmers in 1932, and he sought to raise grain prices in order to save farms from foreclosure. World War II brought a quiet prosperity to North Dakota that lasted into the following decades.

The Arab oil embargo of 1973 and the rise of oil prices throughout the decade spurred drilling for oil, encouraged the mining of lignite for electrical generation, and led to the construction of the nation's first coal gasification plant.

12 STATE GOVERNMENT

Statewide elected officials include governor and lieutenant governor, secretary of state, auditor, treasurer, and attorney general. Commissioners are also elected for the

Photo credit: Dawn Charging/North Dakota Tourism.

A farm outside of Fort Ransom. North Dakota is one of the nation's leading wheat producers.

state's agriculture, insurance, labor, taxation, and public services departments. The legislature has two chambers, with a 53-member senate and a 106-member house of representatives. Senators are elected to four-year terms, while representatives serve for two years. A two-thirds vote of the elected members of each house is required to override a gubernatorial veto.

13 POLITICAL PARTIES

Republicans held the governorship for 58 of the 72 years between 1889 and 1960. From 1960 to 1980, the statehouse was in Democratic hands. In the early and mid-1990s, the Republican party increased its influence at the state level.

In November 1992, North Dakotans cast 44% of the total popular vote for Republican George Bush, 33% for Democrat Bill Clinton, and 25% for Independent Ross Perot. Edward Schafer, a Republican, won the governorship in 1992.

North Dakota's senators in 1994 were Kent Conrad, a Democrat elected in 1992 to fill a seat vacated by the death of Quentin D. Burdick and reelected to a full term in 1994, and Democrat Byron Dorgan, who was also elected in 1992. North Dakota's US Representative is Democrat Earl Pomeroy. Since the November 1994 election, Republicans have controlled both houses of the state legislature.

**North Dakota Presidential Vote
by Major Political Parties, 1948–92**

YEAR	N. DAKOTA WINNER	DEMOCRAT	REPUBLICAN
1948	Dewey (R)	95,812	115,139
1952	*Eisenhower (R)	76,694	191,712
1956	*Eisenhower (R)	96,742	156,766
1960	Nixon (R)	123,963	154,310
1964	*Johnson (D)	149,784	108,207
1968	*Nixon (R)	94,769	138,669
1972	*Nixon (R)	100,384	174,109
1976	Ford (R)	136,078	153,470
1980	*Reagan (R)	79,189	193,695
1984	*Reagan (R)	104,429	200,336
1988	*Bush (R)	127,739	166,559
1992**	Bush (R)	99,168	136,244

*Won US presidential election.
** Independent candidate Ross Perot received 71,084 votes.

14 LOCAL GOVERNMENT

North Dakota in 1992 had 2,795 units of local government, including 53 counties, 366 municipalities designated as cities, and 1,351 townships. Typical elected county officials are the sheriff, court clerk, county judge, and county justice.

15 JUDICIAL SYSTEM

North Dakota has a supreme court of five justices, seven district courts, and a system of municipal courts. According to the FBI Crime Index, in 1994 North Dakota had a total crime rate of 2,735.9 crimes per 100,000 population.

16 MIGRATION

The state reached a peak population in 1930, but then suffered steady losses until well into the 1970s because of out-migration. From 1985 to 1990, North Dakota had a net loss of 44,142 from migration. From 1990 to 1994, the state lost about 17,000 more people who moved to other states. As of 1990, 73.2% of state residents had been born in North Dakota.

17 ECONOMY

North Dakota has been and still is an important agricultural state, especially as a producer of wheat, much of which finds its way onto the world market. Many segments of the economy are affected by agriculture. However, farm numbers have continued to decline, posing a threat to the state's rural life-style. Growth industries include petroleum and the mining of coal, chiefly lignite; North Dakota has more coal resources than any other state.

18 INCOME

In 1994, North Dakota ranked 38th among the 50 states in per capita (per person) income, with $18,621. Total personal income rose to $11.9 billion in 1994. Some 11.2% of all North Dakotans lived below the federal poverty level in 1993.

19 INDUSTRY

By number of employees, the leading manufacturing industries in North Dakota are food products, machinery, printing and publishing, and transportation equipment. Shipments of manufactured goods were valued at over $3.6 billion in 1992.

20 LABOR

North Dakota's labor force numbered 338,000 in 1994, of whom 3.9% were unemployed. As of 1994, 9.4% of all North Dakotans in the work force belonged to labor unions.

A skyline of Fargo, North Dakota's largest city.

21 AGRICULTURE

North Dakota's farm marketings totaled $2.9 billion in 1994 (24th in the US). The state has in some years been the nation's leading wheat producer and is typically the top producer of durum and other spring wheats, as well as of barley, flaxseeds, and sunflowers. The total number of farms has declined over the years as average farm size has increased.

In 1994 crop production included wheat, 356,404,000 bushels; oats, 33,550,000 bushels; corn for grain, 54,000,000 bushels; soybeans, 18,910,000 bushels; hay, 4,510,000 tons; and potatoes, 2.82 billion pounds.

22 DOMESTICATED ANIMALS

Sales of livestock and livestock products accounted for about 21% of North Dakota farm income in 1994. Livestock on North Dakota farms and ranches in that year included 1,920,000 cattle, 127,000 sheep, and 245,000 hogs.

23 FISHING

There is little commercial fishing in North Dakota. In 1992, federal hatcheries distributed over 74,000 pounds of fish.

24 FORESTRY

North Dakota has only 422,000 acres (171,000 hectares) of forestland, or about

1% of its total area. Forestry products are of very minor importance to the economy.

25 MINING

The value of nonfuel minerals produced in North Dakota in 1994 was about $26 million. Construction sand and gravel accounted for more than 70% of the value of North Dakota's nonfuel mineral output. Recovered elemental sulfur is the second most important mineral produced in North Dakota, after coal.

26 ENERGY AND POWER

Power stations in North Dakota generated 28.5 billion kilowatt hours of electricity in 1993. Energy consumption per capita (per person) in 1992 amounted to 516.1 million Btu. Recoverable coal reserves totaled 1.3 billion short tons in 1991. In 1992, North Dakota produced 31,697,000 tons of coal. Proved petroleum reserves in 1991 totaled 232,000,000 barrels; production was 31,000,000 barrels in 1993. In 1991, natural gas reserves totaled 472 billion cubic feet; production was 60 billion cubic feet in 1993. The state has no nuclear power plants. Energy expenditures per capita (per person) were $2,471 in 1992.

27 COMMERCE

North Dakota's wholesale sales for 1992 totaled $7.6 billion; retail sales for 1993 were $5.9 billion; and service establishment receipts for 1992 were $1.8 billion. Exports totaled $336 billion in 1992.

28 PUBLIC FINANCE

Total expenditures for 1991-93 (including federal and special funds) totaled approximately $3.2 billion. General fund revenues for 1993–95 were $1,247,387,540; appropriated expenditures were $1,251,229,967. North Dakota had an outstanding debt of $830 million in 1993, or about $1,303 per capita (per person).

29 TAXATION

North Dakota has personal and corporate income taxes. The state also taxes oil and gas production, gasoline, insurance premiums, alcoholic beverages, tobacco products, mineral leases, and coal severance. There is a general sales and use tax of 5%. In 1992, North Dakotans paid $866 million in federal income tax.

30 HEALTH

Death rates in 1991 for all major causes except cerebrovascular diseases were below the US average, as was infant mortality. As of 1993 the state had 45 community hospitals, with 4,400 beds. Hospital costs per inpatient day in 1993 averaged $507, or $5,403 for an average cost per stay. Medical personnel licensed in the state in 1993 included 1,200 active nonfederal physicians and 6,300 nurses. Some 13.4% of state residents did not have health insurance in 1993.

31 HOUSING

North Dakota had some 240,000 households in 1993, when there were an estimated 282,000 year-round housing units. In 1993, 2,940 new units were authorized at a value of $189.8 million. In 1990, the median home value was $50,800. That year, owners (with a mortgage) and renters had median monthly costs of $608 and $313, respectively.

32 EDUCATION

As of 1990, three-quarters (76.7%) of all adults were high school graduates, and 18.1% had at least four years of college. In 1993/94, 119,115 students were enrolled in public schools, including 84,120 students in prekindergarten to grade 8, and 34,995 in grades 9–12. Expenditures on education averaged $4,404 per pupil (41st in the nation) in 1993. In fall 1993, 41,000 students were enrolled in North Dakota's 19 higher educational institutions. The chief universities are the University of North Dakota (Grand Forks) and North Dakota State University (Fargo).

33 ARTS

The Council on the Arts provides grants to local artists and groups and encourages visits by out-of-state artists and exhibitions. Two popular musical events are the Old Time Fiddlers Contest and the Medora Musical, featuring Western songs and dance. The State of North Dakota generated $3,831,695 from federal and state funds for its arts programs from 1987 to 1991.

34 LIBRARIES AND MUSEUMS

During 1991, North Dakota public libraries had 1,301,707 volumes and a total circulation of 2,882,427. The leading academic library was that of the University of North Dakota (Grand Forks), with 520,538 volumes. Among the most notable of the state's 46 museums are the Art Galleries and Zoology Museum of the University of North Dakota, and the North Dakota Heritage Center at Bismarck, which has an outstanding collection of Native American artifacts.

35 COMMUNICATIONS

In March 1993, 97.1% of North Dakota's 242,000 occupied housing units had telephones. There were 70 radio stations (33 AM, 37 FM) in 1993. As of 1993, 17 commercial television stations and 7 public television stations were in operation. Meredith Cable in Bismarck is the state's major cable service provider.

36 PRESS

As of 1994, there were four morning dailies, and five evening dailies. There were also seven Sunday papers in the state. The leading dailies were the *Fargo Forum,* with an all-day circulation of 55,664, and 70,991 on Sunday; the *Grand Forks Herald,* 40,058 morning, 41,140 Sunday; the *Minot Daily News,* 26,025 evening; and the *Bismarck Tribune,* 31,317 evening, 32,266 Sunday. In addition, there were 67 weekly newspapers and 15 periodicals.

37 TOURISM, TRAVEL, AND RECREATION

In 1993, US travelers spent an estimated $828 million in North Dakota. State parks and other state recreational areas received 954,000 visitors in 1991. Among the leading tourist attractions is the International Peace Garden, commemorating friendly relations between the US and Canada. The most spectacular scenery in North Dakota is part of the Theodore Roosevelt National Park. The so-called badlands, an integral part of the park, consist of strangely colored and interestingly eroded rock formations. Hunting and fishing are major recreational activities in North Dakota.

38 SPORTS

There are no major professional sports teams in North Dakota. In collegiate football, the University of North Dakota Sioux and the North Dakota State University Bison compete in the North Central Conference. The University of North Dakota also competes in collegiate ice hockey. Other annual sporting events include the Governor's Cup Walleye Fishing Tournament in July, and several rodeos throughout the state.

39 FAMOUS NORTH DAKOTANS

Among North Dakota politicians known to the nation was Gerald P. Nye (b.Wisconsin, 1892–1971), a US senator and a leading isolationist opponent of President Franklin D. Roosevelt's foreign policy, as was Senator William Langer (1886–1959). Another prominent senator, Porter J. McCumber (1858–1933), supported President Woodrow Willson in the League of Nations battle. US Representative William Lemke (1878–1950) sponsored farm-relief legislation and in 1936 ran for US president on the Union Party ticket. Usher L. Burdick (1879–1960), a champion of Native Americans, served 18 years in the US House of Representatives.

North Dakota-related writers and commentators include Vilhjalmur Stefansson (b.Canada, 1879–1962) recorded in numerous books his explorations and experiments in the high Arctic; Maxwell Anderson (b.Pennsylvania, 1888–1959), a Pulitzer Prize-winning playwright; Edward K. Thompson (b.Minnesota, 1907), editor of *Life* magazine and founder-editor of *Smithsonian;* radio and television commentator Eric Severeid (1912–92); and novelists Louis L'Amour (1908–88) and Larry Woiwode (b.1941).

To the entertainment world North Dakota has contributed band leaders Harold Bachman (1892–1972); Lawrence Welk (1903–92) and Tommy Tucker (Gerald Duppler, 1908–89); jazz vocalist Peggy Lee (Norma Delores Egstrom, b.1920); country singer Lynn Anderson (b.1947); and actresses Dorothy Stickney (b.1900) and Angie Dickinson (Angeline Brown, b.1931).

Sports personalities associated with the state include outfielder Roger Maris (1934–85), who in 1961 broke Babe Ruth's record for home runs in one season.

40 BIBLIOGRAPHY

Crawford, Lewis F. *History of North Dakota.* 3 vols. Chicago: American Historical Society, 1931.

Federal Writer's Project. *North Dakota: A Guide to the Northern Prairie State.* Reprint. New York: Somerset, 1980 (orig. 1938).

Goodman, L. R., and R. J. Eidem. *The Atlas of North Dakota.* Fargo: North Dakota Studies, Inc., 1976.

North Dakota Economic Development Commission. *North Dakota Growth Indicators.* Bismarck, 1984.

Robinson, Elwyn B. *History of North Dakota.* Lincoln: University of Nebraska Press, 1966.

Tweton, D. Jerome, and Theodore Jelliff. *North Dakota—The Heritage of a People.* Fargo: North Dakota Institute for Regional Studies, 1976.

Tweton, D. Jerome, and Daniel F. Rylance. *The Years of Despair: North Dakota in the Depression.* Grand Forks: Oxcart Press, 1973.

University of North Dakota. Bureau of Business and Economic Research. *Statistical Abstract of North Dakota 1983.* Grand Forks: University of North Dakota Press, 1983.

Wilkins, Robert P., and Wynona H. Wilkins. *North Dakota.* New York: Norton, 1977.

OHIO

State of Ohio

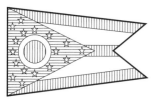

ORIGIN OF STATE NAME: From the Iroquois Indian word *oheo,* meaning "beautiful."

NICKNAME: The Buckeye State.

CAPITAL: Columbus.

ENTERED UNION: 1 March 1803 (17th).

SONG: "Beautiful Ohio."

MOTTO: With God All Things Are Possible.

FLAG: The flag is a burgee, with three red and two white lateral stripes. At the staff is a blue triangular field covered with 17 stars (signifying Ohio's order of entry into the Union), which is grouped around a red disk superimposed on a white circular O.

OFFICIAL SEAL: In the foreground are a sheaf of wheat and a sheaf of 17 arrows; behind, a sun rises over a mountain range, indicating that Ohio is the first state west of the Alleghenies. Surrounding the scene are the words "The Great Seal of the State of Ohio."

ANIMAL: White-tailed deer.

BIRD: Cardinal.

INSECT: Ladybug.

REPTILE: Black racer snake.

FLOWER: Scarlet carnation.

TREE: Buckeye.

GEM: Ohio flint.

BEVERAGE: Tomato juice.

TIME: 7 AM EST = noon GMT.

1 LOCATION AND SIZE

Located in the eastern north-central US, Ohio is the 11th largest of the 12 midwestern states and ranks 35th in size among the 50 states. The state's total area is 41,330 square miles (107,044 square kilometers). Ohio extends about 210 miles (338 kilometers) east-west; its maximum north-south extension is 230 miles (370 kilometers). Ohio's total boundary length is 997 miles (1,605 kilometers). Five important islands lie off the state's northern shore in Lake Erie: the three Bass Islands, Kelleys Island, and Catawba Island.

2 TOPOGRAPHY

Ohio has three distinct topographical regions. The Allegheny Plateau in eastern Ohio consists of rugged hills and steep valleys that recede gradually as the terrain sweeps westward toward the central plains. The Erie lakeshore, a band of level lowlands, runs across the state to the northwestern corner on the Michigan boundary. The central plains extend to the western boundary with Indiana. In the south, undulating hills decline in altitude as they reach the Ohio River, which forms the state's southern boundary with Kentucky and West Virginia. The highest point in the state is Campbell Hill at 1,550 feet (470 meters), northwest of Columbus.

Most of Ohio's 2,500 lakes are situated in the east, and nearly all are reservoirs backed up by river dams. The Maumee, Portage, Sandusky, Cuyahoga, and Grand rivers drain into Lake Erie. The Muskingum, Hocking, Raccoon, Scioto, Olentangy, and Miami rivers drain into the Ohio River.

3 CLIMATE

Lying in the humid continental zone, Ohio has a generally temperate climate. Winters are cold and summers mild in the eastern highlands. The southern region has the warmest temperatures. Among the major cities, Cleveland, in the north, has an annual mean temperature of 50°F (10°C), while the mean temperature in Cincinnati, in the south, is 55°F (13°C). The record low temperature for the state is –39°F (–39°C), set in 1899. The record high is 113°F (45°C), registered in 1934. Cleveland has an average annual snowfall of 52 inches (132 centimeters), while Cincinnati receives 24 inches (61 centimeters).

4 PLANTS AND ANIMALS

More than 2,500 plant species have been found in Ohio. The southeastern hill and valley region supports pitch pine, bigleaf magnolia, and sourwood, with undergrowths of sassafras, witch-hazel, and pawpaw. Other trees include maple,

Ohio
Population Profile

Estimated 1995 population:	11,203,000
Population change, 1980–90:	0.5%
Leading ancestry group:	German
Second leading group:	Irish
Foreign born population:	2.4%
Hispanic origin†:	1.3%
Population by race:	
White:	87.8%
Black:	10.6%
Native American:	0.2%
Asian/Pacific Islander:	0.8%
Other:	0.6%

Population by Age Group

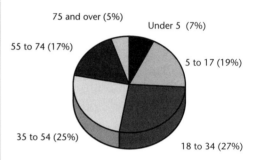

75 and over (5%)
Under 5 (7%)
55 to 74 (17%)
5 to 17 (19%)
35 to 54 (25%)
18 to 34 (27%)

Top Cities with Populations Over 25,000

City	Population	National rank	% change 1980–90
Columbus	642,987	16	12.0
Cleveland	502,539	24	–11.9
Cincinnati	364,278	46	–5.6
Toledo	329,325	49	–6.1
Akron	223,621	73	–6.0
Dayton	183,189	95	–10.5
Youngstown	94,387	219	–17.1
Parma	86,631	245	–5.0
Canton	84,788	258	–11.2
Lorain	71,483	327	–5.5

Notes: †A person of Hispanic origin may be of any race. NA indicates that data are not available.
Sources: Economic and Statistics Administration, Bureau of the Census. *Statistical Abstract of the United States, 1994–95.* Washington, DC: Government Printing Office, 1995; Courtenay M. Slater and George E. Hall. *1995 County and City Extra: Annual Metro, City and County Data Book.* Lanham, MD: Bernan Press, 1995.

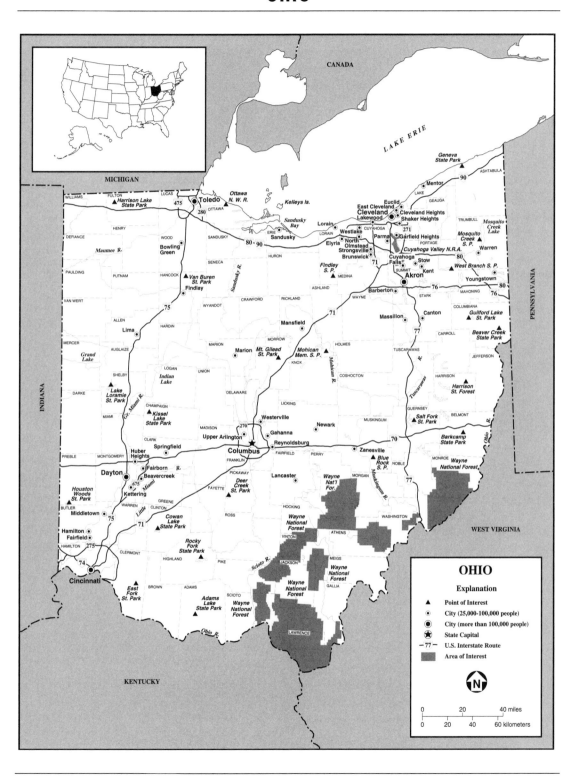

OHIO

Explanation

▲ Point of Interest
⊙ City (25,000-100,000 people)
◉ City (more than 100,000 people)
★ State Capital
–77– U.S. Interstate Route
▬ Area of Interest

poplar, pine, and sycamore. The buckeye—first called the Ohio buckeye and now the official state tree—is characterized by its clusters of cream-colored flowers that bloom in spring and later form large, brown, thick-hulled nuts.

The Buckeye State is rich in mammals. White-tailed deer, badger, and eastern cottontail are mammals found throughout the state's five wildlife districts. The bobcat is among many species with more restricted habitats. Common birds include the mourning dove, eastern belted kingfisher, and eastern horned lark; the cardinal is the state bird. Perch, carp, pike, trout, and other species thrive in Ohio's lakes and streams.

The Division of Wildlife of the Department of Natural Resources has instituted an ambitious endangered species program. Among the numerous animals categorized by the state as endangered are the river otter, bobcat, and upland sandpiper.

5 ENVIRONMENTAL PROTECTION

In recent years, the state's major environmental concerns have been to reverse the pollution of Lake Erie, to control the air pollution caused by industry and automobiles, and to clean up dumps for solid and hazardous wastes. Of recent concern is the problem with so-called "brown fields"—polluted industrial sites whose cleanup costs equal or exceed the cost of the property, thus making future restoration and development unprofitable. The state's regulatory agency for environmental matters is the Ohio Environmental Protection Agency.

Since 1972, anti-pollution efforts in Lake Erie have focused on reducing the discharge of phosphorus into the lake from sewage and agricultural wastes. Sewage treatment facilities have been upgraded with the aid of more than $750 million in federal grants, and efforts have been made to promote reduced-tillage farming to control runoff. By the early 1980s, numerous beaches had been reopened, and sport fishing was once again on the increase. From 1967 to 1983, through the efforts of local health departments and with the eventual help of the federal EPA, over 1,300 open garbage dumps were closed down and more than 200 sanitary landfills constructed to replace them.

By early 1985, with the aid of more than $11 million in federal Superfund grants, cleanup had been completed or begun at 16 major sites. In 1994, there were 38 hazardous waste sites in Ohio.

Another agency, the Ohio Department of Natural Resources, is responsible for the development and use of the state's natural resources. The department also assists in soil conservation, issues permits for dams, promotes conservation of oil and gas, and allocates strip-mining licenses.

6 POPULATION

Ohio ranked seventh in population among the 50 states at the 1990 census, with a population of 10,847,115. The estimated 1995 population was 11,203,000. In 1990, Ohio's population density was 265 persons per square mile (102 persons per square kilometer).

Photo credit: Greater Columbus Convention & Visitors Bureau.

Columbus skyline.

During the 1980s, Columbus increased its population by 12%, whereas Cleveland lost population by 11.9%. As of 1992, Columbus was Ohio's largest city, with a population of 642,987, as compared with Cleveland's 502,539 residents. In 1992, Cincinnati's population was 364,278, followed by Toledo, 329,325; Akron, 223,621; Dayton 183,189; and Youngstown, 94,387.

Ohio's three most populated cities and their suburbs ranked among the 30 largest metropolitan areas in the US in 1990. In that year, metropolitan Cleveland (including Akron and Lorain) had a population of 2,759,823, ranking 13th.

7 ETHNIC GROUPS

By 1990, only about 2.4% of Ohioans were foreign-born, the major places of origin being Germany, Italy, and the United Kingdom. Ethnic clusters persist in the large cities, and some small communities retain a specific ethnic flavor, such as Fairport Harbor on Lake Erie, with its large Finnish population.

As of 1990, there were 1,155,000 blacks, representing 10.6% of the population. Most lived in the larger cities, especially Cleveland, which in 1990 was 46.6% black. Some 140,000 people in Ohio were of Hispanic origin in 1990. The largest number were of Mexican descent, but there were also many Puerto Ricans. Native Americans numbered about 20,000. In 1990, 16,829 Chinese, 12,726 Filipinos, 13,999 Japanese, and 13,041 Koreans were living in Ohio.

8 LANGUAGES

Ohio English reflects three post-Revolutionary migration paths. Into the Western Reserve south of Lake Erie came Northern speech from New York and Connecticut. Most of rural Ohio has North Midland speech from Pennsylvania, and from Kentucky, South Midland speakers took *you-all* into Ohio River towns. Recent northward migration has introduced South Midland speech and black English into such industrial centers as Cleveland, Toledo, and Akron.

Of Ohioans aged five years or older, 94.6% spoke only English at home in 1990. Other languages spoken at home, and the number of speakers, included Spanish, 139,194; German, 80,975; and Italian, 41,179.

9 RELIGIONS

In 1990, Ohio had a Roman Catholic population of 2,141,777. During the same year, the state's Jewish population was estimated at 124,832. Members of all Protestant groups totaled 3,171,021 in 1990. The largest Protestant denominations and their memberships in 1990 were United Methodist, 656,107; Presbyterian, 205,721; United Church of Christ, 195,349; and Lutheran Church—Missouri Synod, 86,336.

10 TRANSPORTATION

Sandwiched between two of the country's largest inland water systems, Lake Erie and the Ohio River, Ohio has long been a leader in water transport. With its numerous terminals on the Ohio River and deep-water ports on Lake Erie, Ohio ranks as one of the major US states for shipping.

In 1992, Class I railroads operated 4,051 rail miles (6,518 kilometers) of track in the state. In 1991, the state handled 4,189,387 rail carloads, second only to Illinois. In 1991/92, Amtrak operated five regularly scheduled trains through Ohio, with a total of 205,562 passengers in the state. In 1992, Ohio had 113,823 miles (183,141 kilometers) of roads (ninth highest in the nation). In 1993, 7,482,837 automobiles, 1,764,425 trucks, and 233,449 motorcycles were registered in the state.

Ohio's ports rank among the busiest of the 50 states in volume. In 1991, the state's two most active ports, Lorain and Cleveland, together handled over $26.7 million tons of cargo, including 84,104 tons of exports.

Ohioans consider Dayton to be the birthplace of aviation because it was there that Wilbur and Orville Wright built the first motor-powered airplane in 1903. The major air terminal is the Greater Cincinnati airport (actually located across the Ohio River in Kentucky), which boarded 4,314,474 passengers on 69,574 departing flights in 1991.

11 HISTORY

The first European travelers in Ohio, during the 17th century, found four Native

American tribes of nomadic hunters: the Wyandot and Delaware in northern Ohio; the Miami and Shawnee in the south. European exploration was begun by a French nobleman, Robert Cavelier, Sieur de la Salle, who voyaged from the St. Lawrence River to the Ohio River in 1669–70.

Both the French and the English claimed possession of Ohio. The French claim rested on La Salle's exploration, while the British claimed all territory extending westward from their coastal colonies. The clash of ambitions eventually brought on the French and Indian War—during which Native Americans fought on both sides. The war ended in 1763 with French defeat and the ceding of the vast western territory to the British. During the Revolutionary War, the American militiaman George Rogers Clark, with a small company of woodsmen-soldiers, seized British posts and trading stations in Ohio. In the Battle of Piqua, Clark's forces defeated Native Americans allied with the British.

To provide for the development of the territory northwest of the Ohio River, the US Congress enacted the Land Ordinance of 1785 and the Northwest Ordinance of 1787. The first permanent settlement in Ohio, the historic town of Marietta, was established in 1788 by an organization of Revolutionary War veterans. Access to the fertile Ohio Valley was provided by the westward-flowing Ohio River, which carried pioneer settlers and frontier commerce.

Increasing settlement of the Ohio Valley aroused Indian resistance, which persisted until Major General "Mad Anthony"

Wayne routed Miami and Shawnee tribesmen in 1794 in the decisive Battle of Fallen Timbers. Native American leaders surrendered claim to the southern half of Ohio, opening that large domain to uncontested American occupation.

Statehood

In 1800, Connecticut ceded to the US a strip of land along Lake Erie (claimed by its colonial charter and called the Western Reserve), and that region became a part of the Northwest Territory. A great wave of migration from the older colonies followed. By 1802, Ohio had enough population to seek statehood, and in November, a constitutional convention assembled at Chillicothe to frame a constitution. On 1 March 1803, Ohio joined the Union as the 17th state.

Within ten years, the new state was confronted by conflicts on two different fronts. In the battle of Tippecanoe on 7 November 1811, Ohio militia regiments led by General William Henry Harrison repulsed an invasion by Native Americans from beyond Ohio's western border. Control of Lake Erie and of Great Lakes commerce was at stake when Commodore Oliver Hazard Perry won a decisive naval victory over a British fleet in western Lake Erie during the War of 1812.

With peace restored in 1815, "Ohio fever" spread through New England as migrants streamed westward, to be joined by immigrants from across the Atlantic, especially England, Ireland, and Germany. By 1850, Ohio was the third most populous state in the Union. The Ohio canal system, created between 1825 and 1841, linked the Ohio River and Lake Erie, providing a waterway to the Atlantic. By 1850, when farm and factory production outstripped the capacity of mule teams and canal barges, railroad building had begun. In the next decade, railroads crisscrossed the state.

1860s–1950s

In 1861, Ohio, like the nation, was divided. The northern counties, teeming with former New Englanders, were filled with abolitionist zeal in opposing slavery. But Ohio's southern counties had close ties with Virginia and Kentucky across the river and gathered enough political support to nominate pro-Confederacy "Copperhead" Clement L. Vallandigham for state governor in 1863. (He was defeated by Unionist John Brough.) Ohio surpassed its quota by providing a total of 320,000 Union Army volunteers and gave the Union its greatest generals—Ulysses S. Grant, William Tecumseh Sherman, and Philip H. Sheridan.

War demands stimulated Ohio manufacturing, and in the decade following the war, the state's industrial products surpassed the value of its rich farm production. In the 1870s, John D. Rockefeller of Cleveland formed the Standard Oil Company, which soon controlled oil refining and distribution throughout the nation. At the same time, B. F. Goodrich of Akron began making fire hose, the first rubber product in an industry whose tremendous growth would make Akron the "rubber capital of the world."

In the 1920s, Ohio's oil, rubber, and glass industries benefited from growing automobile production. Yet none of these industries was immune to the prolonged depression of the 1930s. Widespread unemployment and a stagnant economy were not relieved until the outbreak of World War II, which swept 641,000 Ohioans into military service.

The state's economy prospered after the war, with highway building, truck and tractor production, aircraft manufacture, and airport construction leading the field. The completion of the St. Lawrence Seaway in 1959 made Toledo and Cleveland active ocean ports. Major problems during this period involved pollution created by the dumping of industrial wastes (especially in Lake Erie), as well as urban decay resulting from the departure of middle-class families to the suburbs.

1960s–1990s

Deteriorating neighborhoods produced inadequate revenues for schools and public services, and attempts at racial integration brought controversy and disturbance. When political office went to minority leaders—in 1967, Carl Stokes of Cleveland became the first black mayor of any major US city—friction and tension continued. A further shock was the shooting of 13 students, 4 of whom died, at Kent State University on 4 May 1970 by the National Guard. They had been sent to the campus to preserve order during a series of student demonstrations against US involvement in Indochina.

During the early 1980s, Ohio was still beset by serious social and economic problems. The decline in manufacturing jobs was only partly offset by employment in the growing service area. Ohio's huge coal reserves were of limited use because of their content of sulfur, an atmospheric pollutant.

Ohio has begun to address its problems. It has strengthened its state universities and developed a system of community colleges that have brought vocational training within the reach of most of its citizens. In 1983, the state established the Thomas Edison Program, which provides start-up companies with venture capital funds. Ohio has also taken measures to protect and preserve its natural resources, reversing, to a significant extent, the pollution of Lake Erie.

12 STATE GOVERNMENT

Ohio's General Assembly consists of a 99-member house of representatives, elected for two years; and a senate of 33 members serving four-year terms. Each house may introduce legislation, and both houses must approve a bill before it can be signed into law by the governor. The governor's veto of a bill can be overridden by three-fifths majority votes of both houses.

Officials elected statewide are the governor and lieutenant governor (elected jointly), secretary of state, attorney general, auditor, and treasurer, all of whom serve four-year terms.

13 POLITICAL PARTIES

After the Civil War, 7 of the country's next 12 presidents were Ohio-born Republicans, beginning with Ulysses S. Grant and ending with Warren G. Harding. From

Ohio Presidential Vote by Political Parties, 1948–92

YEAR	OHIO WINNER	DEMOCRAT	REPUBLICAN	PROGRESSIVE	COMMUNIST	LIBERTARIAN
1948	*Truman (D)	1,452,791	1,445,684	37,487	—	—
1952	*Eisenhower (R)	1,600,367	2,100,391	—	—	—
1956	*Eisenhower (R)	1,439,655	2,262,610	—	—	—
1960	Nixon (R)	1,944,248	2,217,611	—	—	—
1964	*Johnson (D)	2,498,331	1,470,865	—	—	—
				AMERICAN IND.		
1968	*Nixon (R)	1,700,586	1,791,014	467,495	—	—
				AMERICAN		
1972	*Nixon (R)	1,558,889	2,441,827	80,067	6,437	—
1976	*Carter (D)	2,011,621	2,000,505	15,529	7,817	8,961
				CITIZENS		
1980	*Reagan (R)	1,745,103	2,203,139	8,979	5,030	49,604
1984	*Reagan (R)	1,825,440	2,678,560	—	—	5,886
					NEW ALLIANCE	
1988	*Bush (R)	1,939,629	2,416,549	—	12,017	11,989
				IND. (Perot)		
1992	*Clinton (D)	1,984,942	1,894,310	1,036,426	6,411	7,252

* Won US presidential election.

1856 to 1992, Ohioans voted for the Republican candidate in all presidential elections except those in which the following six Democrats were elected: Woodrow Wilson (twice), Franklin D. Roosevelt (three times), Harry S Truman, Lyndon B. Johnson, Jimmy Carter, and Bill Clinton. Overall, between 1946 and 1992, Republican governors served seven terms and Democrats, eight terms.

With the November 1994 elections, there were 6 Democrats and 13 Republicans serving as US Representatives. In 1992 both Ohio senators—John Glenn, elected to a fourth term in 1992, and Howard Metzenbaum, elected to a third term in 1988—were Democrats. However, in 1994 Metzenbaum retired and a Republican, Mike DeWine, won the seat. Republican George Voinovich won the governorship in 1990 and again in 1994. In the November 1994 elections, Republicans remained dominant in the state senate, with 20 seats as opposed to the Democrats' 13; and for the first time in 22 years Republicans took control of the house, 55 seats to 43.

In general, third parties have fared poorly in Ohio. Exceptions were the 1968 presidential election, in which American Independent Party candidate George Wallace earned nearly 12% of Ohio's popular vote, and the 1992 presidential election, when Independent Ross Perot captured 21% of the vote. Democrat Bill Clinton captured 40% of the vote to Bush's 38% in that election.

14 LOCAL GOVERNMENT

Local government in Ohio is exercised by the 88 counties, 942 cities and villages, and more than 1,300 townships. Each county is administered by a board of three commissioners. The county government is run by eight officials elected to four-year terms: the auditor or financial officer, whose duties include levying taxes; the clerk of courts, who is elected as clerk of the court of common pleas and also serves as clerk of the county court of appeals; the coroner, who must be a licensed physician; an engineer; a prosecuting attorney; the recorder, who keeps records of deeds, mortgages, and other legal documents; a sheriff; and the treasurer, who collects and disburses public funds.

There are three types of city government: the mayor-council plan, the form adopted by a majority of the state's approximately 200 cities; the city-manager form, under which the city council appoints a professional manager; and the commission type, in which a board of elected commissioners administers the city government.

In practice, most large cities have adopted a home-rule charter which permits them to select the form of government best suited to their requirements. Townships are governed by three trustees and a clerk, who oversee zoning ordinances, parks, road maintenance, fire protection, and other matters within their jurisdiction.

15 JUDICIAL SYSTEM

The supreme court of Ohio, the highest court in the state, reviews proceedings of the lower courts and of state agencies. Below the supreme court are 12 courts of appeals, which exercise jurisdiction over their respective judicial districts. Trial courts include 88 courts of common pleas, one in each county.

Probate courts, domestic relations courts, and juvenile courts often function as divisions of the common pleas courts. In 1957, a system of county courts was established by the legislature to replace justices of the peace and mayor's courts at the local level. Large cities have their own municipal, juvenile, and police courts. Ohio's crime rates rank well below the national averages. In 1993, state and federal prisons in Ohio had 40,641 inmates. The state's 1994 crime rate per 100,000 population was 4,461.4.

16 MIGRATION

The industrialization of Ohio in the late 19th and the 20th centuries encouraged the migration of Ohioans from the farms to the cities. A more recent development has been the exodus of urbanites from Ohio's largest cities. From 1970 to 1990, Cleveland lost 245,000 residents; Cincinnati, 90,000; Akron, 50,000; and Toledo, 50,000. During this period, Columbus was the only major city to gain residents (93,000). Ohio lost more than 72,000 people through migration during the period from 1985 to 1990. As of 1990, 74.1% of state residents had been born in Ohio.

17 ECONOMY

Ohio diversified its industries and enjoyed prosperity during and after World War II. In the 1970s, however, growth began to lag, as manufacturing shrank due to a decline in the demand for durable goods. With unemployment reaching peak levels, the state was forced to borrow from the federal government to fund the soaring cost of unemployment benefits. Recessionary trends in 1980 led to widespread layoffs in the auto parts industry. This bad economic news was partially offset when in 1983 the Honda Motor Company opened Japan's first US automobile assembly plant at Marysville near Columbus.

Despite its shrinking size, manufacturing remains the dominant industry in Ohio. Transportation equipment and industrial machinery are the largest employers.

18 INCOME

Ohio placed 22d in per capita (per person) income in 1994, with an average of $20,883. Total personal income was $231.8 billion. An estimated 13% of all Ohioans lived below the national poverty level in 1993.

19 INDUSTRY

Ohio has been a leading manufacturing state since the mid-1800s. In recent decades, the state has become important as a manufacturer of glassware, soap, matches, paint, business machines, refrigerators—and even comic books and Chinese food products. In 1992, the value of manufacturing shipments was estimated at $184.6 billion. Of this total value, transportation equipment accounted for 19%. Of the leading US industrial corporations listed by *Fortune* magazine for 1992, seven had their headquarters in Ohio.

20 LABOR

In 1994, Ohio's civilian labor force averaged 5,537,000. In that year, there was an unemployment rate of 5.5%. Of all Ohioans employed in 1993, most worked in the state's major metropolitan areas. In 1994, 19.1% of all workers in the state belonged to labor unions.

21 AGRICULTURE

Despite increasing urbanization and industrialization, agriculture retains its economic importance in Ohio. In 1994, the state ranked 13th in farm value (per acre) and 16th in agricultural income among the 50 states. In that year, the state's production of crops, dairy products, and livestock was valued at over $4.4 billion. The average size of farms increased from 94 acres (38 hectares) in 1940 to 203 acres (82 hectares) in 1994.

Ohio was the third-leading producer of tomatoes for processing in 1994 with 343,000 tons. Field crops in 1994 (in bushels) included corn for grain, 486,500,000; soybeans, 175,560,000; wheat, 68,440,000; and oats, 6,720,000. Ohio farmers also produced 4,384,000 tons of hay and 264,000 tons of sugar beets in 1994.

22 DOMESTICATED ANIMALS

In 1994, marketing of livestock and livestock products was valued at more than $1.5 billion. Ohio ranked second among the states in production of eggs, fifth in butter, ninth in milk, and ninth in hog production.

Cattle and hogs are raised in the central and western regions. In 1994, Ohio had 1,800,000 hogs, 1,490,000 head of cattle, and 162,000 sheep. Dairying is common in most regions of the state, but especially in the east and southeast. In 1994, nearly 4.5 billion pounds of milk was produced. Ohio poultry farmers raised 27,000,000 chickens and 6,000,000 turkeys in 1994. Egg production totaled over 5.6 billion.

23 FISHING

Commercial fishing, which once flourished in Lake Erie, has declined during the 20th century. Only 4,985,000 pounds of fish, worth $2,555,000, were landed in 1992. In 1991, a statewide fish hatchery system produced and stocked up to 30 million fish—mostly walleye, saugeye, trout, catfish, bass, sunfish, muskellunge, and pike.

24 FORESTRY

In 1991, Ohio had 7,864,100 acres (3,182,429 hectares) of forestland, representing 30% of the state's total land area. The state's lumber and wood products industry supplies building materials, household furniture, and paper products. In 1992, shipments of paper and allied products were valued at $4.4 billion; lumber and wood products at $1.4 billion; and furniture at $541 million. Reforestation programs involve the planting of more than 5,000 acres (2,000 hectares) per year.

25 MINING

The value of nonfuel mineral production in Ohio in 1994 was $893 million. Sand,

Photo credit: Greater Columbus Convention and Visitors Bureau.

The Ohio State Fair in Columbus, an annual event featuring agricultural produce and livestock exhibits.

gravel, and crushed stone were the leading mineral commodities produced in Ohio. The combined production of about 87 million tons of these commodities accounted for 50% or about $340 million of the state's nonfuel mineral value. In 1992, Ohio ranked second in the lime production (1,809,000 short tons worth $87,230,000), accounting for about 10% of the U.S. total.

26 ENERGY AND POWER

In 1993, electrical output totaled 133.7 billion kilowatt hours. Total energy consumption amounted to 3,733 trillion Btu. Coal was the source of about 39% of all energy consumed; petroleum, 30%;

dry natural gas, 22%; nuclear power, 1%; and other sources, about 8%. Energy expenditures per capita (per person) were $1,920 in 1992.

In 1993, the state produced eight million barrels of crude petroleum. Proven reserves were estimated in 1991 at approximately 66,000,000 barrels. About 137 billion cubic feet of natural gas were extracted in 1993, with reserves estimated in 1991 at 1.1 trillion cubic feet. In 1992, Ohio ranked 11th in the US in coal production, with a total output of 29,889,000 tons. As of 1993, two nuclear facilities, Perry in Lake County and Davis-Besse in Ottawa County, were in operation.

27 COMMERCE

Wholesale sales totaled $127.3 billion for 1992; retail sales were $92.4 billion for 1993; service establishment receipts were $45.2 billion for 1992. Ohio ranked seventh in the US as an exporter of goods, with exports worth $16.3 billion, in 1992.

28 PUBLIC FINANCE

The general assembly has nearly total authority in allocating general revenues, which are used primarily to support education, welfare, mental health facilities, law enforcement, property tax relief, and government operations. The state general revenues for the fiscal year 1994/95 were $30,670 million; expenditures were $30,696.5 million. Ohio had an outstanding debt of $1.1 billion as of 1993.

29 TAXATION

Ohio ranked ninth among the 50 states in total state tax revenues collected during the 1993 fiscal year. The state imposes a personal income tax and a corporate franchise tax. The sales and use tax was 5% on retail sales. Other taxes include those on cigarettes, alcoholic beverages, and gasoline. The state also imposes taxes on estates, banks, and insurance companies. In 1993, Ohio's state tax receipts from its own sources totaled $12.2 billion. Ohio residents paid more than $43.8 billion in federal income taxes in 1993.

30 HEALTH

Ohio ranks above the national average in deaths due to heart disease and cancer, but below the US average for deaths caused by accidents, cerebrovascular diseases, and suicide. Ohio had 192 community hospitals with 41,100 beds in 1993. The state had 23,000 active nonfederal physicians and 89,800 nurses in 1993. The average hospital expense per inpatient day was $940 in 1993, or $5,923 for an average cost per stay. Some 11.1% of state residents did not have health insurance in 1993.

31 HOUSING

In 1993, Ohio had an estimated 4,478,000 housing units. The median monthly mortgage and selected carrying costs for owner-occupied housing units was $625. The median monthly rent was $379. In 1990, the median home value was $63,500. In 1994, the state authorized construction of 47,152 new privately owned housing units, valued at $4.8 billion.

32 EDUCATION

Of the total adult population age 25 years and over in 1993, 82.8% were high school graduates, and 19.5% had completed at least four years of postsecondary study. In 1993/94, the state's 3,818 public elementary and secondary schools enrolled an estimated 1,806,981 pupils. In 1994, there were 103,929 public school teachers. Expenditures on education averaged $5,260 per pupil (28th in the nation) in 1993.

There are 12 state universities, including Ohio State University (Columbus); Ohio University (Athens); Miami University (Oxford); and other state universities at locations including Akron, Bowling Green, Cincinnati, Cleveland, Kent, and

The Cleveland Museum of Art.

Toledo. The largest is Ohio State. Ohio has 45 public two-year colleges. Well-known private colleges and universities include Antioch (Yellow Springs); Case Western Reserve (Cleveland); Kenyon (Gambier); Oberlin; Wittenberg (Springfield); and Wooster.

33 ARTS

The Cleveland Museum of Art was founded in 1913. Other notable centers for the visual arts include the Akron Art Institute, Columbus Museum of Art, and Toledo Museum of Art. Ohio also has three professional theatrical companies: the Cincinnati Playhouse, the Cleveland Playhouse, and the Great Lakes Shakespeare Festival. The Ohio Community Theater Association included groups in Akron, Canton, Columbus, Mansfield, Toledo, and Youngstown.

The Cleveland Orchestra is considered one of the finest in the world, especially since 1946, when George Szell began his 24-year tenure as conductor and music director. The Cincinnati Symphony was reorganized in 1909 with Leopold Stokowski as conductor. Operas are performed by resident companies in Cleveland, Columbus, and other cities.

The Cincinnati Pops Orchestra acquired a new summer home in 1984 at the newly opened Riverbend Music Center. Blossom

The Rock and Roll Hall of Fame and Museum opened in 1995.

Music Center, the Cleveland Orchestra's summer home in Peninsula, draws thousands of concert-goers annually for classical and popular programming. The State of Ohio generated $73,418,813 from federal and state sources in support of its arts programs from 1987 to 1991.

34 LIBRARIES AND MUSEUMS

In 1994, the state public library system had 39,581,381 volumes and a circulation of 130,862,641. Major public library systems include those of Cincinnati, Cleveland, Dayton, and Columbus. Columbus also has the library of the Ohio Historical Society, with 134,500 volumes. Leading academic libraries include those of Ohio

State University and Case Western Reserve University.

Among the state's more than 254 museums are the Museum of Art, Natural History Museum, Western Reserve Historical Society Museum, and Rock and Roll Hall of Fame and Museum in Cleveland; the Art Museum and Taft Museum in Cincinnati; the Dayton Art Institute; and the Center of Science and Industry and Wexner Center for the Arts in Columbus. The Zanesville Art Center has collections of ceramics and glass made in the Zanesville area. Also noteworthy are the US Air Force Museum near Dayton, the Neil Armstrong Air and Space Museum in Wapakoneta, and the Ohio River Museum in Marietta.

Photo credit: Greater Columbus Convention and Visitors Bureau.

The magnificent Ohio Theatre in Columbus.

Schoenbrunn Village State Memorial is a reconstruction of the state's first settlement by Moravian missionaries, near New Philadelphia. Archaeological sites include the "great circle" mounds, built by the Hopewell Indians at present-day Newark, and Inscription Rock on Kelleys Island.

35 COMMUNICATIONS

In March 1993, 95% of Ohio's 4,262,000 occupied housing units had telephones. In 1993 there were 129 AM stations and 241 FM stations. There were 40 commercial and 12 noncommercial television stations. There were also 26 large cable television systems serving the state.

36 PRESS

In 1994 there were 15 morning daily newspapers, 68 daily evening papers, one all-day daily, and 30 Sunday papers. Leading Ohio newspapers with their daily circulation in 1994 were *The Plain Dealer* in Cleveland (432,449); the *Columbus Dispatch* (264,858); the *Cincinnati Enquirer* (198,832); and the *Dayton Daily News* (184,464).

37 TOURISM, TRAVEL, AND RECREATION

Leading tourist attractions include Ohio's presidential memorials and homes: the William Henry Harrison Memorial at North Bend; Ulysses S. Grant's birthplace at Point Pleasant; the James A. Garfield home at Mentor; the Rutherford B. Hayes home at Fremont; the William McKinley Memorial at Canton; the Taft National Historic Site in Cincinnati; and the Warren G. Harding home in Marion. Also of interest is the Thomas A. Edison birthplace at Milan.

Among the many attractions in the northern region are the reconstructions of Auglaize Village near Defiance and of Harbour Town in Vermilion. The Cuyahoga Valley Natural Recreation Area is a popular attraction.

The eastern Allegheny region has several ski resorts for winter sports enthusiasts. Popular tourist attractions include the Amish settlement around Millersburg and the restored Roscoe Village on the Ohio-Erie Canal. The showboat *Majestic*, the last of the original floating theaters, is a popular Cincinnati attraction. The Wright brothers' early flying machines can be viewed in Dayton's Carillon Park. At Columbus are a recreated 19th century Ohio village and a restored German district, as well as the Exposition Center, site of the annual Ohio State Fair.

Ohio's state parks comprise 208,000 acres (84,000 hectares). Among the most visited state parks are Kelleys Island on Lake Erie, Mohican, Pymatuning, and Salt Fork. Anglers there fish for bass, catfish, and rainbow trout. Popular amusement parks include Kings Island (near Cincinnati), Cedar Point (near Sandusky), and Sea World (near Cleveland).

38 SPORTS

There are five major league professional sports teams in Ohio: the Cleveland Indians and the Cincinnati Reds of Major League Baseball; the Cleveland Browns (scheduled to move to Baltimore after the 1995/96 season), and the Cincinnati Bengals of the National Football League and the Cleveland Cavaliers of the National Basketball Association.

Akron has been headquarters for the Professional Bowlers Association (PBA) since its founding in 1958. The World Series of Golf is played annually in Akron, and the Memorial Golf Tournament in Columbus. Major horse-racing tracks include Cleveland's Thistledown, Cincinnati's River Downs, and Columbus's Scioto Downs.

In collegiate sports, Ohio State University has long been a football power, winning 24 Big Ten titles (through 1994). Ohio State also has won NCAA championships in baseball, basketball, fencing, golf, gymnastics, and swimming, while Cincinnati and Dayton universities have had highly successful basketball teams. The Pro Football Hall of Fame is located in Canton, where the sport was first organized professionally in 1920.

39 FAMOUS OHIOANS

Ohio has been the native state of seven US presidents and the residence of another. Inventions by Ohioans include the incandescent light, the arc light, and the airplane.

As the territorial delegate to Congress, William Henry Harrison (b.Virginia,

1773–1841), who later became the ninth US president, fostered the Harrison Land Act, which stimulated new settlements. Harrison died of pneumonia exactly one month after his presidential inauguration. From 1869 to 1881, the White House was occupied by three Ohioans, all Republicans who had served with distinction as Union Army generals. The first, Ulysses Simpson Grant (1822–85), became the nation's hero after victories at Shiloh and Vicksburg and then became the 18th US president, elected in 1868 and reelected in 1872.

Rutherford B. Hayes (1822–93), the 19th US president, defeated New York's Governor Samuel J. Tilden in a close and disputed election. Hayes chose not to run for reelection, returning instead to Ohio to work on behalf of humanitarian causes. James A. Garfield (1831–81), 20th US president, held office only a few months before being assassinated. Benjamin Harrison (1833–1901), 23d US president, moved toward annexation of Hawaii and enlarged the civil-service system.

US presidents in the 20th century include three more native Ohioans. William McKinley (1843–1901), elected in 1896 as the 25th president, established the gold standard and maintained tariff protection for US manufactures. Early in his second term, he was shot to death by a young anarchist. William Howard Taft (1857–1930), the 27th US president, gained a national reputation in 1904 as President Theodore Roosevelt's secretary of war. Five years later, he succeeded Roosevelt in the White House. In 1921, under President Warren G. Harding (1865–1923), Taft became US chief justice.

Harding, the last Ohioan to win the White House, became the 29th US president. Harding died in office amidst corruption in his own cabinet.

Charles W. Fairbanks (1852–1918) served as vice-president under Theodore Roosevelt during 1905–09. Charles Gates Dawes (1865–1951) became vice-president under Calvin Coolidge in 1925, the same year the Dawes Plan for reorganizing German finances brought him the Nobel Peace Prize. Three Ohioans served as chief justice on the Supreme Court: Salmon P. Chase (b.New Hampshire, 1808–73), Morrison R. Waite (b.Connecticut, 1816–88), and Taft. Most notable among nearly 40 cabinet officers from Ohio were Treasury Secretaries Salmon P. Chase and John Sherman (1823–1900), and Secretary of War Edwin M. Stanton (1814–69). William Tecumseh Sherman (1820–91) was a renowned Union general in the Civil War.

Nobel Prize winners from Ohio include Charles G. Dawes and physicists Arthur Compton (1892–1962) and Donald Glaser (b.1926). Notable Pulitzer Prize winners include novelist Louis Bromfield (1896–1956) and historian and biographer Arthur Schlesinger, Jr. (b.1917). Ohio writers of enduring fame are fiction writers Zane Grey (1875–1939) and Sherwood Anderson (1876–1941); poet Hart Crane (1899–1932); and humorist James Thurber (1894–1961). Toni Morrison (b. 1931), winner of the 1988 Pulitzer Prize for literature and the 1993 Nobel Prize for literature, was born in Lorain, Ohio. Rita Dove (b.1952), poet laureate of the US from 1993 to 1995, was the first African American to receive that designation.

Among Ohio's eminent journalists are satirist Ambrose Bierce (1842–1914), columnist James Reston (b.Scotland, 1909), and author-commentator Lowell Thomas (1892–1981). Important in the art world include painters Thomas Cole (b.England, 1801–48) and George Bellows (1882–1925). Defense lawyer Clarence Darrow (1857–1938) was also an Ohioan.

Horace Mann (b.Massachusetts, 1796–1859) was the first president of innovative Antioch College. Among Ohio-born inventor-scientists, Thomas A. Edison (1847–1931) produced the incandescent lamp, the phonograph, and the movie camera. Charles Brush (1849–1929) invented the arc light. The Wright brothers, Orville (1871–1948) and Wilbur (b.Indiana, 1867–1912), made the first flight in a powered aircraft. Ohio's leading industrialist was John D. Rockefeller (b.New York, 1839–1937), founder of Standard Oil of Ohio. Edward "Eddie" Rickenbacker (1890–1973), an ace pilot in World War I, was president of Eastern Airlines.

The most notable Ohioans in the entertainment field are movie actor Clark Gable (1901–60); movie director Stephen Spielberg (b.1947); comedian Bob Hope (Leslie Townes Hope, b.England, 1903); television host Phil Donahue (b.1935); actor Paul Newman (b.1925); singer and actor Dean Martin (Dino Crocetti, 1917–95); jazz pianist Art Tatum (1910–56); and composer Henry Mancini (1924–94).

Leading sports figures from Ohio are baseball pitcher Cy Young (1867–1955), baseball star Peter "Pete" Rose (b.1941), track star Jesse Owens (b.Alabama, 1912–80), and golfer Jack Nicklaus (b.1940). James "Buster" Douglas (b.1960), is a boxer who knocked out Mike Tyson. Astronauts from Ohio include John Glenn (b.1921), the first American to orbit the earth, who was elected US senator from Ohio in 1974; Neil Armstrong (b.1930), the first man to walk on the moon; and James Lovell (b.1928).

40 BIBLIOGRAPHY

Condon, George E. *Cleveland: The Best Kept Secret.* Garden City, N.Y.: Doubleday, 1967.

Havighurst, Walter. *Ohio: A Bicentennial History.* New York: Norton, 1976.

Hopkins, Charles E. *Ohio the Beautiful and Historic.* Boston: Page, 1931.

OKLAHOMA

State of Oklahoma

ORIGIN OF STATE NAME: Derived from the Choctaw Indian words *okla humma*, meaning "land of the red people."

NICKNAME: The Sooner State.

CAPITAL: Oklahoma City.

ENTERED UNION: 16 November 1907 (46th).

SONG: "Oklahoma!"

POEM: "Howdy Folks."

MOTTO: *Labor omnia vincit* (Labor conquers all things).

FLAG: On a blue field, a peace pipe and an olive branch cross an Osage warrior's shield, which is decorated with small crosses and from which seven eagle feathers descend. The word "Oklahoma" appears below.

OFFICIAL SEAL: Each point of a five-pointed star incorporates the emblem of a Native American nation: (clockwise from top) Chickasaw, Choctaw, Seminole, Creek, and Cherokee. In the center, a frontiersman and Native American shake hands before the goddess of justice; behind them are symbols of progress, including a farm, train, and mill. Surrounding the large star are 45 small ones and the words "Great Seal of the State of Oklahoma 1907."

ANIMAL: American buffalo (bison).

BIRD: Scissor-tailed flycatcher.

FISH: White bass (sand bass).

FLORAL EMBLEM: Mistletoe.

TREE: Redbud.

STONE: Barite rose (rose rock).

REPTILE: Collared lizard (mountain boomer).

GRASS: Indian grass.

TIME: 6 AM CST = noon GMT.

1 LOCATION AND SIZE

Situated in the western south-central US, Oklahoma ranks 18th in size among the 50 states. The total area of Oklahoma is 69,903 square miles (181,049 square kilometers). Oklahoma extends 464 miles (747 kilometers) east-west including the panhandle in the northwest, which is about 165 miles (266 kilometers) long. The maximum north-south extension is 230 miles (370 kilometers). The total estimated boundary length of Oklahoma is 1,581 miles (2,544 kilometers).

2 TOPOGRAPHY

Four mountain ranges cross this Great Plains state: the Ouachitas in the southeast, the Ozark Plateau in the northeast, the Arbuckles in the southcentral part of the state, and the Wichitas in the southwest. Much of the northwest belongs to the High Plains, while northeastern Oklahoma consists mainly of buttes and valleys. The state is drained by the Arkansas River, the Red River, the Little River, and Lee Creek. There are few natural lakes but many artificial ones.

3 CLIMATE

Oklahoma has a continental climate with cold winters and hot summers. Normal daily mean temperatures in Oklahoma City range from 37°F (3°C) in January to 82°F (28°C) in July. The record low temperature of –27°F (–33°C) was set on 18 January 1930; the record high, 120°F (49°C), occurred in 1943. Precipitation varies from an average of 15 inches (38 centimeters) annually in the panhandle to over 50 inches (127 centimeters) in the southeast. Oklahoma ranks fourth in the US in annual number of tornadoes sighted.

4 PLANTS AND ANIMALS

Grasses grow in abundance in Oklahoma, with buffalo grass most common in the western counties. Deciduous hardwoods stand in eastern Oklahoma, and red and yellow cactus brighten the Black Mesa. The white-tailed deer is found in all counties, and Rio Grande wild turkeys are hunted across much of the state. A few herds of American buffalo (bison) are also preserved. The bobwhite quail and prairie chicken are common game birds. Native sport fish include bass and catfish. Among the state's endangered species are the leopard darter, red wolf, and Indiana bat.

Oklahoma Population Profile

Estimated 1995 population:	3,271,000
Population change, 1980–90:	4.0%
Leading ancestry group:	German
Second leading group:	Irish
Foreign born population:	2.1%
Hispanic origin†:	2.7%
Population by race:	
White:	82.1%
Black:	7.4%
Native American:	8.0%
Asian/Pacific Islander:	1.1%
Other:	1.4%

Population by Age Group

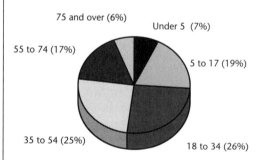

75 and over (6%)
Under 5 (7%)
55 to 74 (17%)
5 to 17 (19%)
35 to 54 (25%)
18 to 34 (26%)

Top Cities with Populations Over 25,000

City	Population	National rank	% change 1980–90
Oklahoma City	453,995	29	10.3
Tulsa	375,307	41	1.8
Lawton	87,168	240	0.6
Norman	83,678	266	17.8
Broken Arrow	62,604	386	62.3
Edmond	57,128	431	51.0
Midwest City	52,845	493	5.5
Enid	45,076	590	–10.0
Moore	41,659	648	15.0
Muskogee	38,329	710	–5.8

Notes: †A person of Hispanic origin may be of any race. NA indicates that data are not available.
Sources: Economic and Statistics Administration, Bureau of the Census. *Statistical Abstract of the United States, 1994–95.* Washington, DC: Government Printing Office, 1995; Courtenay M. Slater and George E. Hall. *1995 County and City Extra: Annual Metro, City and County Data Book.* Lanham, MD: Bernan Press, 1995.

OKLAHOMA

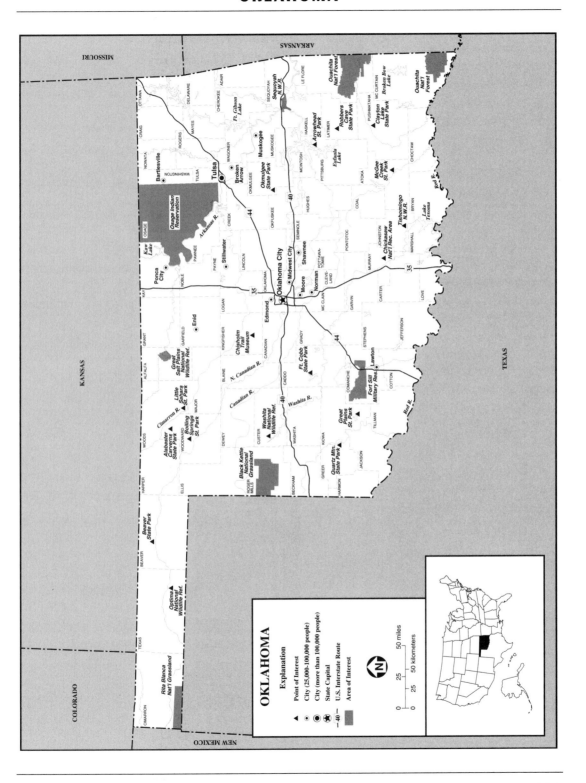

5 ENVIRONMENTAL PROTECTION

Toxic industrial wastes remain an environmental concern, and old mines in the Tar Creek area of northeastern Oklahoma still exude groundwater contaminated by zinc, iron, and cadmium. Three hazardous waste sites are on the EPA's National Priorities List for Superfund cleanup. The state has instituted municipal curbside recycling programs and has 11 municipal landfills. There were 11 hazardous waste sites in Oklahoma as of 1994.

6 POPULATION

Oklahoma ranked 28th among the states in the 1990 census with a total population of 3,145,585. The estimated 1995 population was 3,271,000; a population of 3,382,000 is projected for the year 2000. In 1990, Oklahoma had a population density of 45.8 persons per square mile (17.6 persons per square kilometer). The largest city is Oklahoma City, with 958,839 people in the metropolitan area. The city itself had a population of 453,995 in 1992. Tulsa, the second-largest city, had a 1992 population of 375,307; Lawton had 87,168.

7 ETHNIC GROUPS

According to the 1990 Census, Oklahoma has more Native Americans—252,420—than any other state. More than 51% of the state's black population, 234,000 in 1990, lived in Oklahoma City and Tulsa. Most first- and second-generation Mexicans live in Oklahoma City, Tulsa, and Lawton. Most of the 86,000 persons classified as of Hispanic origin in the 1990 census were of Mexican descent.

8 LANGUAGES

Oklahoma English is diverse, with an uneven blending of features of North Midland, South Midland, and Southern dialects. In 1990, 2,775,957 Oklahomans—95% of the resident population five years old or older—spoke only English at home. Other languages spoken at home, and the number of people who spoke them, included Spanish, 64,562; various Native American languages, 19,158; and German, 15,195.

9 RELIGION

The leading Protestant groups in 1990 included Southern Baptist, 964,615; United Methodist, 326,294; Assembly of God, 88,780; Church of Christ, 85,193; Christian Church (Disciples of Christ), 58,901; and Episcopal, 18,908. There were 143,640 Roman Catholics and an estimated 9,980 Jews in 1990. Buddhism, Islam, and shamanism are also practiced in the state.

10 TRANSPORTATION

As of 31 December 1992, there were 3,423 rail miles (5,508 kilometers) of track. In 1979, Amtrak terminated the state's last passenger train, but is currently considering reestablishing service. Interurban transit needs are supplied by buses. Overall in 1993, Oklahoma had 112,467 miles (180,959 kilometers) of roadway. A total of 2,771,353 motor vehicles were registered in 1993, including 1,758,903 automobiles and 998,407 trucks.

Oklahoma's chief port, the Tulsa Port of Catoosa on the Verdigris River, handled 2,069,090 tons of cargo in 1991.

American Indian Exposition in Anadarko.

Tulsa International Airport, which boarded 1,399,342 passengers in 1991, and Will Rogers World Airport in Oklahoma City, which boarded 1,456,747 passengers, are the state's largest airports.

11 HISTORY

At the time the Spanish *conquistadores*, led by Hernando de Soto and Francisco Vásquez de Coronado, arrived in Oklahoma in the 16th century, only a few scattered Native American tribes inhabited the region. Two centuries later, French trappers moved up the rivers of Oklahoma.

Except for the panhandle, all of present-day Oklahoma became part of US territory with the Louisiana Purchase in 1803. Under the Indian Removal Act of 1830, many Native American tribes from the southeastern US were ordered to resettle in Oklahoma in what was then known as Indian Territory. The Cherokees, Chickasaw, Choctaw, Creek, and Seminole prospered in the new land, which offered rich soil and abundant vegetation. Military posts such as Fort Gibson and Fort Towson were established between 1824 and the 1880s, with settlements growing up around them.

During the early Civil War period, Native Americans allied with the Confederacy. After Union troops captured Fort Gibson in 1863, the Union Army controlled half their lands. Congress opened western Oklahoma—formerly reserved for the Cherokee, Cheyenne, Fox, and other tribes—to homesteaders in 1889. The western region became Oklahoma Territory in 1890, while most of eastern Oklahoma remained under Native American control. Oklahoma became the 46th state on 16 November 1907 after a vote of the residents of both territories. Oklahoma City was named the state capital in 1910.

State Development

Oil wells were producing more than 40 million barrels annually when Oklahoma entered the Union, and the state led all others in oil production until 1928. The decade of the 1920s was a period of racial unrest in Oklahoma—close to 100,000 Oklahomans belonged to the Ku Klux Klan 1921. The 1930s brought a destructive drought, dust storms, and an exodus of unemployed "Okies," many of them to California.

Under post-World War II governors Roy Turner, Johnston Murray, and Raymond Gary, tax reductions attracted industry, major highways were built, and Oklahoma's higher educational facilities were integrated. Oil and gas again brought increased wealth to the state in the 1960s, 1970s, and early 1980s, as state revenues from oil and gas increased from $72 million in 1972 to $745 million in 1982.

In 1983, the oil boom suddenly ended, as oil prices fell in the face of a growing worldwide oil glut. The failure of 24 banks and mounting distress among the state's farmers added to Oklahoma's financial woes. However, those industries with a national rather than a regional base, such as transportation, food processing, and light manufacturing, continued to prosper.

12 STATE GOVERNMENT

The Oklahoma legislature consists of two chambers: a 48-member senate and a 101-member house of representatives. Elected executive officials include the governor, lieutenant governor, attorney general, and state treasurer. Any member of either house may introduce legislation. A bill passed by the legislature becomes law if signed by the governor, or if left unsigned by the governor for five days while the legislature is in session, or if passed over the governor's veto by two-thirds of the elected members of each house (or three-fourths in the case of emergency bills).

13 POLITICAL PARTIES

When Oklahoma was admitted to the Union in 1907, Democrats outnumbered Republicans, as they have ever since. Democrats have dominated the lesser state offices, but the Republicans won the governorship three times between 1962 and 1990. Also, the Republican presidential nominee outpolled his Democratic counterpart in ten of twelve presidential elections between 1948 and 1992.

As of 1994, the Democratic Party had 1,452,949 registered voters, or 63% of the total; while registered Republicans numbered 775,754, or 34% of the total. There were 73,576 registered independents, or 3% of the total.

Oklahomans cast 42% of the popular vote for Republican George Bush in 1992; 33% for Bill Clinton; and 25% for Ross Perot. Democrat Don Nickles won election to his third term in the Senate in 1992. Republican David Boren's seat in the Senate, which came open in 1994, was won by Republican James M. Inhofe.

Of the six-member delegation of US Representatives, five are Republicans and one is Democrat. (Republicans gained two seats in the 1994 election.) In November 1994, Republicans also won the governor's office when Frank Keating, a former official in the administration of President Ronald Reagan, was elected. There are 37 Democrats and 11 Republicans in the state senate and 70 Democrats and 31 Republicans in the state house.

Oklahoma Presidential Vote by Political Parties, 1948–92

YEAR	OKLAHOMA WINNER	DEMOCRAT	REPUBLICAN
1948	*Truman (D)	452,782	687,817
1952	*Eisenhower (R)	430,939	518,045
1956	*Eisenhower (R)	385,581	473,769
1960	Nixon (R)	370,111	533,039
1964	*Johnson (D)	519,834	412,665
1968	*Nixon (R)	301,658	449,697
1972	*Nixon (R)	247,147	759,025
1976	Ford (R)	532,442	545,708
1980	*Reagan (R)	402,026	695,570
1984	*Reagan (R)	385,080	861,530
1988	*Bush (R)	483,423	678,367
1992**	Bush (R)	473,066	592,929

* Won US presidential election.
** Independent candidate Ross Perot received 319,878 votes.

14 LOCAL GOVERNMENT

As of 1992, local governmental units in Oklahoma included 78 counties, 589 incorporated cities and towns, and several hundred unincorporated areas. County government consists of three commissioners elected by districts, as well as a county clerk, assessor, treasurer, and other officials. Any city of 2,000 or more people may vote to become a home-rule city, determining its own form of government. Cities electing not to adopt a home-rule charter operate under aldermanic, mayor-council, or council-manager systems.

15 JUDICIAL SYSTEM

The supreme court, the state's highest court, consists of nine justices. The court's appeals jurisdiction includes all civil cases except those which it assigns to the courts of appeals. The highest appeals court for criminal cases is the court of criminal appeals. District courts have original jurisdiction over legal matters and some review powers over administrative actions. Municipal courts hear cases arising from local ordinances. In 1994, the FBI reported a crime index total of 5,570.1 crimes per 100,000 population.

16 MIGRATION

The trend toward out-migration that began during the dust bowl era of the 1930s continued after World War II. From 1940 through 1960, Oklahoma's net loss from migration was 653,000. Migration patterns were reversed, however, after 1960. From 1960 to the mid-1980s, more people moved into the state than out of it. From 1985 to 1990, however, a net migration loss of about 95,500 was reported.

17 ECONOMY

Manufacturing heads the list of growth areas, followed by wholesale and retail

Oklahoma City, the state capital.

trade, services, finance, insurance, and real estate. Oil and gas extraction continues to play a major role. The oil industry boomed from the mid-1970s through the mid-1980s. In 1985, however, the boom ended, and Oklahoma's unemployment rate, which had averaged about 3% in the early 1980s, jumped to 9%. Since 1986, the economy has undergone a slow but steady recovery.

18 INCOME

In 1994 the average per capita (per person) income in Oklahoma was $17,602 (45th among the states). Total personal income increased to $57.3 billion in 1994. Some 19.9% of all state residents were below the federal poverty level in 1993.

19 INDUSTRY

Resource-related industries dominate the economy, but manufacturing has become increasingly diversified. The total value of shipments of manufactured goods in 1991 was more than $28.4 billion. Among the nation's largest industrial corporations with headquarters in Oklahoma are Phillips Petroleum and Kerr-McGee Oil.

20 LABOR

The civilian labor force in 1994 was estimated at 1,540,000 persons, of whom 5.8% were unemployed. Some 8.8% of all workers in the state were labor union members in 1994, and three national labor unions operating in the state in 1993.

21 AGRICULTURE

Agriculture remains an important economic activity in Oklahoma, even though its share of personal income and employment has declined since 1950. Total farm income, estimated at $3.8 billion, ranked 18th in the US in 1994. The state ranked fourth in the US for wheat production in 1994, with 143,100,000 bushels, worth $494 million. Peanut production was 258,000,000 pounds. Other 1994 crop figures include hay, 4,128,000 tons; sorghum for grain, 14,000,000 bushels; soybeans, 7,280,000 bushels; corn for grain, 16,500,000 bushels; oats, 1,110,000 bushels; and barley, 222,000 bushels.

22 DOMESTICATED ANIMALS

In 1994, there were 5,700,000 cattle (fourth in the US); 98,000 milk cows; 590,000 hogs; and 96,000 sheep on Oklahoma farms and ranches. In 1994, cattle products accounted for 57.7% of agricultural receipts; broilers, 7.8%; and dairy products, 4.3%.

23 FISHING

Commercial fishing is of minor importance in Oklahoma. The white bass (sand bass), Oklahoma's state fish, is abundant in most large reservoirs. Rainbow trout are stocked year-round in the Illinois River, and walleye and sauger are stocked in most reservoirs. In 1991, four state fish hatcheries produced 30 million fish.

24 FORESTRY

Forests cover about 10 million acres (4 million hectares), or nearly one-fourth of the state's land area. In 1993, nearly 90 million cubic feet of roundwood was being harvested in the eastern 18 counties. From this, approximately 150 million board feet of hardwood and 250 million board feet of softwood lumber were produced. The remaining 30 million cubic feet were processed into poles, posts, and paper products.

25 MINING

Large deposits of limestone are found throughout northeastern Oklahoma, while gypsum is extracted in several regions. The value of nonfuel mineral production in Oklahoma in 1994 was estimated at $338 million. Oklahoma remained the only state producing crude iodine, and was first of 20 states producing crude gypsum.

26 ENERGY AND POWER

Electric power production in Oklahoma in 1993 was 48.8 billion kilowatt hours. Coal-fired steam units accounted for 59.4% of electricity produced. The state has no nuclear power plants. Oklahoma is rich in fossil fuel resources, producing oil, natural gas, and coal. Crude oil production was 97 million barrels in 1993. In 1993, Oklahoma's natural gas production was 2.1 trillion cubic feet (third in the US). Production of bituminous coal was 1.9 million tons in 1992. Energy expenditures were $1,887 per capita (per person) in 1992.

Photo credit: Oklahoma Tourism. Photo by Fred W. Marvel.

"Riding into the Sunset" by Electra A. Waggoner. Will Rogers Memorial, Claremore.

27 COMMERCE

Oklahoma's wholesale sales totaled $26.4 billion for 1992; retail sales were $20.8 billion for 1993; and service establishment receipts were $11.2 billion for 1992. The value of foreign exports in 1992 was $2 billion.

28 PUBLIC FINANCE

Article 10, section 23, of the Oklahoma Constitution requires a balanced budget. The consolidated state revenues for the period 1992/93 were $7,758.1 million; expenditures were $7,268.4 million.

The total indebtedness of state and local governments in Oklahoma surpassed $3.7 billion in mid-l993.

29 TAXATION

In 1991, Oklahoma ranked 22d in the US in state taxes per capita (per person). As of 1994, the state taxed personal and corporate income, and levied a sales and use tax of 4.5%. Property taxes remain the principal source of revenue for local governments. Other taxes include a motor fuels tax; a tax on extraction of oil and gas, uranium, and other minerals; and a gas conservation excise tax. Oklahoma's federal income tax burden in 1990 was $4.3 billion.

30 HEALTH

The leading causes of death in 1992 were heart disease, cancer, cerebrovascular disease, and accidents. Oklahoma had 110 community hospitals in 1993, providing 11,700 beds. The average hospital expense per inpatient day was $797 for 1993, or $5,093 for an average cost per stay. Oklahoma had 4,900 licensed nonfederal physicians in 1993 and 17,000 nurses. Some 23.6% of state residents did not have health insurance in 1993.

31 HOUSING

Oklahomans continue to prefer single-family dwellings, despite a recent trend toward condominiums. In 1993 there were an estimated 1,415,000 year-round housing units. As of 1990, the median home value was $48,100, with a median monthly cost for an owner (including mortgage) of $573. The median monthly rent was $340 in 1990.

32 EDUCATION

About 76.7% of all Oklahomans 25 years of age or older were high school graduates in 1990. During the same year, 31.2% of adult state residents had at least one year of college, almost the same as the US average. In 1993, Oklahoma's public school enrollment totaled 602,000. Expenditures on education averaged $4,085 per pupil (45th in the nation) in 1993.

Public higher education institutions include 2 comprehensive institutions, 6 regional campuses, 18 senior and junior colleges, and a professional college. The University of Oklahoma (Norman) and Oklahoma State University (Stillwater), have more than 20,800 students each. The 16 private colleges and universities in Oklahoma increased their enrollment to

19,270 in 1990. Well-known institutions include Oral Roberts University and the University of Tulsa.

33 ARTS

Major arts centers are located in Tulsa and Oklahoma City, but there are many art and crafts museums throughout the state. Oklahoma City's leading cultural institution is the Oklahoma Symphony. The Tulsa Philharmonic, Tulsa Ballet Theater, and Tulsa Opera all appear at the Tulsa Performing Arts Center. The Myriad Center in Oklahoma City and the Lloyd Noble Center in Norman host rock, jazz, and country music concerts.

34 LIBRARIES AND MUSEUMS

Oklahoma has 200 libraries operated by 8 library systems around the state. In 1992, a total of 5,522,919 volumes occupied public library shelves; total circulation was 16,300,147. Oklahoma has 110 museums and historic sites. The Philbrook Art Center in Tulsa houses important collections of Native American, Renaissance, and Oriental art. Other museums of special interest include the Museum of the Great Plains in Lawton, the Cowboy Hall of Fame and Western Heritage Center in Oklahoma City, and the Will Rogers Memorial in Claremore.

35 COMMUNICATIONS

In March 1993, 91.9% of Oklahoma's occupied housing units had telephones. In 1993, Oklahoma had 65 AM and 116 FM radio stations, 21 commercial and 5 educational television channels, and 2 major cable television systems.

36 PRESS

In 1994, Oklahoma had 8 morning dailies, 27 evening dailies, and 37 Sunday newspapers. Leading dailies and their daily circulation in 1994 were the *Oklahoma City Oklahoman* (231,653); and the *Tulsa World* (133,902). As of 1994, there were 148 newspapers that appeared weekly or up to three times a week.

37 TOURISM, TRAVEL, AND RECREATION

Tourism has become a growing area of Oklahoma's economy. Tourists from across the US spent almost $2.7 billion in the state in 1993. Oklahoma's 62 state parks draw some 16 million visitors annually. Chickasaw National Recreation Area centers on artificial Lake Arbuckle. The state also maintains and operates the American Indian Hall of Fame, in Anadarko; the Pioneer Woman Statue and Museum, in Ponca City; and the Chisholm Trail Museum, in Kingfisher.

38 SPORTS

Oklahoma has no major league professional sports teams. The class-AAA baseball 89ers play in Oklahoma City. Sports on the college level are still the primary source of pride for Oklahomans. As of 1994, the University of Oklahoma Sooners had won six national football titles in season-ending polls. They have also produced championships in wrestling, baseball, and gymnastics. The Oklahoma State University Cowboys have captured NCAA and Big Eight titles in basketball, baseball, and golf, and are a perennial national contender in wrestling.

39 FAMOUS OKLAHOMANS

Congressman Carl Albert (b.1908), Speaker of the House from 1971 until his retirement in 1976, held the highest public position of any Oklahoman.

John Berryman (1914–72) won the 1965 Pulitzer Prize in poetry for *77 Dream Songs, 1964*; and Ralph Ellison (1914–94) won the 1953 National Book Award for his novel *Invisible Man*. The popular musical *Oklahoma!*, by Richard Rodgers and Oscar Hammerstein II, is based on *Green Grow the Lilacs* by Oklahoman Lynn Riggs (1899–1954). N(avarre) Scott Momaday (b.1934), born in Lawton, received a Pulitzer Prize in 1969 for *House Made of Dawn*. Woodrow Crumbo (b.1912) and Allen Houser (b.1914) are prominent Native American artists born in the state.

Just about the best-known Oklahoman was William Penn Adair "Will" Rogers (1879–1935), the beloved humorist and writer. James Francis "Jim" Thorpe (1888–1953) became known as the "world's greatest athlete" after his pentathlon and decathlon performances at the 1912 Olympic Games. Baseball star Mickey Mantle (1931–95) was a native Oklahoman.

40 BIBLIOGRAPHY

Fischer, John. *From the High Plains*. New York: Harper & Row, 1978.

Gibson, Arrell M. *The Oklahoma Story*. Norman: University of Oklahoma Press, 1978.

Morgan, H. Wayne, and Anne Hodges. *Oklahoma: A Bicentennial History*. New York: Norton, 1977.

OREGON

State of Oregon

ORIGIN OF STATE NAME: Unknown; name first applied to the river now known as the Columbia, possibly from the Algonquian for "beautiful water."

NICKNAME: The Beaver State.

CAPITAL: Salem.

ENTERED UNION: 14 February 1859 (33d).

SONG: "Oregon, My Oregon."

DANCE: Square dance.

MOTTO: She flies with her own wings.

COLORS: Navy-blue and gold.

FLAG: The flag consists of a navy-blue field with gold lettering and illustrations. Obverse: the shield from the state seal, supported by 33 stars, with the words "State of Oregon" above and the year of admission below. Reverse: a beaver.

OFFICIAL SEAL: A shield, supported by 33 stars and crested by an American eagle, depicts mountains and forests, an elk, a covered wagon and ox team, wheat, a plow, a pickax, and the state motto. In the background, as the sun sets over the Pacific, an American merchant ship arrives as a British man-o'-war departs. The words "State of Oregon 1859" surround the whole.

ANIMAL: American beaver.

BIRD: Western meadowlark.

FISH: Chinook salmon.

FLOWER: Oregon grape.

TREE: Douglas fir.

ROCK: Thunderegg (geode).

INSECT: Oregon swallowtail butterfly.

TIME: 5 AM MST = noon GMT; 4 AM PST = noon GMT.

1 LOCATION AND SIZE

Located on the Pacific coast of the northwestern US. Oregon ranks tenth in size among the 50 states. The total area of Oregon is 97,073 square miles (251,419 square kilometers). Oregon extends 395 miles (636 kilometers) east-west; the state's maximum north-south extension is 295 miles (475 kilometers). The total boundary length of Oregon is 1,444 miles (2,324 kilometers).

2 TOPOGRAPHY

The Cascade Range, extending north-south, divides Oregon into distinct eastern and western regions. At the state's western edge, the Coast Range rises from the beaches, bays, and rugged headlands of the Pacific coast. Between the Coast and Cascade ranges lie fertile valleys, notably the Willamette Valley. The two-thirds of the state lying east of the Cascade Range consists generally of arid plateaus cut by river canyons. The Great Basin lies in the southeast.

The Cascades, Oregon's highest mountains, contain nine snow-capped volcanic peaks more than 9,000 feet (2,700 meters) high, of which the highest is Mt. Hood, at 11,235 feet (3,424 meters).

The Columbia, forming most of the northern border with Washington, is by far the largest and most important of the state's rivers. The largest of the Columbia's tributaries in Oregon, and longest river entirely within the state, is the Willamette. More than half of Oregon's eastern boundary with Idaho is formed by the Snake River. Oregon has 19 natural lakes with a surface area of more than 3,000 acres (1,200 hectares), and many smaller ones. Crater Lake—at 1,932 feet (589 meters) the deepest in the US—is a natural wonder.

3 CLIMATE

Oregon has a generally temperate climate, but there are marked regional variations. The western third of the state has relatively heavy precipitation and moderate temperatures. The eastern two-thirds have little precipitation and more extreme temperatures.

In January, normal daily mean temperatures range from 25°F (–4°C) to 45°F (7°C). In July, the normal daily means range between 65°F (18°C) and 78°F

Oregon Population Profile

Estimated 1995 population:	3,141,000
Population change, 1980–90:	7.9%
Leading ancestry group:	German
Second leading group:	English
Foreign born population:	4.9%
Hispanic origin†:	4.0%
Population by race:	
White:	92.8%
Black:	1.6%
Native American:	1.4%
Asian/Pacific Islander:	2.4%
Other:	1.8%

Population by Age Group

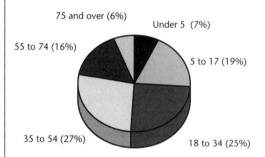

75 and over (6%)
Under 5 (7%)
55 to 74 (16%)
5 to 17 (19%)
35 to 54 (27%)
18 to 34 (25%)

Top Cities with Populations Over 25,000

City	Population	National rank	% change 1980–90
Portland	445,458	30	19.3
Eugene	115,963	159	6.7
Salem	112,050	171	20.8
Gresham	74,434	306	106.7
Beaverton	57,232	429	74.3
Medford	49,518	534	18.6
Springfield	46,281	570	7.4
Corvallis	44,810	593	9.3
Hillsboro	41,177	657	35.6
Tigard	32,235	870	105.4

Notes: †A person of Hispanic origin may be of any race. NA indicates that data are not available.
Sources: Economic and Statistics Administration, Bureau of the Census. *Statistical Abstract of the United States, 1994–95.* Washington, DC: Government Printing Office, 1995; Courtenay M. Slater and George E. Hall. *1995 County and City Extra: Annual Metro, City and County Data Book.* Lanham, MD: Bernan Press, 1995.

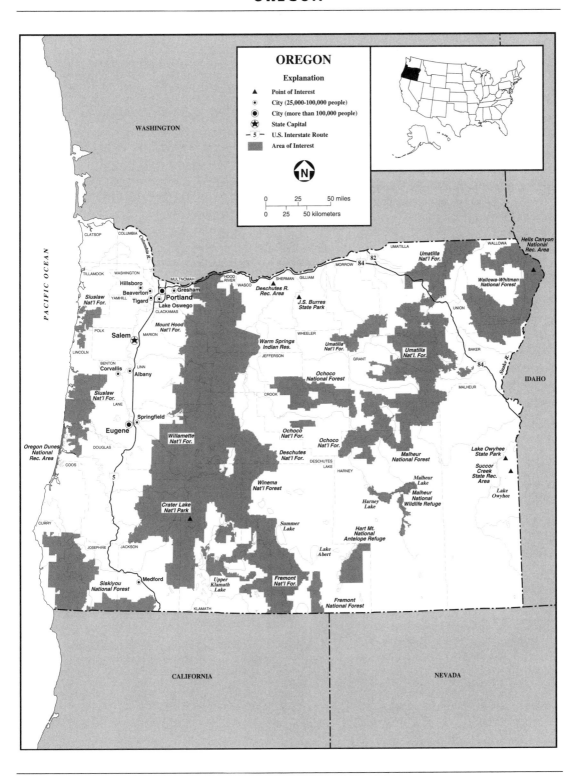

OREGON

Explanation

▲ Point of Interest
⊙ City (25,000-100,000 people)
◉ City (more than 100,000 people)
★ State Capital
— 5 — U.S. Interstate Route
▨ Area of Interest

N

0   25   50 miles
0   25   50 kilometers

WASHINGTON

PACIFIC OCEAN

CLATSOP
COLUMBIA
Columbia R.
TILLAMOOK
WASHINGTON
Siuslaw Nat'l For.
Hillsboro
Beaverton
Tigard
YAMHILL
MULTNOMAH
Portland
Gresham
Lake Oswego
CLACKAMAS
HOOD RIVER
WASCO
SHERMAN
GILLIAM
Deschutes R. Rec. Area
J.S. Burres State Park
UMATILLA
MORROW
84
82
Umatilla Nat'l For.
WALLOWA
Hells Canyon National Rec. Area
Wallowa-Whitman National Forest
Mount Hood Nat'l For.
POLK
Salem
MARION
Warm Springs Indian Res.
WHEELER
JEFFERSON
Umatilla Nat'l For.
GRANT
UNION
Umatilla Nat'l For.
BAKER
Snake R.
84
IDAHO
LINCOLN
BENTON
Corvallis
LINN
Albany
Ochoco National Forest
CROOK
MALHEUR
Siuslaw Nat'l For.
LANE
Springfield
Eugene
Ochoco Nat'l For.
Ochoco Nat'l For.
Malheur National Forest
Lake Owyhee State Park
Succor Creek State Rec. Area
Oregon Dunes National Rec. Area
DOUGLAS
Willamette Nat'l For.
Deschutes Nat'l For.
DESCHUTES
LAKE
HARNEY
Malheur National Wildlife Refuge
Malheur Lake
Lake Owyhee
COOS
5
Winema Nat'l Forest
Crater Lake Nat'l Park
Summer Lake
Harney Lake
Hart Mt. National Antelope Refuge
CURRY
Lake Abert
JOSEPHINE
JACKSON
Medford
Upper Klamath Lake
Fremont Nat'l For.
Fremont National Forest
Siskiyou National Forest
KLAMATH

CALIFORNIA

NEVADA

(26°C). The record low temperature, −54°F (−48°C), was registered in 1933; the all-time high, 119°F (48°C), occurred in 1938. The average annual rainfall varies from less than 8 inches (20 centimeters) in the drier plateau regions to as much as 200 inches (508 centimeters) on the upper west slopes of the Coast Range.

4 PLANTS AND ANIMALS

Oregon has a diverse assortment of vegetation and wildlife. The coastal region is covered by a rainforest of spruce, hemlock, and cedar rising above dense underbrush. A short distance inland, areas of Douglas fir—Oregon's state tree and dominant timber resource—begin. In the high elevations of the Cascades, Douglas fir gives way to pines and true firs. Ponderosa pine predominates on the eastern slopes. The state's many species of smaller native plants include Oregon grape—the state flower—as well as many types of berries.

More than 130 mammal species are native to Oregon, of which 28 are found throughout the state. Many species, such as the cougar and bear, are protected, either entirely or through hunting restrictions. Deer and elk are popular game mammals, with herds managed by the state: mule deer predominate in eastern Oregon, black-tailed deer in the west. At least 60 species of fish are found in Oregon, including 5 different salmon species, of which the Chinook is the largest and the coho most common.

Hundreds of species of birds inhabit Oregon, either year-round or during particular seasons. The state lies in the path of the Pacific Flyway, a major route for migratory waterfowl. Extensive bird refuges have been established in various parts of the state. The brown pelican, short-tailed albatross, and California condor are among species classified as endangered.

5 ENVIRONMENTAL PROTECTION

A vehicle inspection program has been instituted to reduce exhaust emissions in the Portland area and in Rogue Valley. The Department of Environmental Quality (DEQ) also operates an asbestos program to protect the public from asbestos in buildings that are being demolished or remodeled. In 1973, the legislature enacted what has become known as the Oregon Bottle Bill, the first state law prohibiting the sale of nonreturnable beer or soft-drink containers. There were 13 hazardous waste sites in the state as of 1994.

6 POPULATION

Oregon ranked 29th among the 50 states at the 1990 census, with a population of 2,842,321. Like other western states, Oregon experienced a more rapid population growth than that of the US as a whole in the 1970s, when population expanded 26%. The estimated 1995 population was 3,141,000. The Census Bureau population projection for the year 2000 is 3,404,000. Oregon's estimated population density in 1990 was 29.6 persons per square mile (11.3 persons per square kilometer). The city of Portland had 445,458 residents in 1992. The population of Eugene was 115,963; Salem, 112,050.

7 ETHNIC GROUPS

Oregon's Native Americans numbered some 38,000 in 1990, with most of the population living in urban areas. About 46,000 black Americans lived in Oregon in 1990. People of Hispanic descent numbered about 113,000 in the same year. In 1990 there were 14,796 Chinese, 14,142 Japanese, 9,355 Koreans, 9,114 Filipinos, 8,130 Vietnamese, 3,287 Laotians, and 2,726 Asian Indians. French Canadians have lived in Oregon since the opening of the territory, and they have continued to come in a small but steady migration.

8 LANGUAGES

The Midland dialect dominates Oregon English, except for a Northern dialect influence in the Willamette Valley. In 1990, 2,448,772 Oregonians—92.7% of the population five years old or older—spoke only English at home. Other languages spoken at home, and number of speakers, included Spanish, 83,087; German, 19,289; French, 10,854; Chinese, 10,099; and Vietnamese, 7,468.

9 RELIGION

Just over one-third of Oregon's population is affiliated with an organized religion, well below the national average. The leading Christian denominations were the Roman Catholic church, with 279,650 members in 1990; and the Church of Jesus Christ of Latter-day Saints (Mormon), with 89,601 members in 1994. Other major Protestant groups, with their 1990 memberships, were United Methodist, 42,209; Assemblies of God, 46,902; and Presbyterian, 38,086. Jewish Oregonians were estimated to number 10,691 in 1990.

10 TRANSPORTATION

The state's major deepwater port and international airport, Portland, is the transportation hub of Oregon. The state has 2,478 rail miles (3,987 kilometers) of track and is served by several major rail systems, including the Southern Pacific, Union Pacific, and Burlington Northern. The number of Amtrak riders in the state in 1991/92 totaled 496,929.

Starting with pioneer trails and toll roads, Oregon's roads and highways had become a network extending 96,036 miles (154,522 kilometers) by 1993. At the beginning of 1994, there were 2,624,127 motor vehicles (including 2,000,645 passenger cars) registered in Oregon.

The Columbia River forms the major inland waterway for the Pacific Northwest. The Port of Portland operates five major cargo terminals, and handled over 29.2 million tons of cargo in 1991. Oregon also has several important coastal harbors, including Astoria, Newport, and Coos Bay, the largest lumber export harbor in the US. The largest and busiest airfield, Portland International Airport, handled 83,617 departures in 1991 and boarded 3,164,431 passengers.

11 HISTORY

The first European to see Oregon was probably Sir Francis Drake in 1578, while on a raiding expedition against the Spanish. For most of the next 200 years, European contact was limited to occasional

Photo credit: Esther Mugar & David Ryan.

Portland, viewed from River Place Marina.

sightings by mariners, who considered the coast too dangerous for landing. In 1778, however, British Captain James Cook visited the Northwest and named several Oregon capes.

The first overland trek to Oregon was the Lewis and Clark Expedition, which traveled from St. Louis to the mouth of the Columbia River, where it spent the winter of 1805–06. In 1811, Oregon's first permanent white residents established a trading post at the mouth of the Columbia River. For the next 20 years, European and US interest in Oregon focused on the quest for beaver pelts. In 1834 Jason Lee, a Methodist missionary,

started a mission in the Willamette Valley, near present-day Salem.

Oregon became a territory in 1849, three years after the Oregon Treaty between Great Britain and the US established the present US-Canadian boundary. Ten years later, after a delay caused by North-South rivalries, Congress voted to make Oregon the 33d state.

State Development

Oregon remained relatively isolated until the completion of the first transcontinental railroad link in 1883. Its population grew steadily in the 20th century as migration into the state continued. Improved transportation helped make the state the nation's leading lumber producer and a major exporter of agricultural products. Development was also aided by hydroelectric projects.

The principal economic changes since World War II have been the growth of the aluminum industry, a rapid expansion of the tourist trade, and the creation of a growing electronics industry. The dominant industries in the Oregon economy, however, remained those centered on its abundant natural resources— timber, agriculture, and coal. These industries suffered in the late 1970s and 1980s when interest rates skyrocketed, reducing demand for houses and therefore for wood. Fewer people moved to Oregon and, in 1982 and 1983, the state's population declined.

It was hoped that construction of high-technology plants, planned for the mid-1980s, would help stabilize Oregon's economy, but a slump in the computer industry delayed the proposed projects.

12 STATE GOVERNMENT

The constitution establishes a 60-member house of representatives, elected for two years, and a senate of 30 members, serving four-year terms. Major executive officials include the governor, secretary of state, attorney general, and state treasurer. Much policy in Oregon is set by boards and commissions whose members are appointed by the governor.

Bills become law when approved by a majority of house and senate and either signed by the governor, or left unsigned for 5 days when the legislature is in session, or for 20 days after it has adjourned. The governor may veto a legislative bill, but the legislature may override a veto by a two-thirds vote of those present in each house.

13 POLITICAL PARTIES

Oregon has a strong tradition of political independence. In 1976 the state gave independent presidential candidate Eugene McCarthy a higher percentage of votes than any other state. Another independent, John Anderson, won 112,389 votes (9.5%) in the 1980 presidential election.

As of 1994, there were 792,115 registered Democrats (45% of the total number of registered voters) and 641,914 registered Republicans (36%). There were also 340,420 independents and minor-party members (19%). Dr. John Kitzhaber, a Democrat who designed Oregon's health care rationing system, defeated Republican congressman Denny Smith to become governor in 1994. Mark Hatfield and Robert Packwood, both Republicans, were both elected to a fifth term in the Senate in 1990 and 1992, respectively. Packwood resigned in 1995 due to pressure from a congressional committee investigating charges of sexual harassment against him. All but one of the five US Representatives are Democrats.

As of November 1994, there are 16 Democrats and 14 Republicans in the state senate, and 32 Republicans and 28 Democrats in the state house. Oregon voters gave Democratic presidential nominee Bill Clinton 43% of the popular vote in November 1992, while incumbent George Bush received 33% and Independent Ross Perot captured 24%.

14 LOCAL GOVERNMENT

As of 1992, Oregon had 36 counties and 240 municipal governments. Towns and cities enjoy home rule, the right to choose their own form of government and to enact legislation on matters of local concern. Most of Oregon's larger cities have council-manager forms of government. Typical elected county officials are three to five commissioners, and an assessor, district attorney, sheriff, and treasurer.

15 JUDICIAL SYSTEM

Oregon's highest court is the supreme court, consisting of seven justices. It accepts cases on review from the ten-judge court of appeals, which has exclusive jurisdiction over all criminal and civil appeals from lower courts. Circuit courts are the trial courts for civil and criminal matters. The more populous counties also have district courts, which hear minor civil, criminal, and traffic matters.

Oregon's crime rate was above the national average in 1994, with 6,296.4 crimes reported per 100,000 population. There were 6,657 inmates in state and federal correctional facilities in 1993, or about 175 per 100,000 in population.

16 MIGRATION

Most immigration to Oregon has come from other states, although Canadians have also arrived in significant numbers. From 1985 to 1990, the net migration gain was 123,500. In 1990, 46.6% of state residents had been born in Oregon.

17 ECONOMY

Since early settlement, Oregon's natural resources have formed the basis of its

Oregon's Presidential Vote by Political Parties, 1948–92

YEAR	OREGON WINNER	DEMOCRAT	REPUBLICAN	PROGRESSIVE	SOCIALIST	LIBERTARIAN
1948	Dewey (R	243,147	260,904	14,978	5,051	—
1952	*Eisenhower (R)	270,579	420,815	3,665	—	—
1956	Eisenhower (R)	329,204	406,393	—	—	—
1960	Nixon (R	367,402	408,065	—	—	—
1964	*Johnson (D)	501,017	282,779	—	—	—
					AMERICAN IND.	
1968	*Nixon (R)	358,866	408,433	—	49,683	—
					AMERICAN	
1972	*Nixon (R)	392,760	486,686	—	46,211	—
1976	Ford (R	490,407	492,120	—	—	—
					CITIZENS	
1980	*Reagan (R)	456,890	571,044	—	13,642	25,838
1984	*Reagan (R)	536,479	685,700	—	—	—
				NEW ALLIANCE		
1988	Dukakis (D)	678,367	483,423	2,985	—	6,261
					IND. (Perot)	
1992	*Clinton (D)	621,314	475,757	3,030	354,091	4,277

* Won US presidential election.

economy. Vast forests have made lumber and wood products the leading industry in the state. Since World War II, however, the state has striven to diversify its job base. The aluminum industry has been attracted to Oregon, along with computer and electronics firms, which now constitute the fastest-growing manufacturing area. The state's economy has traditionally been dependent on the health of the US construction industry. Jobs are plentiful when US housing starts rise, but unemployment increases when nationwide construction drops off.

18 INCOME

Per capita (per person) income in Oregon in 1994 was $20,468, 26th among the 50 states. Total personal income rose to $63.2 billion in 1994. About 11.8% of all Oregonians were living below the federal poverty level during 1993.

19 INDUSTRY

Manufacturing in Oregon is dominated by the lumber and wood products industry. More than half of Oregon's industrial workers are employed in the Portland area. Computer and electronics firms constitute the state's fastest-growing industry. Development, principally in the "Silicon forest" west of Portland, brought many jobs during the early 1980s. The value of manufactured shipments from Oregon was $32.2 billion in 1992.

20 LABOR

Oregon's civilian labor force numbered 1,643,000 in 1994, with an unemployment rate of 5.4%. Some 21.5% of all workers in the state were union members in 1994.

21 AGRICULTURE

Oregon ranked 28th in the US in agricultural output in 1994, with cash receipts of $2.6 billion. Crops accounted for 73% of the total. Wheat has been Oregon's leading crop since the state was first settled, but more than 170 farm and ranch commodities are now commercially produced. Oregon leads the nation in the production of winter pears, filberts (hazelnuts), peppermint oil, a variety of berries, and several grass and seed crops.

Farmland covers about 17.5 million acres (7 million hectares), or 28% of Oregon's total area. Quantity of selected crops in 1994 was as follows: wheat, 58,580,000 bushels; hay, 2,840,000 tons; potatoes, 2,578 million pounds; pears, 258,000 tons; and strawberries, 702,000 tons. In recent years, the growth of Oregon's wine industry has become noteworthy.

22 DOMESTICATED ANIMALS

Cattle production is Oregon's leading agricultural activity in terms of value, although income varies greatly with market conditions. In 1994, Oregon's cattle production accounted for 13% of agricultural sales. There were 100,000 dairy cows, providing the basis for a dairy industry that includes a major cheese industry on the northern Oregon coast. The 1994 dairy output accounted for 8.2% of agricultural receipts.

Photo credit: Esther Mugar & David Ryan.

Vineyards in Yamhill county.

23 FISHING

Oregon's fish resources have long been of great importance to its inhabitants. In 1992, Oregon ranked sixth among the states in the total amount of its commercial catch. The catch included salmon, especially chinook and silver; groundfish such as flounder, rockfish, and lingcod; shellfish such as shrimp and oysters; and albacore tuna. About four million fish were distributed by federal hatcheries in 1992.

24 FORESTRY

Oregon's total land area is 62 million acres (25 million hectares). Almost half of this, 27.3 million acres (11 million hectares), is forested. Douglas-fir is a primary conifer species in western Oregon, with western hemlock and sitka spruce found along the coast. In eastern Oregon, ponderosa pine is the main species. Several species of true fir, larch, and lodgepole pine also grow east of the Cascades. The Oregon Department of Forestry manages about 786,000 acres (318,000 hectares) of forest land.

Private forest lands have gained importance as Oregon's timber supplier due to harvest limitations placed on federal forest land. Oregon law has required reforestation following timber harvesting since

1941. About 100 million seedlings are planted in Oregon each year.

25 MINING

The estimated value of Oregon's nonfuel mineral production in 1994 was $253 million. Oregon was the nation's sole producer of nickel. In 1992, Oregon produced 576,000 short tons of portland cement, while construction sand and gravel production fell to 13,600,00 short tons. The state ranked first nationally in the quantity of pumice produced.

26 ENERGY AND POWER

Oregon ranks second in the US in hydroelectric power development, and hydropower supplies nearly half of the state's energy needs. In recent decades, nuclear and coal-fired steam plants have been built to supply additional electric power. The state has no nuclear power plants. Oregon's total electric power production in 1993 was 40.7 billion kilowatt hours. Energy consumption per capita (per person) was 317.1 million Btu in 1992. Energy expenditures were $1,716 per capita (per person) in 1992.

27 COMMERCE

Oregon's wholesale sales for 1992 totaled $42.4 billion; retail sales for 1993 were $27.8 billion; and service establishment receipts for 1992 were $12.4 billion. Oregon shipped $4.9 billion worth of goods abroad in 1992.

28 PUBLIC FINANCE

The Oregon constitution prohibits a state budget deficit. The revenues budgeted for the 1993–95 period were $23,723.7 million; expenditures were $20,012.6 million.

As of mid-1994, the total state and local government debt was $11.3 billion.

29 TAXATION

Oregon's chief source of general revenue is the personal income tax. A corporate income tax is also levied. Local governments rely on the property tax. Oregon does not have a general sales tax, although it does tax sales of gasoline and cigarettes. In 1990, Oregon had a federal income tax burden of $4,667 million.

30 HEALTH

Major causes of death were heart disease, cancer, cerebrovascular diseases, accidents, and suicide. In 1993, Oregon had 63 community hospitals, with 7,400 beds. The average hospital expense per inpatient day in 1993 was $1,053, or $5,309 for an average cost per stay. There were 6,400 active nonfederal physicians in 1993 and 24,000 nurses. Some 14.7 of state residents did not have health insurance in 1993.

31 HOUSING

In general, owner-occupied homes predominate in Oregon, and there are few urban slums. In 1993 there were an estimated 1,262,000 housing units in Oregon. In 1990, the median home value was $67,100. The median 1990 monthly costs for owners (with a mortgage) and renters were $650 and $408, respectively.

Photo credit: Shirley Petersen.

*Deady Hall at the University of Oregon
in Eugene.*

32 EDUCATION

Oregon's 1991 Educational Act for the 21st Century set into motion an extensive restructuring of the state's kindergarten through 12th-grade public school system. As of 31 December 1992, there were 893 public elementary schools and 222 public secondary schools. In 1993, there was a total public school enrollment of 521,000. Expenditures on education in that year averaged $6,088 per pupil (15th in the nation).

Higher education in Oregon comprises 16 community colleges, 19 independent institutions, and a state system of 8 institutions. The state system had a fall 1993 total enrollment of 59,545 students. University of Oregon in Eugene had the highest regular enrollment (16,593), followed by Portland State University in Portland (14,486) and Oregon State University in Corvallis (14,101).

Major private higher education institutions include Willamette University, Salem; the University of Portland, and Reed College, Portland; and Pacific University, Forest Grove.

33 ARTS

The Portland Art Museum, with an associated art school, is the city's center for the visual arts. The state's most noted theatrical enterprise is the annual Shakespeare Festival in Ashland. The Oregon Symphony is situated in Portland, and Salem and Eugene have small symphony orchestras of their own. The Oregon Arts Commission operates a program of direct-mail marketing of fine art prints created by artists from the Northwest. The total amount of federal and state aid to Oregon for the support of its arts programs was $12,593,542 from 1987–91.

34 LIBRARIES AND MUSEUMS

In 1991/92, Oregon had over 600 academic, public, and special libraries, including branches. The total book stock of all public libraries was 7,209,558, and their combined circulation was 24,588,412. Most cities and counties in Oregon have public library systems. The State Library

Photo credit: Esther Mugar & David Ryan.

Crater Lake National Park, Crater Lake

in Salem, with over 1.3 million volumes in 1991/92, serves as a reference agency for the state government.

Oregon has 76 museums, historic sites, botanical gardens and arboretums. Fort Clatsop National Memorial—featuring a replica of Lewis and Clark's winter headquarters—is among the state's notable attractions. The Oregon Historical Society operates a major historical museum in Portland and issues the *Oregon Historical Quarterly*.

35 COMMUNICATIONS

As of March 1993, 92.8% of Oregon's 1,214,000 households had telephones.

Oregon had 89 AM and 104 FM commercial radio stations in 1993. Six of the state's 23 commercial television stations were in Portland. A state-owned broadcasting system, which includes seven television stations, provides educational radio and television programming. As of 1993, seven large cable television systems served Oregon.

36 PRESS

As of 1994, 19 daily and 89 weekly newspapers were published in Oregon. The state's largest newspaper, the *Oregonian*, published in Portland, is owned by the Newhouse group. Leading Oregon newspapers with their 1994 daily circulations include the *Oregonian* (337,672); the *Eugene Register-Guard* (74,786); and the *Salem Statesman-Journal* (60,992).

37 TOURISM, TRAVEL, AND RECREATION

Oregon's abundance and variety of natural features and recreational opportunities make the state a major tourist attraction. Travel and tourism was the state's third-largest employer in 1991, when more than 15 million out-of-state visitors spent more than $2.97 billion in the state.

Among the leading attractions are the rugged Oregon coast, with its offshore salmon fishing; Crater Lake National Park; the Cascades wilderness; and Portland's annual Rose Festival. Oregon has one national park, Crater Lake, and three other areas managed by the National Park Service. The US Forest Service administers the Hells Canyon National Recreation Area and other sites. Oregon has one of the nation's most extensive state park systems: 225 parks and recreation areas cover 90,000 acres (36,400 hectares).

38 SPORTS

Oregon's lone major professional team, based in Portland, is the Trail Blazers, winners of the National Basketball Association championship in 1977. The Portland Beavers compete in baseball's class–AAA Pacific Coast League. The University of Oregon and Oregon State University belong to the Pacific 10 Conference.

Horse-racing takes place at Portland Meadows and at the Oregon State Fair in Salem. There is greyhound-racing at the Multnomah Kennel Club near Portland.

39 FAMOUS OREGONIANS

Prominent federal officeholders from Oregon include Senator Wayne Morse (b.Wisconsin, 1900–74), an early opponent of US involvement in Viet Nam; Representative Edith Green (1910–84), a leader in federal education assistance; and Representative Al Ullman (b.Montana, 1914–86), chairman of the House Ways and Means Committee until his defeat in 1980. A recent cabinet member from Oregon was former governor Neil Goldschmidt (b.1940), secretary of transportation during the Carter administration.

Oregon's most famous Native American was Chief Joseph (1840?–1904), leader of the Nez Percé in northeastern Oregon. Abigail Scott Duniway (b.Illinois, 1823–1915) was the Northwest's foremost advocate of women's suffrage. Journalist and communist John Reed (1887–1920), author of *Ten Days That Shook the World,* an eyewitness account of the Bolshevik Revolution, was born in Portland. Award-winning science-fiction writer Ursula K. LeGuin (b.California, 1929) is a Portland resident. Linus Pauling (1901–94), two-time winner of the Nobel Prize (for chemistry in 1954, for peace in 1962), was a Portland native.

40 BIBLIOGRAPHY

Cogswell, Philip. *Capitol Names: Individuals Woven into Oregon's History.* Portland: Oregon Historical Society, 1977.

Dodds, Gordon B. *Oregon: A Bicentennial History.* New York: Norton, 1977.

Parkman, Francis, Jr. *The Oregon Trail.* New York: Penguin, 1982.

PENNSYLVANIA

Commonwealth of Pennsylvania

ORIGIN OF STATE NAME: Named for Admiral William Penn, father of the founder of Pennsylvania.

NICKNAME: The Keystone State.

CAPITAL: Harrisburg.

ENTERED UNION: 12 December 1787 (2d).

MOTTO: Virtue, Liberty, and Independence.

SONG: "Pennsylvania."

COAT OF ARMS: A shield supported by two horses displays a sailing ship, a plow, and three sheaves of wheat; an eagle forms the crest. Beneath the shield an olive branch and a cornstalk are crossed, and below them is the state motto.

FLAG: The coat of arms appears in the center of a blue field.

OFFICIAL SEAL: Obverse: A shield displays a sailing ship, a plow, and three sheaves of wheat, with a cornstalk to the left, an olive branch to the right, and an eagle above, surrounded by the inscription "Seal of the State of Pennsylvania." Reverse: A woman representing Liberty holds a wand topped by a liberty cap in her left hand and a drawn sword in her right, as she tramples a lion representing Tyranny. The legend "Both Can't Survive" encircles the design.

ANIMAL: White-tailed deer.

BIRD: Ruffed grouse.

DOG: Great Dane.

FISH: Brook trout.

FLOWER: Mountain laurel.

INSECT: Firefly.

TREE: Hemlock.

FOSSIL: Phacops rana.

BEAUTIFICATION AND CONSERVATION PLANT: Penngift crownvetch.

BEVERAGE: Milk.

TIME: 7 AM EST = noon GMT.

1 LOCATION AND SIZE

Located in the northeastern US, the Commonwealth of Pennsylvania is the second largest of the three Middle Atlantic states and ranks 33d in size among the 50 states. The total area of Pennsylvania is 45,308 square miles (117,348 square kilometers). The state extends 307 miles (494 kilometers) east-west and 169 miles (272 kilometers) north-south. The total boundary length of Pennsylvania is 880 miles (1,416 kilometers).

2 TOPOGRAPHY

Pennsylvania may be divided into more than a dozen distinct regions, ranging from a narrow belt of coastal plain along the lower Delaware River to the Allegheny High Plateau that makes up the western and northern parts of the state. The Piedmont Plateau dominates the southeastern corner of the state, and the Great Valley runs from the middle of the state's eastern border to the middle of its southern border.

Other regions include the Pocono Plateau and the Allegheny Mountains, composed of parallel ridges and valleys. A narrow lowland region, the Erie Plain, borders Lake Erie in the extreme northwestern part of the state. Mount Davis, at 3,213 feet (979 meters), is the state's highest peak.

Pennsylvania contains about 250 natural lakes larger than 20 acres (8 hectares). The largest is Conneaut Lake, about 30 miles (48 kilometers) south of the city of Erie. The largest artificial lake is Lake Wallenpaupack in the Poconos. Major rivers include the Susquehanna, the Delaware, the Allegheny, and the Monongahela.

3 CLIMATE

Although Pennsylvania lies entirely within the humid continental zone, its climate varies according to region and elevation. The region with the warmest temperatures is the low-lying southeast, in the Ohio and Monongahela river valleys. The region bordering Lake Erie receives the moderating effect of the lake, which prevents early spring and late autumn frosts. The rest of

Pennsylvania Population Profile

Estimated 1995 population:	12,134,000
Population change, 1980–90:	0.1%
Leading ancestry group:	German
Second leading group:	Irish
Foreign born population:	3.1%
Hispanic origin†:	2.0%
Population by race:	
White:	89.0%
Black:	9.0%
Native American:	0.1%
Asian/Pacific Islander:	1.2%
Other:	0.7%

Population by Age Group

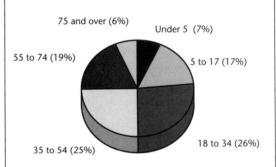

75 and over (6%)
Under 5 (7%)
55 to 74 (19%)
5 to 17 (17%)
18 to 34 (26%)
35 to 54 (25%)

Top Cities with Populations Over 25,000

City	Population	National rank	% change 1980–90
Philadelphia	1,552,572	5	–6.1
Pittsburgh	366,852	45	–12.8
Erie	109,267	176	–8.7
Allentown	106,429	185	1.3
Scranton	79,746	282	–7.2
Reading	79,028	285	–0.4
Bethlehem	72,373	320	1.4
Lancaster	57,171	430	1.5
Harrisburg	53,430	483	–1.7
Altoona	52,477	494	–9.1

Notes: †A person of Hispanic origin may be of any race. NA indicates that data are not available.
Sources: Economic and Statistics Administration, Bureau of the Census. *Statistical Abstract of the United States, 1994–95.* Washington, DC: Government Printing Office, 1995; Courtenay M. Slater and George E. Hall. *1995 County and City Extra: Annual Metro, City and County Data Book.* Lanham, MD: Bernan Press, 1995.

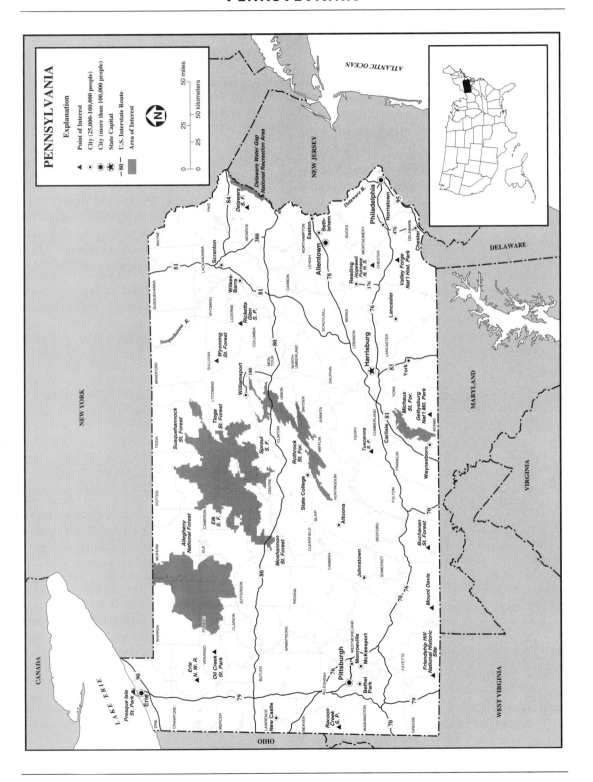

PENNSYLVANIA

Explanation

▲ Point of Interest
⊙ City (25,000-100,000 people)
◉ City (more than 100,000 people)
★ State Capital
—80— U.S. Interstate Route
▨ Area of Interest

0   25   50 miles
0   25   50 kilometers

N

ATLANTIC OCEAN

NEW JERSEY

DELAWARE

MARYLAND

VIRGINIA

WEST VIRGINIA

OHIO

CANADA

NEW YORK

LAKE ERIE

Delaware Water Gap National Recreation Area

Delaware S.F.

Scranton

Wilkes-Barre

Ricketts Glen S.P.

Wyoming St. Forest

Williamsport

Tioga St. Forest

Susquehannock St. Forest

Sproul S.F.

Rothrock St. For.

Allegheny National Forest

Elk S.F.

Moshannon St. Forest

State College

Altoona

Johnstown

Buchanan St. Forest

Mount Davis

Friendship Hill National Historic Site

Pittsburgh

Monroeville

McKeesport

Bethel Park

Raccoon Creek S.P.

New Castle

Erie

Presque Isle St. Park

Erie N.W.R.

Oil Creek St. Park

Easton
Beth-lehem

Allentown

Reading

Hopewell Furnace N.H.S.

Valley Forge Nat'l Hist. Park

Philadelphia

Norristown

Chester

Lancaster

Harrisburg

York

Carlisle

Michaux St. For.

Gettysburg Nat'l Mill. Park

Waynesboro

Susquehanna R.

Delaware R.

WAYNE
PIKE
MONROE
SUSQUEHANNA
BRADFORD
WYOMING
LACKAWANNA
LUZERNE
SULLIVAN
LYCOMING
COLUMBIA
CARBON
NORTHAMPTON
LEHIGH
BUCKS
MONTGOMERY
CHESTER
DELAWARE
BERKS
LEBANON
SCHUYLKILL
NORTHUMBERLAND
MONTOUR
UNION
SNYDER
JUNIATA
DAUPHIN
LANCASTER
YORK
ADAMS
CUMBERLAND
PERRY
FRANKLIN
FULTON
BEDFORD
MIFFLIN
HUNTINGDON
CENTRE
CLINTON
CAMERON
POTTER
TIOGA
MCKEAN
ELK
CLEARFIELD
BLAIR
CAMBRIA
SOMERSET
INDIANA
JEFFERSON
CLARION
FOREST
WARREN
VENANGO
CRAWFORD
ERIE
MERCER
LAWRENCE
BUTLER
ARMSTRONG
WESTMORELAND
ALLEGHENY
WASHINGTON
GREENE
FAYETTE
BEAVER

81 84 380 78 76 176 95 476 83 81 70 76 79 90 80

the state, at higher elevations, has cold winters and cool summers.

Among the major population centers, Philadelphia has an annual mean temperature of 54°F (12°C), and Pittsburgh has an annual mean of 50°F (10°C). In the cooler northern areas, Scranton has a normal annual mean ranging from 41°F (5°C) to 59°F (15°C); Erie, from 42°F (6°C) to 58°F (14°C). The record low temperature for the state is –42°F (–41°C), set in 1904. The record high, 111°F (44°C), was reached in 1936.

Philadelphia has about 41 inches (104 centimeters) of precipitation annually, and Pittsburgh has 36 inches (91 centimeters). Pittsburgh, however, has much more snow—45 inches (114 centimeters), compared with 22 inches (56 centimeters) for Philadelphia. The snowfall in Erie, in the snow belt, exceeds 54 inches (137 centimeters) per year. The state has experienced several destructive floods.

4 PLANTS AND ANIMALS

Maple, walnut, and poplar are among the species that fill Pennsylvania's extensive forests, along with sassafras and sycamore. Mountain laurel (the state flower) and June-berry are among the shrubs and small trees found in most parts of the state. Wintergreen and wild ginger are also common.

Numerous mammals are found in Pennsylvania, among them the white-tailed deer (the state animal), black bear, red and gray foxes, and common cottontail. Native amphibians include the hellbender and Fowler's toad; among reptilian

species are five varieties of lizard. The ruffed grouse, a common game species, is the official state bird. Other game birds are the wood dove and ring-necked pheasant. The robin, cardinal, and English sparrow are common nongame birds.

More than 170 types of fish have been identified in the state, with brook trout, pirate perch, and white bass among the common native varieties. Species on the endangered list include the brown (grizzly) bear, eastern cougar, and bald eagle.

5 ENVIRONMENTAL PROTECTION

The Pennsylvania Department of Environmental Resources regulates mining operations, administers land and water management programs, and oversees all aspects of environmental control. As of the early 1990s, sewage and industrial wastes were the major pollutants in areas with high industrial and population concentrations. In western and parts of central Pennsylvania, drainage from abandoned bituminous coal mines created serious water-quality problems. Oil and gas well operations were additional pollution sources. Pennsylvania has 44 municipal landfills and 603 curbside recycling programs.

The state had 102 hazardous waste sites as of 1994. In March 1979, Pennsylvania suffered the worst nuclear-power accident in US history when a nuclear reactor on Three Mile Island malfunctioned and radioactive gases escaped. The cleanup of radioactive waste cost about $1 billion.

Photo credit: Pennsylvania Office of Travel and Tourism.

Hawk Mountain Bird Sanctuary in Berks County.

6 POPULATION

As recently as 1940, Pennsylvania was the second-most populous state in the US. By the 1990 census, however, Pennsylvania had slipped to fifth place with a population of 11,881,643. The estimated 1995 population was 12,134,000. The population is expected to be 12,296,000 in 2000. The population density in 1990 was 265.1 persons per square mile (102 persons per square kilometer). There are fewer young people and more persons aged 65 or over represented in the state's population than in the US as a whole.

The largest city in the state, Philadelphia, was the fifth-largest US city as of 1992, with a population of 1,552,572. The population of its metropolitan area was 5,899,345 in 1990. Pittsburgh's population was 366,852 in 1992 (40th) in the city proper. The Pittsburgh metropolitan area population (19th in the US) totaled 2,139,000 in 1990. The 1992 populations of some of Pennsylvania's other major cities were Erie, 109,267; Allentown, 106,429; Scranton, 79,746; Reading, 79,028; and Bethlehem, 72,373.

7 ETHNIC GROUPS

The late 19th and early 20th centuries brought waves of immigrants from Ireland, Wales, various Slavic nations, and the eastern Mediterranean and the Balkans.

Pennsylvania had only 15,000 Native Americans as of 1990. Its black population in 1990 was about 1,090,000, amounting to 9.2% of the state's population as a whole. Philadelphia was almost 40% black in 1990; Pittsburgh, 25%.

Hispanic Americans in Pennsylvania numbered 232,000 in 1990. Most were Puerto Ricans, with smaller numbers of Cubans and Central Americans. In 1990, the Asian population included 25,908 Chinese, 25,800 Koreans, 19,769 Asian Indians, 14,474 Filipinos, and 14,126 Vietnamese.

8 LANGUAGES

Although not quite uniform, Pennsylvania's North Midland dialect is significant as the source of much midwestern and western speech. The only non-Midland sector is the northern group of counties, settled from southern New York State, where features of the Northern dialect predominate. In much of central Pennsylvania, descendants of the colonial Palatinate German population retain their speech as Deutsch, often misnamed Pennsylvania Dutch.

In 1990, 10,278,294 Pennsylvanians—92.7% of the population five years old or older—spoke only English at home. Other languages spoken at home included Spanish, 213,096; Italian, 103,844; German, 78,499; and Polish, 55,344.

9 RELIGIONS

With a long history of toleration, Pennsylvania has been a haven for numerous religious groups. William Penn brought the Quakers to Pennsylvania during the 1680s, and the climate of religious liberty soon attracted other dissident groups, including German Mennonites, Moravians, French Huguenots, and English Baptists. The Presbyterians, who built their first church in the state in 1704, played a major role in the development of Pittsburgh and other cities in the western part of the state.

As of 1990, Roman Catholics constituted the largest religious group in the state, with a total population of 3,675,250. The largest Protestant denomination in 1990 was United Methodist, with 722,871 members. Other Protestant groups were the Evangelical Lutheran Church in America, 682,111; Presbyterian, 388,774; Congregationalist (United Church of Christ), 284,275; and Episcopal, 138,152. The historically important Mennonites had 50,009 followers in 1990; Friends USA (Quakers), 12,081; and Moravians, 11,724. The Jewish population living in Pennsylvania as of 1990 was 329,651.

10 TRANSPORTATION

Although Pennsylvania's road and rail networks are showing signs of old age, the state remains an important center of transportation, and its ports are among the busiest in the US. In 1992, Pennsylvania had 58 railroads in operation—more than any other state—on 5,352 rail miles (8,611 kilometers) of track. Amtrak, which operates a total of 55 regularly scheduled trains through the state, had a total of 3,989,919 Pennsylvania riders in 1992.

Photo credit: Pennsylvania Office of Travel & Tourism.

Hugh Moore Park and canal in Easton.

The Philadelphia Rapid Transit System, the state's first subway, was established in 1902 and is operated by the Southeastern Pennsylvania Transportation Authority (SEPTA). In 1985, a 1.1-mile (1.8-kilometer) subway was opened in Pittsburgh as part of a 10.5-mile (16.9-kilometer) light-rail (trolley) transit system linking downtown Pittsburgh with the South Hills section of the city.

Throughout its history, Pennsylvania has been a pioneer in road transportation. The Pennsylvania Turnpike, which opened in 1940, was the first high-speed, multilane highway in the US. In 1993, this 470-mile (756-kilometer) toll highway received $269.8 million from motorists. In the same year, Pennsylvania had 117,038 miles (188,314 kilometers) of public roads. In 1992, total road and highway expenditures from all units of government came to over $3.8 billion. As of 1993 there were 8,282,066 motor vehicles registered, including 6,599,468 automobiles, 1,650,112 trucks, and 32,486 buses.

With access to the Atlantic Ocean and the Great Lakes, and with such navigable waterways as the Delaware, Monongahela, Allegheny, and Ohio rivers, Pennsylvania was an early leader in water transportation. Philadelphia, Pittsburgh, and Erie all developed as major ports. The Philadelphia Harbor handled 37.2 million tons of cargo in 1991. Although no longer

Valley Forge National Historical Park in Montgomery County.

the dominant gateway to the Mississippi, Pittsburgh is still a major inland port, handling 31.2 million tons of cargo in 1991.

Erie is the state's port on the Great Lakes, with just over one million tons of cargo handled in 1991. The busiest air terminal in the state, Greater Pittsburgh Airport, boarded 7,707,903 passengers in 1991. Philadelphia International Airport boarded 6,381,130 passengers.

11 HISTORY

The first Europeans to sail up the Delaware River found the Leni-Lenape (later called the Delaware) and other Algonkian tribes, including the Nanticoke and the Shawnee. The other major Indian language group in Pennsylvania was the Iroquoian, which included the Susquehanna (Conestoga), Wyandot, and Erie tribes. The Iroquoian Confederacy of the Five Nations, located in what is now New York, destroyed the Erie in the 1640s, the Susquehanna by 1680, and conquered the Leni-Lenape by 1720 but failed to destroy them.

The first European to reach Pennsylvania was probably the Dutchman Cornelis Jacobssen, who in 1614 entered Delaware Bay. In 1638, the Swedes began farming along the Delaware River. They established a post at Tinicum Island (1643) and several forts along the Schuylkill River.

The Dutch conquered the Swedish territories in 1655 but surrendered the land to the English in 1664.

British Rule

In 1681 King Charles II granted the region to William Penn, who belonged to the Society of Friends (Quakers), a Protestant sect persecuted for its ideas of equality and pacifism. Penn intended to make the region—named Pennsylvania in honor of his father—a refuge for all persecuted peoples. From the beginning, Penn gave up nearly all his law-making power over the new colony, allowing landowners to vote and establishing a governing council to exercise legislative, executive, and judicial power.

As Pennsylvania's government evolved, its population grew steadily, with most of the first immigrants coming from the British Isles and Germany. A key issue during the pre-Revolutionary period was the size and extent of the colony, of which all boundaries except the Delaware River were disputed. In 1763, after a lengthy struggle, Pennsylvania and Maryland agreed to have Charles Mason and Jeremiah Dixon establish the famous Mason-Dixon line.

Pennsylvania moved rapidly toward independence after the British victory in the French and Indian War. The Continental Congress began meeting in Philadelphia in September 1774, and the Declaration of Independence was proclaimed from Independence Hall in that city on 4 July 1776. General George Washington set up winter headquarters at Valley Forge, remaining there from December 1777 to June 1778. The British, who had occupied Philadelphia since September 1777 evacuated the city by the spring of 1778, and Congress reconvened there on 2 July. Philadelphia would serve as the US capital until 1783, and again from 1790 to 1800.

Statehood

In 1780, Pennsylvania passed the first state law abolishing slavery. Seven years later, Pennsylvania became the second state to ratify the US Constitution and join the Union. In 1790, Pennsylvania adopted a new constitution, modeled on the federal one, allowing all taxpaying males to vote. Four years later, western Pennsylvania settlers, opposed to a federal excise tax on distilled spirits, waged the Whiskey Rebellion, which was soon suppressed by state troops under federal command.

By 1800, the first stages of industrialization were at hand. Pittsburgh's first iron furnace was built in 1792. The completion of the Main Line of Public Works, a canal and rail system connecting Philadelphia with Pittsburgh, was a major development of the early 19th century. The 1840s saw not only an influx of Irish immigrants but also the rise of the Native American (Know-Nothing) Party, an anti-Catholic movement. The antislavery crusade, which gave birth to the Republican Party, influenced state politics during the following decade.

The majority of Pennsylvanians voted for Republican Abraham Lincoln in 1860. Pennsylvania rallied to the Union cause, supplying some 338,000 men, a figure exceeded only by New York. The state was the scene of the Battle of Gettysburg (1–3 July 1863), a turning point in the Civil War. Under General George Gordon Meade, the Union troops defeated Confederate forces under General Robert E. Lee, who was then forced to lead a retreat to Virginia.

Post–Civil War Era

In the post–Civil War years, the state was dominated by industry. Between 1890 and 1900, Pennsylvania was the nation's chief producer of coal, iron, and steel, and for much of that period the main source of petroleum and lumber. Farmers' sons and daughters joined immigrants from abroad in flocking to urban centers to work in mines, mills, and factories. As the state's industrial wealth increased, education, journalism, literature, art, and architecture flourished in Philadelphia and Pittsburgh.

Industrial leaders—supported both by the Republican state government and by popular opinion—smashed labor's efforts to unite, particularly in the great steel strike of 1919. Despite the nationwide economic boom of the 1920s, Pennsylvania's industrial growth rate was low. Coal, textiles, and agriculture—all basic to the state's economy—were depressed during that period.

The disastrous depression of the 1930s brought major changes to Pennsylvania. George H. Earle, the state's first Democratic governor since 1890, successfully introduced a "Little" New Deal, supporting labor, regulating utilities, aiding farmers, and building public works. Full employment and prosperity returned to Pennsylvania with new demands on it for steel, ships, munitions, and uniforms during World War II.

Post–World War II Era

Pennsylvania was in fifth place nationally in manufacturing by 1958. Markets, transportation, banks, factories, machinery, and skilled labor remained abundant, and two Democratic governors were able to attract new industries to the state during the 1950s and early 1960s. Republican Governor Raymond P. Shafer (1967–71), Scranton's Republican successor, was as forward-looking as his predecessors in his efforts to rehabilitate the economy. The 1873 constitution was extensively revised at a constitutional convention held in 1967–68, during Shafer's administration.

During his first term (1971–75), Democratic governor Milton J. Shapp secured passage of a state income tax to pay for new social programs. He also championed the consumer with no-fault auto insurance, adopted in 1974. Shapp's successor, Republican Richard L. Thornburgh, had scarcely been elected before a nuclear reactor at Three Mile Island malfunctioned in March 1979, releasing radioactive gases into the air. The disaster confronted Pennsylvania and the nation with vexing questions concerning the safety and wisdom of atomic power.

In the mid-1980s, Pennsylvania found itself confronted with the problem of completing the transition from a manufacturing to a service economy. Under Governor

Robert Casey, who took office in 1987, Pennsylvania created an organization called the Governor's Response Team, which helped companies to obtain low-interest loans and to retrain their workers. Casey was reelected in 1990.

After US Senator John Heinz died in office, Democrat Harris Wofford was appointed to that seat for the remainder of the term. Wofford campaigned on the issue of health care and was elected in 1991. In 1994, Wofford was defeated by Republican Rick Santorum.

12 STATE GOVERNMENT

The general assembly consists of a 50-member senate, elected to staggered four-year terms, and a 203-member house of representatives, elected every two years.

As head of the executive branch and chief executive offices of the state, the governor of Pennsylvania has the power to appoint heads of administrative departments, boards, and commissions, to approve or veto legislation, to grant pardons, and to command the state's military forces. Other Pennsylvania officials also elected for four years are the lieutenant governor, auditor general, state treasurer, and attorney general.

A bill may be introduced in either house of the general assembly. After the measure is passed by majority vote in each house, the governor has ten days in which to sign it, refuse to sign it (in which case it becomes law), or veto it. Vetoes may be overridden by a two-thirds vote of the

Pennsylvania Presidential Vote by Political Parties, 1948–92

YEAR	PENNSYLVANIA WINNER	DEMOCRAT	REPUBLICAN	PROGRESSIVE	SOCIALIST	PROHIBITION	SOC. LABOR
1948	Dewey (R)	1,752,426	1,902,197	55,161	11,325	10,538	1,461
					SOC. WORKERS		
1952	*Eisenhower (R)	2,146,269	2,415,789	4,222	1,508	8,951	1,377
1956	*Eisenhower (R)	1,981,769	2,585,252	—	2,035	—	7,447
1960	*Kennedy (D)	2,556,282	2,439,956	—	2,678	—	7,158
1964	*Johnson (D)	3,130,954	1,673,657	—	10,456	—	5,092
					PEACE & FREEDOM	AMERICAN IND.	
1968	Humphrey (D)	2,259,403	2,090,017	7,821	4,862	378,582	4,977
							AMERICAN
1972	*Nixon (R)	1,796,951	2,714,521	—	4,639	—	70,593
				COMMUNIST			US LABOR
1976	*Carter (D)	2,328,677	2,205,604	1,891	3,009	25,344	2,744
					LIBERTARIAN	SOC. WORKERS	
1980	*Reagan (R)	1,937,540	2,261,872	5,184	33,263	20,291	—
1984	*Reagan (R)	2,228,131	2,584,323	21,628	6,982	—	—
				CONSUMER		NEW ALLIANCE	POPULIST
1988	*Bush (R)	2,194,944	2,300,087	19,158	12,051	4,379	3,444
							IND. (Perot)
1992	*Clinton (D)	2,239,164	1,791,164		21,477	4,661	902,667

*Won US presidential election.

elected members of each house. A bill becomes effective 60 days after enactment.

13 POLITICAL PARTIES

The Republican Party totally dominated Pennsylvania politics from 1860, when the first Republican governor was elected, to the early 1930s, and again from 1939 through 1955. However, since the mid–1950s Pennsylvania has emerged as a two-party state, and Democrats elected governors in 1954, 1958, 1970, 1974, 1986, and 1990. Republicans won the governorship in 1962, 1966, 1978, 1982, and 1994.

Both US Senate seats were held by Republicans from 1968 to 1991. In November of 1991, a little-known Democrat and former college president named Harris Wofford defeated former governor Richard Thornburgh for the seat of Senator John Heinz, who died in 1991. In 1994, Republican Rick Santorum, a Congressman from the Pittsburgh area, defeated Wofford. The other Senator, Republican Arlan Specter, is currently serving his third term. In 1994, Pennsylvania's 21 US House of Representatives seats were held by 11 Democrats and 10 Republicans.

As of 1994 there were 3,043,757 registered Democrats, or 51% of the total number of registered voters; 2,567,643 Republicans, or 43%; and 381,602 Independents, or 6%. In 1992, Democratic nominee Bill Clinton garnered 45% of the vote in 1992; Bush received 36%; and Independent Ross Perot collected 18%.

14 LOCAL GOVERNMENT

As of 1992, Pennsylvania had 67 counties, 1,022 municipal governments, 1,548 townships, 516 school districts, and 2,244 authorities (special districts). Under home-rule laws, municipalities may choose to draft and amend their own charter.

The chief governing body in each county is a three-member board of commissioners. Other elected officials generally include the sheriff, district attorney, and treasurer. There are four classes of cities, based on population. The only first-class city, Philadelphia, is governed by a mayor and 17-member city council. Both Pittsburgh and Scranton are governed under mayor-council systems.

Boroughs are governed under mayor-council systems giving the council strong powers. Other elected officials are the tax assessor, tax collector, and auditor or controller. The state's first-class townships are governed by elected commissioners. Second-class townships have three supervisors who are elected at large.

15 JUDICIAL SYSTEM

Since 1968, all Pennsylvania courts have been organized under the Unified Judicial System. The highest court in the state is the supreme court, established in 1722, making it the oldest appeals court in the US. In general, the supreme court hears appeals from the commonwealth court. A separate appeals court, called the superior court, hears appeals from the courts of common pleas.

In counties other than Philadelphia, misdemeanors and other minor offenses are tried by district justices, formerly known as justices of the peace. Pennsylvania's overall crime rate in 1994 was 3,271.9 per 100,000 people, well below the national norm.

16 MIGRATION

During the 19th century, more immigrants settled in Pennsylvania than in any other state except New York. By the turn of the century, the urban population surpassed the rural population. During the 20th century, this pattern has been reversed. The trend among whites, particularly since World War II, has been to move out—from the cities to the suburbs, and from Pennsylvania to other states. Blacks continued to migrate to the larger cities until the early 1970s, when a small out-migration began.

Overall, between 1940 and 1980, Pennsylvania lost a net total of 1,759,000 residents through migration. From 1985 to 1990, Pennsylvania had a net migration gain of nearly 21,000. From 1990 to 1994, however, the state lost about 52,000 residents because of migration to other states. As of 1990, 80.2% of state residents were native-born, the highest proportion among all the 50 states.

17 ECONOMY

Dominated by coal and steel, Pennsylvania is an important contributor to the national economy, but its role has diminished considerably in this century. Declines in coal and steel production and the loss of other industries to the Sunbelt have not been entirely counterbalanced by gains in other areas, despite a steady expansion of machinery production, increased tourism, and the growth of service-related industries and trade.

Manufacturing, the second largest employer in Pennsylvania, lost about 350,000 jobs during the 1980s. The outlook for the steel industry remained uncertain in the 1980s and 1990s, as Pennsylvania's aging factories faced severe competition from foreign producers. Services, in contrast, added about 375,000 jobs, reaching a total of 1.4 million in 1990. The fastest-growing service industries were concentrated in the medical and health fields.

18 INCOME

Although Pennsylvania is one of the nation's most industrialized states, its wage earners tend to receive less than their counterparts in other states. Per capita (per person) income in 1994 was $22,195—17th among the 50 states and slightly below the US average. Total personal income increased to $267.5 billion in 1994. In 1993, about 13.2% of all Pennsylvanians were below the federal poverty level.

19 INDUSTRY

At different times throughout its history, Pennsylvania has been the nation's principal producer of ships, iron, chemicals, lumber, oil, textiles, glass, coal, and steel. Although it is still a major manufacturing center, Pennsylvania's industrial leadership has diminished steadily during this century. From 1977 to 1991, the value of shipments of manufactured goods grew from $79.8 billion to $134 billion. Leading

Amish farm in Lancaster County.

industries by value of shipments were primary metals and food products.

Pittsburgh is a popular site for corporate headquarters. Among the leading companies headquartered there are USX (formerly US Steel), Westinghouse Electric, Aluminum Company of America, and H. J. Heinz.

20 LABOR

In 1994, Pennsylvania's civilian labor force averaged 5,829,000. The unemployment rate for the state in 1994 was 6.2%.

The nation's first labor union was organized by Philadelphia shoemakers in 1794. In the 19th century, the state's coal fields were the sites of violent organizing struggles. A major strike in 1919, involving half the nation's steelworkers, shut down the industry for more than three months. As of 1993, there were 24 national labor unions operating in the state. The most important union in the state is the United Steelworkers of America, headquartered in Pittsburgh. Some 19.4% of all workers in the state were union members in 1994.

21 AGRICULTURE

Pennsylvania ranked 19th among the 50 states in agricultural income in 1994, with receipts of nearly $3.8 billion. Most farms in the state produce crops and dairy items for Philadelphia and other major eastern markets. As of 1994, there were about 51,000 farms averaging 160 acres (65 hectares) in size.

This table shows field crops in 1994:

CROP	OUTPUT (BUSHELS)
Hay (tons)	4,528,000
Corn for grain	123,600,000
Oats	8,480,000
Soybeans	13,545,000
Wheat	7,920,000
Barley	4,875,000

In 1994, Pennsylvania was the nation's leading producer of mushrooms, which accounted for 7.6% of the state's agricultural receipts. Roses, carnations, chrysanthemums, and other greenhouse and nursery items contributed 8.3% to 1994 agricultural receipts. Other crops were tomatoes, potatoes, strawberries, apples, pears, peaches, grapes, and cherries (sweet and tart).

22 DOMESTICATED ANIMALS

Most of Pennsylvania's farm income stems from livestock production, primarily in Lancaster County. There were 1,750,000 cattle, 1,090,000 hogs, 639,000 milk cows, and 110,000 sheep on Pennsylvania farms in 1994.

Pennsylvania was a leading producer of chickens in the US during 1994, yielding 597 million pounds of broilers and 202 million pounds of turkeys. Egg production accounted for 6.3% of agricultural receipts in 1994. Over 10 billion pounds of milk (fourth among the 50 states), worth over $1.4 billion, was produced by Pennsylvania dairy farms in 1994. In 1994, dairy products made up 38.4% of the state's agricultural receipts.

23 FISHING

Although there is little commercial fishing in Pennsylvania—the 1992 catch of 485,000 pounds was worth only $395,000—the state's many lakes and streams make it a popular area for sport fishing. Walleye, trout, and salmon were the leading species.

24 FORESTRY

Pennsylvania's forests are richly diverse and dominate the landscape. They cover 59.2% (16,992,700 acres) of the total land area and consist of about 90 different tree species. About 1.1 billion board feet of timber is harvested annually in Pennsylvania, most of it hardwood. Pennsylvania has led the nation in the volume of export grade hardwoods produced for a number of years.

25 MINING

In 1994, Pennsylvania produced nonfuel minerals with a total value of about $964 million. The most valuable was crushed stone (first in US). Other important minerals were portland cement, lime, and construction sand and gravel. Pennsylvania is the nation's third-leading producer of steel and is fourth in coal.

26 ENERGY AND POWER

Total energy consumption in 1992 reached 3,597 trillion Btu. Coal supplied 62% of the state's energy needs; petroleum, 2%; natural gas, less than 1%; nuclear power, 35%; and hydropower and other sources, 1%. The state had nine nuclear power plants in 1993. Energy consumption was 299.9 million Btu per capita (per person). Energy expenditures per capita averaged $1,875.

Pennsylvania's nuclear power production dropped abruptly on 28 March 1979, when a malfunction at the Unit 2 plant at Three Mile Island near Harrisburg caused the reactor's containment building to fill up with radioactive water. Some radioactive steam was vented into the atmosphere, and thousands of residents of nearby areas were temporarily evacuated. Three Mile Island's 819,000-kilowatt Unit 1 plant was also shut down after the accident, but it was reopened in fall 1985.

Oil reserves totaled 15 million barrels in 1991. Crude oil output dropped to two million barrels. The state's natural gas production in 1993 was 132 billion cubic feet; estimated reserves as of 1991 were 1,629 billion cubic feet. Coal is the state's most valuable mineral commodity, accounting for more than two-thirds of all mine income. In 1992, Pennsylvania's mining companies produced 67,612,000 tons of coal. Pennsylvania is the only major US producer of anthracite coal, with an output of 3,543,000 tons in 1992.

27 COMMERCE

Pennsylvania's wholesale sales totaled $126.4 billion in 1992; retail sales were $96.5 billion in 1993; service establishment receipts were $55.4 billion in 1992. Philadelphian John Wanamaker opened the world's first department store in 1876; by 1982, Pennsylvania had 572 department stores. In 1992, total exports of Pennsylvania goods had a value of $10.3 billion (12th in the US).

28 PUBLIC FINANCE

By law, annual operating expenditures may not exceed available revenues and surpluses from prior years. The general revenues for the state government in 1993 were $37,779,000,00; general expenditures were $34,359,000,000.

The state debt at the end of fiscal 1993 exceeded $12.9 billion, or $1,080 per capita (per person).

29 TAXATION

Pennsylvania taxes personal and corporate income, insurance premiums, and financial institutions. The state's 6% sales and use tax exempts essential items such as clothing, groceries, and medicines. Other taxable items are employee wages and real estate transfers. In 1993, Pennsylvanians paid $16.6 billion in state taxes.

30 HEALTH

Death rates for the leading causes of death—heart disease, cancer, and stroke—were well above the US average. The overall death rate in 1991 was 1,025.5 persons per 100,000 population, one of the highest among the states. Statewide in 1993 there were 233 community hospitals, with 53,400 beds. The average expense per inpatient day in Pennsylvania hospitals in 1993 was $861, and the average cost per stay was $6,564. There were 30,700 active nonfederal physicians in 1993 and 109,000 nurses. Some 10.8% of state residents did not have health insurance in 1993. The University of Pennsylvania

School of Medicine, founded in 1765, is the nation's oldest medical school.

31 HOUSING

Faced with a decaying housing stock, Philadelphia during the 1970s and 1980s encouraged renovation of existing units along with the construction of new ones, effectively revitalizing several neighborhoods. Most of Pennsylvania's housing is owner-occupied. The median monthly cost for an owner-occupied housing unit with a mortgage in 1990 was $682; for a non-mortgaged unit, the cost was $226. The median monthly rent was $404. In 1990, the median home value was $69,700.

32 EDUCATION

As of 1990, 78.6% of the population 25 years old and older had completed four years of high school. Some 18.6% had finished four or more years of college. In 1993, 103,715 students graduated from public high schools. During the 1993/94 school year, 968,465 students were enrolled in public elementary schools, and 775,617 in secondary schools. Expenditures on education averaged $6,914 per pupil (sixth in the nation) in 1993.

Enrollment in the 14 state-owned colleges in fall 1993 totaled 95,962. Indiana University of Pennsylvania had 14,062 students as of fall 1993. Four universities have nonprofit corporate charters but are classified as state-related: Pennsylvania State University (State College), Temple University (Philadelphia), the University of Pittsburgh, and Lincoln University. Of these, Penn State is by far the largest, with a fall 1993 enrollment of 68,623. In 1994 there were 14 community colleges.

The nine state-aided private institutions had a combined enrollment of 41,811 in 1993. The largest of these schools is the University of Pennsylvania (Philadelphia), founded in 1740 by Benjamin Franklin. Among its noteworthy professional schools is the Wharton School of Business. The state's many private colleges and universities include Bryn Mawr College, Bucknell University in Lewisburg, Carnegie-Mellon University and Duquesne University in Pittsburgh, Haverford College, Lafayette College (Easton), Lehigh University (Bethlehem), Swarthmore College, and Villanova University. Enrollment at all private colleges and universities in the state totaled 177,194 in fall 1993.

33 ARTS

Philadelphia was the cultural capital of the colonies, and rivaled New York as a theatrical center during the 1800s. In 1984, Philadelphia had five fully developed resident theaters, ranking third in the nation after New York and California. A number of regional and summer-stock theaters are scattered throughout the state, the most noteworthy being in Bucks County, Lancaster, and Pittsburgh. The National Choreographic Center was established in the mid-1980s in Carlisle in conjunction with the Central Pennsylvania Youth Ballet School.

Pennsylvania's most significant contribution to the performing arts has come through music. One of America's first important songwriters, Stephen Foster, grew up in Pittsburgh. The Pittsburgh

Symphony, which began performing in 1896, was temporarily disbanded in 1910 and revived under Fritz Reiner in 1927. Even more illustrious has been the career of the Philadelphia Orchestra, founded in 1900. An important dance company, the Pennsylvania Ballet, is based in Philadelphia, which also is the home of the Curtis Institute of Music, one of the nation's premier music conservatories. Opera companies include the Pennsylvania Opera Theater, Pittsburgh Opera, and Opera Company of Philadelphia.

Expressions '80, a minorities arts festival in Philadelphia that attracted artists from a six-state area, was the first regional festival of its kind in the Northeast. The Pennsylvania Writers Collection, an initiative program of the Pennsylvania Council on the Arts, supports the work of the state's creative writers. The total amount of federal and state funding for Pennsylvania's arts programs from 1987 to 1991 was $85,273,685.

34 LIBRARIES AND MUSEUMS

Pennsylvania's public libraries stocked 26,219,331 volumes during 1993/94, with a total circulation of 53,985,078. The largest public library in the state, and one of the oldest in the US, is the Free Library of Philadelphia, with 5,129,439 volumes in 49 branches. Also noteworthy are the Carnegie Library in Pittsburgh and the State Library of Pennsylvania in Harrisburg.

Philadelphia is the site of the state's largest academic collection, the University of Pennsylvania Libraries, with 3,844,414 volumes. Other major acadezmic libraries are at the University of Pittsburgh,

Pennsylvania State, Lehigh, Temple, Carnegie-Mellon, and Swarthmore.

Pennsylvania has 329 museums and public gardens, with many of the museums located in Philadelphia. The Franklin Institute, established in 1824 as an exhibition hall and training center for inventors and mechanics, is a leading showcase for science and technology. Other important museums are the Philadelphia Museum of Art and the Academy of Natural Sciences.

The Carnegie Institute in Pittsburgh is home to several major museums, including the Carnegie Museum of Natural History and the Museum of Art. Other institutions scattered throughout the state include the US Army Military History Institute, Carlisle; and Pennsylvania Dutch Folk Culture Society, Lenhartsville. Several old forts commemorate the French and Indian War, and George Washington's Revolutionary War headquarters at Valley Forge is now a national historical park. Brandywine Battlefield (Chadds Ford) is another Revolutionary War site. Gettysburg National Military Park commemorates the Civil War.

35 COMMUNICATIONS

In 1993, 97.5% of Pennsylvania's 4,736,000 households had telephones. Pittsburgh's KDKA became the world's first commercial radio station in 1920. By 1993, it was one of 185 AM stations in the state. In addition, there were 259 FM radio stations and 46 television stations. WQED in Pittsburgh pioneered community-sponsored educational television when it began broadcasting in 1954. In 1993, there were 42 large cable television systems in service.

36 PRESS

Benjamin Franklin may have been colonial Pennsylvania's most renowned publisher, but the state's first publisher was Andrew Bradford. His *American Weekly Mercury*, established in 1719, was the third newspaper to appear in the colonies. The *Pennsylvania Gazette*, purchased by Franklin in 1730, served as the springboard for *Poor Richard's Almanack*.

In 1994, Pennsylvania had 37 morning newspapers, 45 evening newspapers, 2 all-day dailies, and 31 Sunday papers. The leading dailies, with daily circulation in 1994, included the *Philadelphia Inquirer* (515,523); the *Philadelphia Daily News* (221,855); and the *Pittsburgh Post-Gazette* (161,514).

Farm Journal and *Current History*, both monthlies, are published in Philadelphia. There also are monthlies named for both Philadelphia and Pittsburgh. Of more specialized interest are the gardening, nutrition, and health magazines and books from Rodale Press in Emmaus and the automotive guides from the Chilton Company in Radnor.

37 TOURISM, TRAVEL, AND RECREATION

Travelers and tourists spent more than $8.9 billion in Pennsylvania in 1985. Travel and tourism was the state's second-largest employer. Philadelphia—whose Independence National Historical Park has been called the most historic square mile in America—offers the Liberty Bell, Independence Hall, and many other sites. North of Philadelphia, in Bucks County, is the town of New Hope, with its numerous crafts and antique shops. The Lancaster area is "Pennsylvania Dutch" country, featuring tours and exhibits of Amish farm life. Gettysburg contains not only the famous Civil War battlefield but also the home of Dwight D. Eisenhower, opened to the public in 1980. Among the most popular sites are Chocolate World and Hersheypark in the town of Hershey, and Valley Forge National Historic Park.

No less of an attraction are the state's outdoor recreation areas. By far the most popular for both skiing and camping are the Delaware Water Gap and the Poconos, also a favorite resort region. The state park system includes 98 parks, 11 state forests, and 3 environmental education centers.

38 SPORTS

Pennsylvania has seven major league professional sports teams: the Philadelphia Phillies and the Pittsburgh Pirates of Major League Baseball; the Philadelphia Eagles and the Pittsburgh Steelers of the National Football League; the Philadelphia 76ers of the National Basketball Association; and the Pittsburgh Penguins and Philadelphia Flyers of the National Hockey League.

Horse-racing is conducted at Keystone Race Track in Bucks County, Penn National Race Course in Dauphin County, and Commodore Downs in Erie County. Each June, Pennsylvania hosts a major auto race, the Pocono 500. The Penn Relays, an important amateur track meet, is held in Philadelphia every April.

In collegiate sports, football is most prominent. The University of Pittsburgh Panthers were named national champions in 1918, 1937, and 1976. Pennsylvania State was named champion in 1982 and 1986 and was a frequent winner of the Lamber Cup as the best independent college team in the East. Villanova won the NCAA basketball championship in 1985.

Other annual sporting events include the US Pro Indoor Tennis Championship in Philadelphia in January and February. Each summer, Williamsport hosts baseball's Little League World Series.

39 FAMOUS PENNSYLVANIANS

Johan Printz (b.Sweden, 1592–1663), the 400-pound, hard-drinking, hard-ruling governor of New Sweden, was Pennsylvania's first European resident of note. The founder of Pennsylvania was William Penn (b.England, 1644–1718), a Quaker of sober habits and deep religious beliefs. Most extraordinary of all Pennsylvanians was Benjamin Franklin (b.Massachusetts, 1706–90), a printer, author, inventor, scientist, legislator, diplomat, and statesman who served the Philadelphia, Pennsylvania, and US governments in a variety of posts.

Only one native Pennsylvanian, James Buchanan (1791–1868), has ever become US president. Entering the White House in 1857, he tried unsuccessfully to maintain the Union by avoiding extremes and preaching compromise. Dwight D. Eisenhower (b.Texas, 1890–1969) retired to a farm in Gettysburg after his presidency was over. George M. Dallas (1792–1864),

Pennsylvania's only US vice-president, was James K. Polk's running mate.

The six Pennsylvanians who have served on the US Supreme Court have all been associate justices: James Wilson (1742–98), Henry Baldwin (1780–1844), Robert C. Grier (1794–1870), William Strong (1808–95), George Shiras, Jr. (1832–1924), and Owen J. Roberts (1875–1955).

Notable historical figures include Betsy Ross (Elizabeth Griscom, 1752–1836), the seamstress who allegedly stitched the first American flag. Pamphleteer Thomas Paine (b.England, 1737–1809); pioneer Daniel Boone (1734–1820); and General Anthony Wayne (1745–96) also distinguished themselves during this period. In the Civil War, General George B. McClellan (1826–85) led the Union army on the Peninsula and at the Battle of Antietam. At the Battle of Gettysburg, Generals George Gordon Meade (b.Spain, 1815–72) and Winfield Scott Hancock (1824–86) both showed their military prowess. Recent state governors of note include George H. Earle (1890–1974); Milton J. Shapp (b.Ohio, 1912); William W. Scranton (b.Connecticut, 1917); and Richard L. Thornburgh (b.1932).

Pennsylvanians have won Nobel Prizes in every category except literature. General George C. Marshall (1880–1959), chief of staff of the US Army in World War II and secretary of state when the European Recovery Program (Marshall Plan) was adopted, won the 1953 Nobel Peace Prize. Simon Kuznets (b.Russia, 1901–85) received the 1971 Nobel Prize in economic science for work on economic growth. In physics, Otto Stern (b.Germany, 1888–1969) won the 1943 prize for work on the magnetic momentum of protons. In chemistry, Theodore W. Richards (1868–1928) won the 1914 Nobel Prize for determining the atomic weight of many elements, and Christian Boehmer Anfinsen (b.1916) won the 1972 award for pioneering studies in enzymes. In physiology or medicine, Haldane K. Hartline (1903–83) won in 1967 for work on the human eye, and Howard M. Temin (b.1934) was honored in 1975 for the study of tumor viruses.

Many other Pennsylvanians were distinguished scientists. John Bartram (1699–1777) and his son William (1739–1823) won international repute as botanists. Nathaniel Chapman (b.Virginia, 1780–1853) was the first president of the American Medical Association. Rachel Carson (1907–64), a marine biologist and writer, became widely known for her crusade against the use of chemical pesticides. Noted inventors born in Pennsylvania include steamboat builder Robert Fulton (1765–1815).

Pennsylvania played a large role in the economic development of the US. Andrew C. Mellon (1855–1937) was an outstanding figure in finance, as well as secretary of the treasury under presidents Warren G. Harding, Calvin Coolidge, and Herbert Hoover. Andrew Carnegie (b.Scotland, 1835–1919) and his associates, including Henry Clay Frick (1849–1919) and Charles M. Schwab (1862–1939), created the most efficient steel-manufacturing company of its time. Frank W. Woolworth (b.New York, 1852–1919) and Sebastian S. Kresge (1867–1966) were pioneer merchandisers. Other prominent businessmen born in Pennsylvania are automobile pioneer Clement Studebaker (1831–1901), chocolate manufacturer Milton S. Hershey (1857–1945), and Chrysler's retired Chairman of the Board, Lee A. Iacocca (b.1924).

Charles Taze Russell (1852–1916), initially a Congregationalist, founded the group that later became Jehovah's Witnesses. Among the state's outstanding scholars are historian Henry Steele Commager (b.1902), anthropologist Margaret Mead (1901–78), behavioral psychologist B(urrhus) F(rederic) Skinner (1904–89), urbanologist Jane Jacobs (b.1916), and language theorist Noam Chomsky (b.1928). Thomas Gallaudet (b.1787–1851) was a pioneer in education of the deaf. Florence Kelley (1859–1932) was an important social reformer, as was Bayard Rustin (1910–87).

Pennsylvania has produced a large number of distinguished journalists and writers. In addition to Benjamin Franklin, journalists include Moses L. Annenberg (1878–1942) and I(sidor) F(einstein) Stone (b.1907). Ida M. Tarbell (1857–1944) was perhaps Pennsylvania's most famous muckraker. Among the many noteworthy Pennsylvania-born writers are Charles Brockden Brown (1771–1810), Bayard Taylor (1825–78), Richard Harding Davis (1864–1916), Gertrude Stein (1874–1946), Donald Barthelme (b.1931), and John Updike (b.1932). James Michener (b.New York, 1907) was raised in the state. Pennsylvania playwrights include

Maxwell Anderson (1888–1959), George S. Kaufman (1889–1961), and Clifford Odets (1906–63). Prominent among Pennsylvania poets is Wallace Stevens (1879–1955).

Composers include Stephen Collins Foster (1826–64) and Samuel Barber (1910–81). Among Pennsylvania painters prominent in the history of American art are Benjamin West (1738–1820), renowned as the father of American painting; Thomas Eakins (1844–1916); Mary Cassatt (1845–1926); Man Ray (1890–1976); Andrew Wyeth (b.1917); and Andy Warhol (1927–87). Outstanding sculptors include William Rush (1756–1833) and Alexander Calder (1898–1976).

Pennsylvania produced and supported a host of actors, notably the illustrious Barrymore family, including Lionel (1878–1954), Ethel (1879–1959), and John (1882–1942). Other actors include W. C. Fields (William Claude Dukenfield, 1880–1946); James Stewart (b.1908); Gene Kelly (b.1912); Charles Bronson (Charles Buchinsky, b.1922); Mario Lanza (1925–59); Shirley Jones (b.1934); and comedian Bill Cosby (b.1937). Film directors Joseph L. Mankiewicz (1909–93), Arthur Penn (b.1922), and Sidney Lumet (b.1924), as well as film producer David O. Selznick (1902–65), also came from Pennsylvania.

Among the state's outstanding musicians are Pennsylvania-born vocalists Marian Anderson (1897–1993), Marilyn Horne (b.1934), and Anna Moffo (b.1934).

Pianists include jazz interpreters Earl "Fatha" Hines (1905–83) and Erroll Garner (1921–77). Popular band leaders include Fred Waring (1900–84), Jimmy Dorsey (1904–57), and his brother Tommy (1905–56). Dancers and choreographers from Pennsylvania include Martha Graham (1893–1991) and Paul Taylor (b.1930).

Of the many outstanding athletes associated with Pennsylvania, Jim Thorpe (b.Oklahoma, 1888–1953) was most versatile, having starred in Olympic pentathlon and decathlon events and football. Baseball Hall of Famers include Stan Musial (b.1920) Roy Campanella (1921–93), and Reggie Jackson (b.1946). Outstanding Pennsylvania football players include John Unitas (b.1933), Joe Namath (b.1943), and Tony Dorsett (b.1954). Other stars include basketball's Wilt Chamberlain (b.1936); golf's Arnold Palmer (b.1929); tennis's Bill Tilden (1893–1953); swimming's Johnny Weissmuller (1904–84); and track and field's Bill Toomey (b.1939).

Pennsylvania has also been the birthplace of a duchess—Bessie Wallis Warfield, the Duchess of Windsor (1896–1986); and of a princess—Grace Kelly, Princess Grace of Monaco (1929–82).

40 BIBLIOGRAPHY

Cochran, Thomas C. *Pennsylvania: A Bicentennial History*. New York: Norton, 1978.

Klein, Philip S., and Ari Hoogenboom. *A History of Pennsylvania*. Rev. ed. University Park: Pennsylvania State University Press, 1980.

Soderland, Jean R., and Richard S. Dunn, eds. *William Penn and the Founding of Pennsylvania, 1680-1684: A Documentary History*. Philadelphia: University of Pennsylvania Press, 1983.

RHODE ISLAND

State of Rhode Island and Providence Plantations

ORIGIN OF STATE NAME: Named for Rhode Island in Narragansett Bay, which was likened to the isle of Rhodes in the Mediterranean Sea.

NICKNAME: The Ocean State. (Also: Little Rhody.)

CAPITAL: Providence.

ENTERED UNION: 29 May 1790 (13th).

SONG: "Rhode Island."

MOTTO: Hope.

COAT OF ARMS: A golden anchor on a blue field.

FLAG: In the center of a white field is a golden anchor and, beneath it, a blue ribbon with the state motto in gold letters, all surrounded by a circle of 13 gold stars.

OFFICIAL SEAL: The anchor of the arms is surrounded by four scrolls, the topmost bearing the state motto: the words "Seal of the State of Rhode Island and Providence Plantations 1636" encircle the whole.

BIRD: Rhode Island Red.

FLOWER: Violet.

TREE: Red maple.

MINERAL: Bowenite.

ROCK: Cumberlandite.

TIME: 7 AM EST = noon GMT.

1 LOCATION AND SIZE

One of the six New England states in the northeastern US, Rhode Island is the smallest of all the 50 states. The total area of Rhode Island is 1,212 square miles (3,139 square kilometers). The state extends 37 miles (60 kilometers) east-west and 48 miles (77 kilometers) north-south. The total boundary length of Rhode Island is 160 miles (257 kilometers). The state has 38 islands, including Block Island, southwest of Point Judith.

2 TOPOGRAPHY

Rhode Island comprises two main regions. The New England Upland Region, which is rough and hilly and marked by forests and lakes, occupies the western two-thirds of the state. The Seaboard Lowland, with its sandy beaches and salt marshes, occupies the eastern third. The highest point in the state is Jerimoth Hill, at 812 feet (247 meters). Rhode Island's rivers include the Blackstone, Providence, Sakonnet, and Pawcatuck. Of the state's 38 islands, the largest is Aquidneck.

3 CLIMATE

Rhode Island has a humid climate, with cold winters and short summers. The average annual temperature is 50°F (10°C). At Providence the temperature ranges from an average of 28°F (–2°C) in January to 72°F (22°C) in July. The record high temperature, 104°F (40°C), was registered in 1975; the record low, –23°F (–31°C), in 1942. In Providence, the average annual precipitation is 45 inches (114 centimeters); snowfall averages 37 inches (94 centimeters) a year.

4 PLANTS AND ANIMALS

Though small, Rhode Island has three distinct life zones; sand-plain lowlands, rising hills, and highlands. Common trees are the tuliptree, pin and post oaks, and red cedar. Cattails are abundant in marsh areas, and 40 types of fern and 30 species of orchid are indigenous to the state. Swordfish, lobsters, and clams populate coastal waters; brook trout and pickerel are among the common freshwater fish. The Indiana bat, peregrine falcon, and bald eagle are on the federal endangered list.

5 ENVIRONMENTAL PROTECTION

The Department of Environmental Management coordinates all of the state's environmental protection and management programs. These include pollution control, hazardous waste management, protection of wildlife resources, forest management, and the enforcement of conservation laws. Rhode Island had 12 hazardous waste sites as of 1994.

6 POPULATION

Rhode Island ranked 43d in population among the 50 states with a 1990 census total of 1,003,464. The 1995 population

Rhode Island Population Profile

Estimated 1995 population:	1,021,000
Population change, 1980–90:	5.9%
Leading ancestry group:	Irish
Second leading group:	Italian
Foreign born population:	9.5%
Hispanic origin†:	4.6%
Population by race:	
White:	91.4%
Black:	3.9%
Native American:	0.4%
Asian/Pacific Islander:	1.8%
Other:	2.5%

Population by Age Group

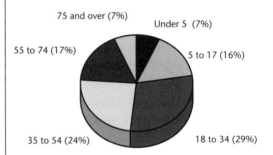

75 and over (7%)
Under 5 (7%)
55 to 74 (17%)
5 to 17 (16%)
35 to 54 (24%)
18 to 34 (29%)

Top Cities with Populations Over 25,000

City	Population	National rank	% change 1980–90
Providence	155,418	113	2.5
Warwick	85,823	251	–1.9
Cranston	76,703	297	5.7
Pawtucket	71,058	330	2.0
East Providence	50,394	519	–1.2
Woonsocket	42,373	634	–4.4
Newport	27,456	1,009	–3.5

Notes: †A person of Hispanic origin may be of any race. NA indicates that data are not available.
Sources: Economic and Statistics Administration, Bureau of the Census. *Statistical Abstract of the United States, 1994–95.* Washington, DC: Government Printing Office, 1995; Courtenay M. Slater and George E. Hall. *1995 County and City Extra: Annual Metro, City and County Data Book.* Lanham, MD: Bernan Press, 1995.

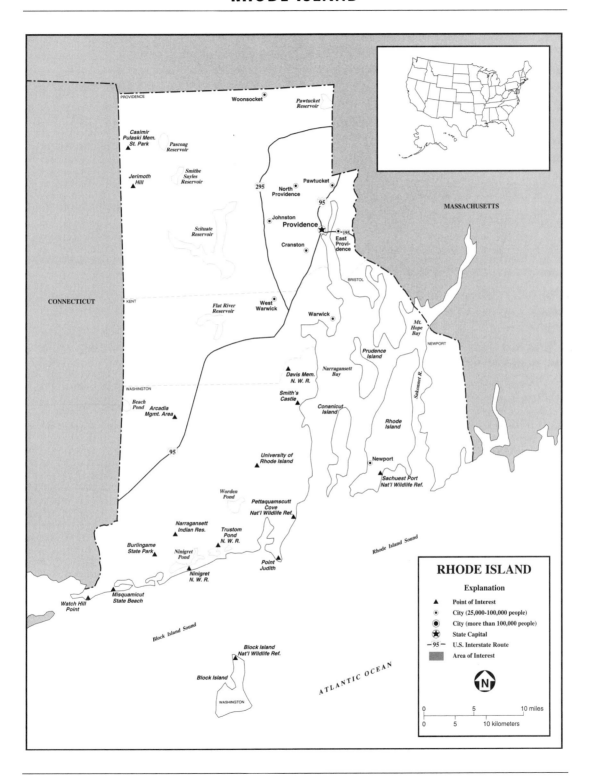

MASSACHUSETTS

CONNECTICUT

PROVIDENCE

Woonsocket

Pawtucket Reservoir

Casimir Pulaski Mem. St. Park

Pascoag Reservoir

Smithe Sayles Reservoir

Jerimoth Hill

295

North Providence

Pawtucket

95

Johnston

Scituate Reservoir

Providence

I-95 East Provi-dence

Cranston

BRISTOL

KENT

Flat River Reservoir

West Warwick

Warwick

Mt. Hope Bay

NEWPORT

Prudence Island

Davis Mem. N. W. R.

Narragansett Bay

Sakonnet R.

WASHINGTON

Smith's Castle

Conanicut Island

Rhode Island

Beach Pond

Arcadia Mgmt. Area

95

University of Rhode Island

Newport

Sachuest Port Nat'l Wildlife Ref.

Worden Pond

Pettaquamscutt Cove Nat'l Wildlife Ref.

Narragansett Indian Res.

Trustom Pond N. W. R.

Rhode Island Sound

Burlingame State Park

Ninigret Pond

Point Judith

Ninigret N. W. R.

Watch Hill Point

Misquamicut State Beach

Block Island Sound

Block Island Nat'l Wildlife Ref.

Block Island

ATLANTIC OCEAN

WASHINGTON

RHODE ISLAND

Explanation

▲ Point of Interest

⊙ City (25,000-100,000 people)

◉ City (more than 100,000 people)

★ State Capital

—95— U.S. Interstate Route

◼ Area of Interest

N

| 0 | | 5 | | 10 miles |

| 0 | 5 | | 10 kilometers |

was estimated to be 1,021,000. Rhode Island was, at 960.3 persons per square mile (369 persons per square kilometer), the nation's second most densely populated state. Providence, the capital, had a population in 1992 of 155,418. The next largest cities were Warwick, with 85,823; and Cranston, with 76,703.

7 ETHNIC GROUPS

Rhode Island's black population numbered 39,000 in 1990, or 3.9% of the state total. Among other minority groups, the 1990 census counted 46,000 persons of Hispanic origin, 4,071 Native Americans, 3,417 Cambodians, 3,037 Chinese, and 2,040 Laotians.

8 LANGUAGES

English in Rhode Island is of the Northern dialect, with the distinctive features of eastern New England. Rhode Island's immigrant past is reflected in the fact that in 1990, 18% of the state's residents reported speaking a language other than English in the home. The leading languages, and the number of people speaking them, were Portuguese, 39,947; Spanish, 35,492; French, 31,669; and Italian, 20,619.

9 RELIGIONS

Contemporary Rhode Island has the largest percentage of Roman Catholics among the US states, reflecting heavy immigration from Italy, Ireland, Portugal, and French Canada. There were 633,427 Roman Catholics and an estimated 16,101 Jews in 1990. The only large Protestant denomi-

nations were Episcopal, 31,865; and American Baptist, 21,703.

10 TRANSPORTATION

As of 1992, Providence & Worcester was the only freight-hauling railroad in operation, utilizing 114 rail miles (183 kilometers) of track. The number of Amtrak riders, at three stops, was 385,616 in 1991/92. In 1993, there were 6,057 miles (9,746 kilometers) of public highways and roads, and 695,310 motor vehicles were registered. The port at Providence handled over six million tons of cargo in 1991. Theodore Francis Green Airport is the major air terminal, with 954,208 boarded passengers in 1991.

11 HISTORY

Before the arrival of the first white settlers, the Narragansett Indians inhabited the area from what is now Providence south along Narragansett Bay. Their principal rivals, the Wampanoag, dominated the eastern shore region. In 1524, Florentine navigator Giovanni da Verrazano became the first European to explore Rhode Island. The earliest permanent settlement was established at Providence in 1636 by English clergyman Roger Williams and a small band of followers who left the Massachusetts Bay Colony to seek freedom of worship.

Other nonconformists followed, settling Portsmouth (1638), Newport (1639), and Warwick (1642). In 1644, Williams journeyed to England, where he secured parliamentary permission to unite the four original towns into a single colony, the Providence Plantations. In 1663, a royal

Providence skyline.

charter was obtained. Between 1675 and 1676, a Native American uprising known as King Philip's War was soundly defeated.

Statehood

The early 18th century was marked by significant growth in agriculture and commerce, including the rise of the slave trade. Having the greatest degree of self-rule, Rhode Island had the most to lose from British efforts after 1763 to increase supervision and control over the colonies. On 4 May 1776, Rhode Island became the first colony formally to renounce all allegiance to King George III. Favoring the weak central government established by the Articles of Confederation, the state quickly ratified them in 1778, but later resisted the strong central government of the federal constitution. Rhode Island withheld ratification until 29 May 1790, making it the last of the original 13 states to join the Union.

The principal trends in 19th-century Rhode Island were industrialization, immigration, and urbanization. During the first half of the century, the state's royal charter, which remained in effect, gave disproportionate influence to landowners and rural towns. Political reformers, led by Thomas Wilson Dorr, drafted a "People's Constitution," ratified in a popular referendum in December 1841.

The latter half of the 19th century was marked by continued industrialization and urbanization.

Politically the state was dominated by the Republican Party until the 1930s, when Democrats seized power during the New Deal and have mostly kept it since then. Present-day Rhode Island is predominantly Catholic and Democratic, but it retains an ethnic and cultural diversity surprising in view of its size but consistent with its heritage. The Rhode Island economy has seen little growth since the 1950s. Manufacturing jobs, once held by 30% of the work force, have declined recently.

12 STATE GOVERNMENT

Legislative authority is vested in the general assembly, a two-chamber body composed of 50 senators and 100 representatives. All legislators are elected for two-year terms. The assembly may override the governor's veto by a three-fifths vote, and, in joint session, name justices to the supreme court.

The chief officers of the executive branch are the governor, lieutenant governor, attorney general, secretary of state, and general treasurer. Until 1994, all were then elected for two-year terms in even-numbered years. The term length was increased to four years starting with the 1994 elections.

13 POLITICAL PARTIES

For nearly five decades, Rhode Island has been one of the nation's most solidly Democratic states. It has voted for the Republican presidential candidate only four times since 1928. In 1980, Rhode Island was one of only six states to favor Jimmy Carter. However, in 1984, Republican Edward DiPrete was elected governor, and Ronald Reagan narrowly carried the state in the presidential election. In the 1992 presidential election, Democratic nominee Bill Clinton captured 47% of the popular vote; incumbent George Bush received 29%; and Ross Perot collected 23%. In 1994, Republican Lincoln C. Almond was elected governor and Republican John H. Chafee won a fourth term to the US Senate. Both US Representatives were Democrats in 1994.

Rhode Island Presidential Vote by Major Political Parties, 1948–92

YEAR	RHODE ISLAND WINNER	DEMOCRAT	REPUBLICAN
1948	*Truman (D)	188,736	135,787
1952	*Eisenhower (R)	203,293	210,935
1956	*Eisenhower (R)	161,790	225,819
1960	*Kennedy (D)	258,032	147,502
1964	*Johnson (D)	315,463	74,615
1968	Humphrey (D)	246,518	122,359
1972	*Nixon (R)	194,645	220,383
1976	*Carter (D)	227,636	181,249
1980	Carter (D)	198,342	154,793
1984	*Reagan (R)	197,106	212,080
1988	Dukakis (D)	225,123	177,761
1992**	*Clinton (D)	213,299	131,601

*Won US presidential election.
** Independent candidate Ross Perot received 105,045 votes.

14 LOCAL GOVERNMENT

As of 1995, Rhode Island was subdivided into 8 cities and 31 towns, the main units of local government. The state's five counties are merely units of judicial administration. Many smaller communities retain the New England town meeting form of government. Larger cities and towns are governed by a mayor and/or city manager and a council.

Photo credit: Jim McElholm, Greater Providence Convention & Visitors Bureau.

The Rhode Island State House, built in 1900, was designed by the notable architectural firm of McKim, Mead and White.

15 JUDICIAL SYSTEM

The five-member supreme court is the state's highest appeals court. It may also issue advisory opinions on the constitutionality of actions by the governor or either house of the legislature. The second judicial level consists of the 19-member superior court and the 11-member family court. The former, the state's trial court, hears all jury trials in criminal cases and in civil matters involving more than $5,000, but can also hear nonjury cases. The family court deals with divorce, custody, juvenile crime, adoption, and related cases. Superior, family, and district court judges are appointed by the governor with the consent of the senate.

Civil matters involving $5,000 or less, small claims procedures, and nonjury criminal cases are handled at the district level. All cities and towns appoint judges to operate probate courts for wills and estates. Providence and a few other communities each have a municipal or police court. The 1994 crime rate of 4,119.1 per 100,000 persons was slightly below the national average. There were 2,783 prisoners in state and federal prisons in 1993.

16 MIGRATION

During the 19th and early 20th centuries, immigrants of many nationalities, including Irish, Italian, French-Canadian, British, Portuguese, Swedish, Polish, and

German came to work in the state's growing industries. Between 1940 and 1970, 2,000 more people left the state than moved to it. However, from 1985 to 1990, there was a net gain from migration of nearly 34,000. As of 1990, 63.4% of state residents had been born in Rhode Island.

17 ECONOMY

Rhode Island's economy is based overwhelmingly on industry. Agriculture, mining, forestry, and fishing make only small contributions. Unemployment rates, which had exceeded those of the US throughout the 1970s, fell dramatically in 1983 and 1984, but rose to 8.7% in 1992. Rhode Island's chief economic problem, its concentration of manufacturing industries paying low wages, persists. Manufacturing employment declined 23% between 1983 and 1992, while service jobs increased 36%.

18 INCOME

With a per capita (per person) income of $21,948 in 1994, Rhode Island ranked ninth among the 50 states. Total personal income grew to $21.9 billion in 1994. In 1993, 11.2% of the population lived below the federal poverty level.

19 INDUSTRY

The Industrial Revolution began early in Rhode Island. In 1790, Samuel Slater opened a cotton mill in Pawtucket, one of the first modern factories in America. Today, the state's leading manufactured products are jewelry, silverware, machinery, primary metals, textiles, and rubber products. Over 1,000 manufacturers in the state produce finished jewelry and jewelry parts. Hasbro, one of the world's largest toy manufacturers, is headquartered in Pawtucket and had sales exceeding $2.5 million in 1992.

20 LABOR

In 1994, the civilian labor force for the state totaled 505,000. The unemployment rate was 7.1%. Some 16.3% of all workers in the state belonged to labor unions in 1994.

21 AGRICULTURE

The state's total receipts from farm marketings were $80.7 million in 1994, 49th in the US. Rhode Island had only about 700 farms in 1994, with an average size of just 76 acres (31 hectares). Nursery and greenhouse products were the main agricultural commodity, accounting for 58.2% of agricultural receipts in 1994.

22 DOMESTICATED ANIMALS

Marketings from livestock and livestock products totaled $12,287,000 in 1994, of which dairy products accounted for about $4.3 million. In 1994, the state had about 7,500 cattle, 3,300 hogs, and 2,100 milk cows.

23 FISHING

The commercial catch in 1992 was 141.6 million pounds, valued at $85.6 million. The most valuable edible fish and shellfish caught in 1991 were whiting, fluke and yellowtail flounders, cod, scup lobster, squid, and clams. In 1991, the state developed restoration stocks of 160,500 fish, and maintenance stocks of 118,000 fish.

24 FORESTRY

In 1993, forests and woodlands covered 465,000 acres (188,000 hectares), 60% of the state's land area. Some 372,000 acres (160,000 hectares) were usable as commercial timberland.

25 MINING

The value of nonfuel mineral production in Rhode Island in 1994 was estimated to be $27 million. Crushed stone (1.4 million short tons, worth $8.8 million) and construction sand and gravel (1.2 million short tons, worth $5.7 million) accounted for nearly all of the state's production.

26 ENERGY AND POWER

Rhode Island's power production totaled 171 million kilowatt hours in 1991, the lowest in the US. In 1992, energy expenditures per capita (per person) were $1,865. Energy consumption in that year was 246.5 million Btu per capita. The state, as of 1993, had no nuclear power plants.

27 COMMERCE

Wholesale sales totaled $19.5 billion for 1992; retail sales were $7.6 billion for 1993; service establishment receipts were $4.2 billion for 1992. Foreign exports of manufactured goods were $859 million in 1992.

28 PUBLIC FINANCE

The general revenues for 1993 were $3,765,000,000; expenditures were $4,176,000,000. The total outstanding debt was $5.1 billion as of 1993, or $5,150 per capita (per person).

29 TAXATION

As of 1994, Rhode Island levied a state income tax, a corporate tax rate, and a sales and use tax of 7% on most items.

30 HEALTH

Death rates from heart disease and cancer —the leading causes of death in 1991— were well above the national averages. There were 11 community hospitals in 1993 with 3,000 beds. The state had 2,700 active nonfederal physicians in 1993 and 9,700 nurses. The average hospital expense per inpatient day was $885 in 1993, with an average cost per stay of $5,672. Some 10.3% of state residents did not have health insurance in 1993.

31 HOUSING

In 1993, there were an estimated 422,000 housing units. The state authorized 2,579 privately owned new housing units worth $235.1 million in 1993. In 1990, Rhode Island ranked sixth in median home value, at $133,500. Owners with a mortgage who occupied their houses had a median monthly cost of $891, while owners without a mortgage paid a median of $290 in costs per month. Median monthly rent in 1990 was $489.

32 EDUCATION

Only 73.2% of adult Rhode Islanders were high school graduates in 1990, the lowest such percentage for any northern state. As of 1993, 147,000 students were enrolled in public schools. Expenditures on education averaged $6,649 per pupil (eighth in the nation) in 1993. Some 23,036 were in private schools in the fall

Newport Harbor, Newport.

of 1991, most of them in Catholic schools. More than 78,273 students were enrolled in the state's 13 institutions of higher education in fall 1990. Leading institutions included Brown University (founded 1764) as well as Johnson and Wales University in Providence; the University of Rhode Island in Kingston; Roger Williams College in Bristol; and Providence College. The Rhode Island School of Design is located in Providence.

33 ARTS

Newport and Providence have notable art galleries and museums. Theatrical groups include the Trinity Square Repertory Company, the Sock and Buskin Players of Brown University, and the Players, all in Providence. The Rhode Island Philharmonic performs throughout the state. Newport is the site of the internationally famous Newport Jazz Festival. The State of Rhode Island's Arts funding from 1987 to 1991 amounted to $10,251,115.

34 LIBRARIES AND MUSEUMS

In 1991, Rhode Island had 120 public, academic, and special libraries. In 1991, public libraries had a book stock of 3,253,298, and a combined circulation of 5,657,359. The Brown University Libraries include the Annmary Brown Memorial Library, with its collection of rare manuscripts; and the John Carter Brown

Library, with an excellent collection of early Americana.

Among the state's more than 47 museums and historic sites are the Haffenreffer Museum of Anthropology in Bristol, the Museum of Art of the Rhode Island School of Design in Providence, and the Slater Mill Historic Site in Pawtucket.

35 COMMUNICATIONS

As of March 1993, 94.7% of the state's 391,000 occupied housing units had telephones. In 1993, the state had 15 AM and 18 FM radio stations. Rhode Island had seven television stations, including one public broadcasting affiliate. The state had three large cable television systems in 1993.

36 PRESS

In 1994, Rhode Island had seven daily newspapers, with a combined circulation of 947,154. The largest was the *Providence Journal-Bulletin*.

37 TOURISM, TRAVEL, AND RECREATION

Travelers from other states spent $708 million in Rhode Island during 1993. Historic sites—especially the mansions of Newport and Providence—and water sports (particularly the America's Cup yacht races) are the main tourist attractions. Block Island is a popular resort. Rhode Island's state parks and recreational areas total 9,000 acres.

38 SPORTS

Rhode Island has no major league professional sports teams. Pawtucket has a AAA minor league baseball team. Providence College has competed successfully in collegiate basketball. The Newport Yacht Club hosted the America's Cup, international sailing's most prestigious event, from 1930 until 1983. Newport is also the site of the International Tennis Hall of Fame and the Yachting Hall of Fame.

39 FAMOUS RHODE ISLANDERS

Important federal officeholders from Rhode Island were US Senators Nelson W. Aldrich (1841–1915), Theodore Francis Green (1867–1966), John O. Pastore (b.1907), and Claiborne DeBorda Pell (b.1918). Foremost among Rhode Island's historical figures is Roger Williams (b.England, 1603?–83), founder of Providence. Other significant pioneers, also born in England, include Anne Hutchinson (1591–1643), religious leader and cofounder of Portsmouth; and William Coddington (1601–78), founder of Newport. Important in the War for Independence was General Nathanael Greene (1742–86).

The 19th century brought to prominence reformer Thomas Wilson Dorr (1805–54). Also important were naval officers Oliver Hazard Perry (1785–1819), who secured important US victories in the War of 1812; and his brother, Matthew C. Perry (1794–1858), who led the expedition that opened Japan to foreign trade in 1854. Samuel Slater (b.England, 1768–1835) was a pioneer in textile manufacturing. Other significant public figures include Unitarian theologian William Ellery Channing (1780–1842).

Rhode Island's best-known creative writer is Gothic novelist H. P. Lovecraft

(1890–1937). The state was also home to portrait painter Gilbert Stuart (1755–1828) and composer George M. Cohan (1878–1942). Important sports personalities include Baseball Hall of Famers Napoleon "Nap" Lajoie (1875–1959) and Charles "Gabby" Hartnett (1900–72).

40 BIBLIOGRAPHY

Conley, Patrick T. *Rhode Island Profile.* Providence: Rhode Island Publications Society, 1983.

Providence Journal-Bulletin. *Journal-Bulletin Rhode Island Almanac.* 99th ed. Providence, 1985.

Steinberg, Sheila, and Cathleen McGuigan. *Rhode Island: An Historical Guide.* Providence: Rhode Island Bicentennial Commission, 1976.

SOUTH CAROLINA

State of South Carolina

ORIGIN OF STATE NAME: Named in honor of King Charles I of England.

NICKNAME: The Palmetto State.

CAPITAL: Columbia.

ENTERED UNION: 23 May 1788 (8th).

SONG: "Carolina."

MOTTO: *Animis opibusque parati* (Prepared in mind and resources); *Dum spiro spero* (While I breathe, I hope).

COAT OF ARMS: A palmetto stands erect, with a ravaged oak (representing the British fleet) at its base; 12 spears, symbolizing the first 12 states, are bound crosswise to the palmetto's trunk by a band bearing the inscription "Quis separabit" (Who shall separate?). Two shields bearing the inscriptions "March 26" (the date in 1776 when South Carolina established its first independent government) and "July 4," respectively, hang from the tree. Under the oak are the words "Meliorem lapsa locavit" (Having fallen, it has set up a better one) and the year "1776." The words "South Carolina" and the motto *Animis opibusque parati* surround the whole.

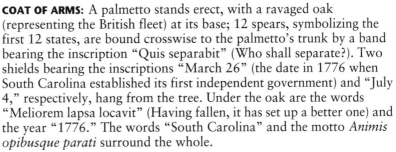

FLAG: Blue field with a white palmetto in the center and a white crescent at the union.

OFFICIAL SEAL: The official seal consists of two ovals showing the original designs for the obverse and the reverse of South Carolina's great seal of 1777. Left (obverse): same as the coat of arms. Right (reverse): as the sun rises over the seashore, Hope, holding a laurel branch, walks over swords and daggers. The motto *Dum spiro spero* is above her, the word "Spes" (Hope) below.

ANIMAL: White-tailed deer.

BIRD: Carolina wren.

WILD GAME BIRD: Wild turkey.

FISH: Striped bass.

FLOWER: Yellow jessamine.

TREE: Palmetto.

GEM: Amethyst.

STONE: Blue granite.

TIME: 7 AM EST = noon GMT.

1 LOCATION AND SIZE

Situated in the southeastern US, South Carolina ranks 40th in size among the 50 states. The state's total area is 31,113 square miles (80,583 square kilometers). South Carolina extends 273 miles (439 kilometers) east-west; its maximum north-south extension is 210 miles (338 kilometers). Its total boundary length is 824 miles

(1,326 kilometers). The state includes 13 major Sea Islands in the Atlantic.

2 TOPOGRAPHY

South Carolina is divided into two major regions: the upcountry, which lies within the Piedmont Plateau, and the low country to the southeast, which forms part of the Atlantic Coastal Plain. In the extreme northwest, the Blue Ridge Mountains cover about 500 square miles (1,300 square kilometers). The highest elevation, at 3,560 feet (1,085 meters), is Sassafras Mountain. Many artificial lakes are associated with electric power plants. Three river systems—the Pee Dee, Santee, and Savannah—drain most of the state.

3 CLIMATE

South Carolina has a humid, subtropical climate. Average temperatures range from 68°F (20°C) on the coast to 58°F (14°C) in the northwest, with colder temperatures in the mountains. The record high temperature is 111°F (44°C) set in 1954; the record low for the state is −20°F (−29°C), set in 1977. The daily mean temperature at Columbia is 44°F (7°C) in January and 81°F (27°C) in July. Rainfall is ample throughout the state, ranging from 38 inches (97 centimeters) in the central region to 52 inches (132 centimeters) in the upper Piedmont.

4 PLANTS AND ANIMALS

Principal trees of South Carolina include palmetto (the state tree), balsam fir, and beech. Rocky areas of the Piedmont contain a mixture of moss and lichens. The coastal plain has a wide variety of grasses,

South Carolina Population Profile

Estimated 1995 population:	3,772,000
Population change, 1980–90:	11.7%
Leading ancestry group:	African American
Second leading group:	German
Foreign born population:	1.4%
Hispanic origin†:	0.9%
Population by race:	
White:	69.0%
Black:	29.8%
Native American:	0.2%
Asian/Pacific Islander:	0.6%
Other:	0.4%

Population by Age Group

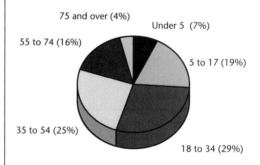

75 and over (4%)
Under 5 (7%)
55 to 74 (16%)
5 to 17 (19%)
35 to 54 (25%)
18 to 34 (29%)

Top Cities with Populations Over 25,000

City	Population	National rank	% change 1980–90
Columbia	98,832	202	−3.1
Charleston	81,301	274	15.7
North Charleston	74,379	307	12.3
Greenville	59,042	413	0.1
Spartanburg	45,113	587	−0.8
Rock Hill	44,384	600	17.7
Sumter	42,461	632	68.5
Mount Pleasant	32,038	878	117.6
Florence	30,740	913	−1.0
Anderson	27,931	992	−4.1

Notes: †A person of Hispanic origin may be of any race. NA indicates that data are not available.
Sources: Economic and Statistics Administration, Bureau of the Census. *Statistical Abstract of the United States, 1994–95.* Washington, DC: Government Printing Office, 1995; Courtenay M. Slater and George E. Hall. *1995 County and City Extra: Annual Metro, City and County Data Book.* Lanham, MD: Bernan Press, 1995.

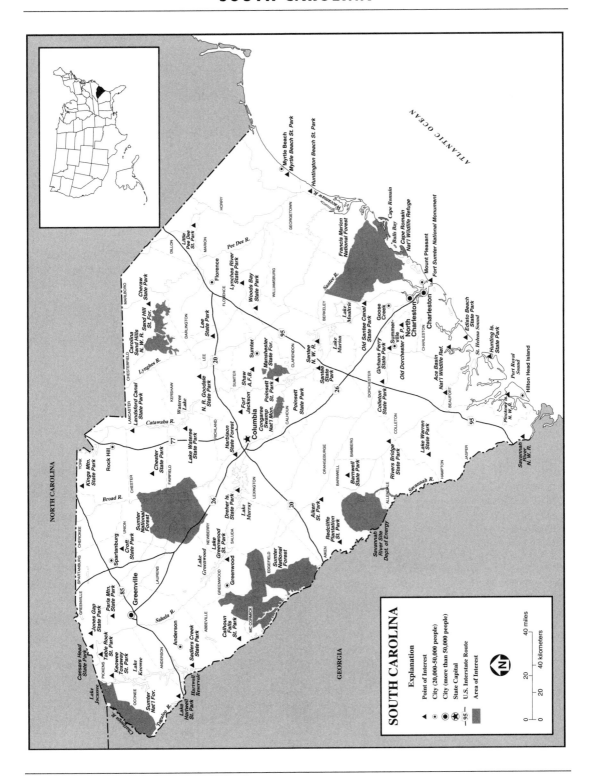

SOUTH CAROLINA

Explanation

▲ Point of Interest
⊙ City (20,000-50,000 people)
◉ City (more than 50,000 people)
★ State Capital
—95— U.S. Interstate Route
▨ Area of Interest

ATLANTIC OCEAN

NORTH CAROLINA

GEORGIA

Myrtle Beach
Myrtle Beach St. Park
Huntington Beach St. Park

Cape Romain
Cape Romain
Nat'l Wildlife Refuge

Mount Pleasant
Fort Sumter National Monument

Francis Marion
National Forest

Bulls Bay

Santee R.

Georgetown

HORRY

Little
Pee Dee
St. Park

Pee Dee R.

MARION

Florence
Lynches River
State Park

FLORENCE

DILLON

MARLBORO

Cheraw
State Park

Carolina
Sand Hills
N. W. R. Sand Hill
St. For.

CHESTERFIELD

DARLINGTON

Lynches R.

Lee
State Park

LEE

Woods Bay
State Park

WILLIAMSBURG

Lake
Moultrie

BERKELEY

Goose
Creek

North
Charleston
Charleston

CHARLESTON

Edisto Beach
State Park

St. Helena Sound

Hunting Is.
State Park

Old Santee Canal
State Park

Summer-
ville

Old Dorchester S. P.
Girhans Ferry
State Park

DORCHESTER

Colleton
State Park

COLLETON

Ace Basin
Nat'l Wildlife Ref.

BEAUFORT

Port Royal
Sound

Hilton Head Island

Pinckney Is.
N. W. R.

JASPER

Savannah
River
N. W. R.

Savannah R.

HAMPTON

Lake Warren
State Park

Rivers Bridge
State Park

ALLENDALE

BAMBERG

Barnwell
State Park

BARNWELL

ORANGEBURGE

Sumter
MSumter
Manchester
State For.

Santee
N. W. R.

Santee
State Park

CLARENDON

Lake
Marion

Shaw
A.F.B.

Poinsett
St. Park

Poinsett
State Park

CALHOUN

Fort
Jackson

Congaree
Swamp
Nat'l Mon.

Columbia

RICHLAND

N. R. Goodale
State Park

KERSHAW

SUMTER

Waterree
Lake

Catawba R.

LANCASTER

Landsford
Canal
State Park

Harbison
State Forest

Lake Wateree
State Park

FAIRFIELD

Chester
State Park

CHESTER

Rock Hill

Kings Mtn.
State Park

YORK

Broad R.

Sumter
National
Forest

Croft
State Park

Spartanburg

UNION

SPARTANBURG

CHEROKEE

GREENVILLE

Paris Mtn.
State Park

Greenville

Jones Gap
State Park

Caesars Head
State Park

Table Rock
St. Park

PICKENS

Keowee
Toxaway
St. Park

Lake
Keowee

Lake
Jocassee

OCONEE

Sumter
Nat'l For.

Lake
Hartwell
St. Park

Toxaway R.

Chattooga R.

ANDERSON

Anderson

Sadlers Creek
State Park

ABBEVILLE

Saluda R.

Calhoun
Falls
State Park

MCCORMICK

Hartwell
Reservoir

Sumter
National
Forest

EDGEFIELD

GREENWOOD

Greenwood

Lake
Greenwood

Lake
Greenwood
St. Park

NEWBERRY

SALUDA

Lake
Murray

Dreher Is.
State Park

LEXINGTON

AIKEN

Aiken
St. Park

Redcliffe
Plantation
St. Park

Savannah
River Site
Dept. of Energy

LAURENS

85

77

20

26

20

95

95

26

40 miles

40 kilometers

0 20

0 20

N

Courtesy: the Charleston Area Convention & Visitors Bureau.

A scenic country lane in Charleston.

shrubs, and vines. South Carolina mammals include white-tailed deer (the state animal), cottontail and marsh rabbits, and woodchuck. Common birds include the mockingbird and Carolina wren (the state bird). Among endangered animals are the brown pelican, eastern cougar, and American alligator.

5 ENVIRONMENTAL PROTECTION

The Department of Health and Environmental Control is South Carolina's primary environmental protection agency. The Department's areas of responsibility include programs dealing with surface and ground water protection; air quality; and solid, hazardous, and nuclear waste. The state has implemented an innovative river basin planning program for the protection of its surface water resources. The state had 26 hazardous waste sites as of 1994.

6 POPULATION

South Carolina in 1990 ranked 25th in population among the 50 states, with 3,486,703 residents. The estimated 1995 population was 3,772,000. The population density in 1990 was 115.8 persons per square mile (44.5 persons per square kilometer). The largest cities, with 1992 populations, were Columbia, 98,832; Charleston, 81,031; North Charleston, 74,379; and Greenville, 59,042.

7 ETHNIC GROUPS

The population of South Carolina is mainly of Northern European heritage. Black Americans made up about 30% of the state's population in 1990, when the census also counted 8,246 Native Americans. There were also 8,316 Mexicans, 6,028 Filipinos, 4,282 Puerto Ricans, 3,279 Japanese, and 3,198 Koreans in South Carolina.

8 LANGUAGES

South Carolina English is marked by a division between the South Midland of the upcountry and the plantation Southern of the coastal plain. Along the coast and on the Sea Islands, some blacks still use the Gullah dialect, based on a Creole mixture of pre-Revolutionary English and African speech. In 1990, 96.5% of all state residents five years of age and older reported speaking English at home. Other languages spoken at home, and number of speakers, included Spanish, 44,427; French, 22,339; and German, 14,053.

9 RELIGIONS

South Carolina is predominantly Protestant, and has been since colonial days. The Protestant denominations with more than 100,000 members in 1990 were Southern Baptist; Baptist Educational and Missionary Convention (black), 894,390; and United Methodist, 308,915. In 1990, the Episcopal Church had 48,655 members. As of 1990, the state also had 78,768 Roman Catholics and an estimated 8,558 Jews.

10 TRANSPORTATION

Most freight service is furnished by Norfolk Southern and CSX Transportation. In 1991/92, the number of Amtrak riders was 250,310. The state road network in 1993 was made up of 53,637 miles (86,302 kilometers) of rural roads, 10,521 miles (16,928 kilometers) of urban roads, including 810 miles (1303 kilometers) of interstate highways. There were 1,997,482 passenger vehicles and 686,229 trucks and buses registered in 1993. Charleston is one of the major ports on the Atlantic, handling over 9.4 million tons of cargo in 1991. Charleston, Columbia, and Greenville–Spartanburg are the major airports.

11 HISTORY

Prior to European settlement, the region now called South Carolina was populated by several Native American groups, including Iroquoian, Siouan, and Muskogean tribes. In the early 1500s, long before the English claimed the Carolinas, Spanish sea captains explored the coast. The English established their first permanent settlement in 1670 under the supervision of the eight lords who had been granted rights to "Carolana" by King Charles II. At first the colonists settled at Albemarle Point on the Ashley River. Ten years later, they moved across the river to the present site of Charleston.

The colony flourished, as rice cultivation began in the coastal swamps, and black slaves were imported as field hands. The original royal grant had created a very large colony, but eventually the separate provinces of North Carolina and Georgia were established. The colonists were successful in having the lords' control overthrown in 1719 and the government transferred to royal rule by 1721.

Statehood

South Carolina opposed the Stamp Act of 1765 and took an active part in the American Revolution. The first British property seized by American Revolutionary forces was Fort Charlotte in McCormick County in 1775. Delegates from South Carolina were leaders at the federal constitutional convention of 1787. On 23 May 1788, South Carolina became the eighth state to ratify the Constitution.

Between the Revolutionary War and the Civil War, two issues dominated South Carolinians' political thinking: tariffs and slavery. Large farms became profitable by using slave labor, and with more than half its population consisting of black slaves, the state seceded from the Union on 20 December 1860. The first battle of the Civil War took place at Fort Sumter in Charleston Harbor on 12 April 1861. In the closing months of the war, Union troops under General William Tecumseh Sherman burned Columbia and caused widespread destruction elsewhere. South Carolina contributed about 63,000 soldiers to the Confederacy out of a white population of some 291,000.

Given the right to vote and hold office during Reconstruction, blacks attained the offices of lieutenant governor and US representative. Former Confederate General Wade Hampton was elected governor in 1876, and the following year President Rutherford B. Hayes declared an end to Reconstruction and withdrew federal troops from the state.

1880s–1990s

For the next 100 years, South Carolina suffered through political turmoil, crop failures, and recessions. The political reign of Benjamin Ryan "Pitchfork Ben" Tillman, who served as governor from 1890 to 1894 and then as US senator until his death in 1918, inaugurated a period of political and racial repression that sought to exclude black voters.

The main economic transformation since 1890 has been the replacement of rice and cotton farming by tobacco and soybean cultivation, along with the movement of tenant farmers, or sharecroppers, from the land to the cities. There they found jobs in textile mills, and textiles became the state's leading industry after 1900. With the devastation of the cotton crop by the boll weevil in the 1920s, farmers were compelled to diversify their crops. Labor shortages in the North during and after World War II drew many thousands of blacks to Philadelphia, Washington, D.C., New York, and other cities.

Public school desegregation after 1954 proceeded peacefully, and racial integration at the workplace became the standard. In 1983, for the first time in 95 years, a black state senator was elected. Most South Carolinians remain conservative in political and social matters.

12 STATE GOVERNMENT

The general assembly consists of a senate of 46 members, elected for four-year terms; and a house of representatives of 124 members, elected for two years. Officials elected statewide include the governor and lieutenant governor (who run separately), attorney general, secretary of state, comptroller general, and treasurer.

Bills may be introduced in either house, except for revenue measures, which are reserved to the house of representatives. The governor has a regular veto and an item veto on appropriation matters, either of which may be overridden by a two-thirds vote of those present in each house of the legislature. Bills automatically become law after five days if the governor takes no action.

13 POLITICAL PARTIES

From the end of Reconstruction, the Democratic Party dominated state politics. In 1948 the States' Rights Democrat (or "dixiecrat") faction was formed and its

candidate, South Carolina Governor J. Strom Thurmond, carried the state. Thurmond's switch to the Republicans while in the US Senate boosted support for the state's Republican Party, which since 1964 has captured South Carolina's eight electoral votes in seven of the eight presidential elections.

In 1992, incumbent George Bush won 48% of the popular vote, to Democrat Bill Clinton's 40%, and Independent Ross Perot's 12%. As of 1994, there were two Democrats and four Republicans serving as US Representatives. The state senate contained 30 Democrats and 16 Republicans. In the state house there were 73 Democrats, 50 Republicans, and 1 Independent.

14 LOCAL GOVERNMENT

As of 1992, South Carolina had 46 counties, 270 incorporated municipalities, 91 school districts, and 297 special districts

South Carolina Presidential Vote by Political Parties, 1948–92

YEAR	SOUTH CAROLINA WINNER	DEMOCRAT	REPUBLICAN	STATES' RIGHTS DEMOCRAT	LIBERTARIAN
1948	Thurmond (SRD)	34,423	5,386	102,607	—
1952	Stevenson (D)	172,957	168,043	—	—
				UNPLEDGED	—
1956	Stevenson (D)	136,278	75,634	88,509	—
1960	*Kennedy (D)	198,121	188,558	—	—
1964	Goldwater (R)	215,723	309,048	—	—
				AMERICAN IND.	
1968	*Nixon (R)	197,486	254,062	215,430	—
				AMERICAN	
1972	*Nixon (R)	186,824	477,044	10,075	—
1976	*Carter (D)	450,807	346,149	2,996	—
1980	*Reagan (R)	430,385	441,841	—	4,975
1984	*Reagan (R)	344,459	615,539	—	4,359
1988	*Bush (R)	370,554	606,443	—	4,935
				IND. (Perot)	
1992	Bush (R)	479,514	577,507	138,872	2,719

* Won US presidential election.

Photo credit: South Carolina Department of Parks, Recreation, and Tourism.

State house in Columbia.

of various types. Most municipalities operate under the mayor-council or city manager system. More than half the counties have a county administrator or manager. Customarily, each county has a council or commission, attorney, auditor, clerk of court, coroner, tax collector, treasurer, and sheriff.

15 JUDICIAL SYSTEM

South Carolina's unified judicial system is headed by the chief justice of the five-member supreme court, which is the final court of appeal. A five-member intermediate court of appeals became a permanent constitutional court in 1984. Sixteen circuit courts hear major criminal and civil

cases. South Carolina's total crime rate for 1994 exceeded the national average at 6,000.8 reported crimes per 100,000 inhabitants. In 1993 there were 18,704 inmates in state and federal correctional institutions.

16 MIGRATION

In the 20th century, many blacks left the state for cities in the North. Between 1940 and 1970, South Carolina's net loss from migration was 601,000. In the 1980s, however, the net gain from migration was nearly 200,000. During 1990–94, South Carolina gained about 44,000 more residents due to interstate migration.

17 ECONOMY

Textiles and farming completely dominated the economy until after World War II, when efforts toward economic diversification attracted paper, chemical, and other industries to the state. By 1992, manufacturing had become the most important part of the South Carolina economy. Two military bases, Westinghouse Savannah River Site and Charleston Naval Shipyard, account for a significant portion of the state's manufacturing. Employment at those facilities grew significantly during the 1980s when military expenditures increased. In the early 1990s, however, the federal government began cutting staff at the bases and was considering phasing them out.

Largely because of its legacy of low-wage industries and an unorganized and poorly educated work force, the state continues to fall below national norms by most economic measures. Since the end of World War II, rising foreign and domestic investment, coupled with an abundance of first-class tourist facilities along the coast, have contributed to the continuing growth of South Carolina's economy. The state was only temporarily hurt by the national recession of the early 1990s.

18 INCOME

South Carolina ranked 43d among the 50 states in 1994 with a per capita (per person) income of $17,712. Total personal income increased to $64.9 billion in 1994. In 1993, 18.7% of all residents were living below the federal poverty level.

19 INDUSTRY

Many textile mills were closed during the 1970s and early 1980s because of the importation of cheaper textiles from abroad. The economic slack was made up, however, by the establishment of new industries, especially paper and chemical manufactures. South Carolina's major manufacturing centers are concentrated in the northern part of the state and in the Piedmont area.

20 LABOR

In 1994, South Carolina had a civilian labor force of 1,828,000. There was an unemployment rate of 6.3%. Only 3.8% of all workers in the state were union members in 1994, which was the lowest percentage of any state.

21 AGRICULTURE

In 1994, South Carolina ranked 35th among the 50 states in farm income with nearly $1.4 billion. For most of the 19th century, cotton was the primary cash crop, but today tobacco outranks cotton in annual cash value. South Carolina leads the nation in the sale of fresh peaches, which are produced mainly in the sand hills and Piedmont. Production of leading crops in 1994 included tobacco, 110,450,000 pounds; soybeans, 15,660,000 bushels; wheat, 18,000,000 bushels; cotton, 380,000 bales; and peaches, 250,000,000 pounds.

22 DOMESTICATED ANIMALS

In 1994, livestock and livestock products were valued at $614.9 million, or 45% of the state's farm income. At the close of 1994, there were 540,000 cattle, 28,000

Photo credit: South Carolina Department of Parks, Recreation, and Tourism.

Thoroughbreds grazing, Aiken.

milk cows, and 350,000 hogs. Broilers and cattle products accounted for 15.1% and 9.1%, respectively, of the state's agricultural receipts.

23 FISHING

Major commercial fishing is restricted to saltwater species of fish and shellfish, mainly shrimp, crabs, clams, and oysters. In 1992, the commercial catch totaled 19,272,000 pounds and was valued at $25,621,000. In 1992, federal hatcheries distributed 4.1 million fish within the state.

24 FORESTRY

In 1990 the forest products industry was the third largest industry in South Carolina. The state had 12,645,557 acres (5,117,657 hectares) of forestland in 1993—about 66% of the state's area. Shipments of lumber and wood products were valued at $1.4 billion in 1990. Shipments of paper and related products were valued at $2.8 billion.

25 MINING

The estimated 1994 value of nonfuel mineral commodities produced in South Carolina was $415 million. Cement was the leading mineral commodity produced in the state in 1992; almost 2.4 million short tons were produced. Crushed stone, which accounted for 24.4% of the total mineral value, continued to lead gold as the second-most valuable commodity.

26 ENERGY AND POWER

Although it lacks fossil fuel resources, South Carolina produces more electricity than it consumes. In 1993, power production reached 75.6 billion kilowatt hours. Energy expenditures for that year were $1,869 per capita (per person). The state had seven nuclear power plants as of 1993.

27 COMMERCE

Wholesale sales totaled $21.3 billion for 1992; retail sales were $27.9 billion for 1993; service establishment receipts were $12.2 billion for 1992. Foreign exports of South Carolina's own products were valued at $4.2 billion in 1992.

28 PUBLIC FINANCE

The state constitution requires that budget appropriations not exceed expected revenues. The state shares tax collections with its subdivisions—counties and municipalities—which determine how their share of the money will be spent. The General Fund revenues for fiscal year 1992/93 were $3,672,593,567; expenditures were $3,521,238,395.

As of 1993, South Carolina's public debt totaled $4.9 billion, or $1,350 per capita (per person).

29 TAXATION

South Carolinians bear a lighter tax burden than most other states. As of 1994, the chief levies were personal and corporate

Courtesy: the Charleston Area Convention & Visitors Bureau.

A historic Charleston house.

income taxes; a 5% sales tax; and taxes on gasoline, alcoholic beverages, business licenses, insurance, and gifts and estates. Taxes paid to the state government totaled $4.3 billion in 1993.

30 HEALTH

As of 1992, the leading causes of death were heart disease, cancer, stroke, and accidents. The state has mounted major programs to detect heart disease and high blood pressure, reduce infant mortality, and expand medical education. In 1993, South Carolina had 68 community hospitals with 11,400 beds. The average hospital expense was $838 per inpatient day, or $5,955 for an average cost per stay. Nonfederal medical personnel included 6,205 active physicians in 1993 and 20,700 nurses. Some 16.9% of state residents did not have health insurance in 1993.

31 HOUSING

In 1993 there were an estimated 1,501,000 year-round housing units. The median value of an owner-occupied house was $61,100 in 1990. In 1990, over 16.5% of the state's housing units consisted of mobile homes or trailers, a greater proportion than in any other state except Wyoming. In 1993, 21,068 new units, valued at almost $1.7 billion, were authorized.

32 EDUCATION

For decades, South Carolina ranked below the national averages in most phases of education. During the 1970s, however, significant improvements were made, and South Carolina high school graduates now score only slightly lower than the national averages on standardized examinations. As of 1990, more than 68.9% of all residents 25 years or older had completed high school and 16.2% had attended college. In 1993, there were 638,000 pupils enrolled in public schools. Expenditures on education averaged $4,669 per pupil (37th in the nation) in 1993.

Higher education institutions in 1991/92 enrolled 164,907 students. The state has three major universities: the University of South Carolina, with 26,131 students (1991/92) at its main campus in Columbia; Clemson University in Clemson; and the Medical University of South Carolina in Charleston. In addition, there are 6 four-year state colleges, 21 four-year private colleges and universities, and 8 private junior colleges.

33 ARTS

South Carolina's three major centers for the visual arts are the Gibbes Art Gallery in Charleston, the Columbia Museum of Art and Science, and the Greenville County Museum of Art. Columbia's Town Theater claims to be the nation's oldest continuous community playhouse.

Perhaps South Carolina's best-known musical event is the Spoleto Festival. It is held annually in Charleston during May and June (modeled on the Spoleto Festival in Italy), and artists of international repute perform in original productions of operas and dramas. The State of South Carolina generated $25,714,562 in federal and state funds for its arts programs from 1987 to 1991.

34 LIBRARIES AND MUSEUMS

Public libraries in South Carolina had a combined book stock of 5,832,747 volumes and a total circulation of 13,406,973 in 1990/92. The State Library in Columbia supervises the 39 county and regional libraries and also provides reference and research services for the state government. The University of South Carolina and Clemson University libraries have the most outstanding academic collections.

There are 123 museums and historic sites, notably the Charleston Museum specializing in history, natural history, and anthropology. Charleston is also famous for its many old homes, streets, churches, and public facilities. At the entrance to Charleston Harbor stands Fort Sumter, where the Civil War began.

35 COMMUNICATIONS

In March 1993, 89.1% of South Carolina's 1,300,000 occupied housing units had telephones. The state had 213 radio stations (100 AM, 113 FM) and 21 commercial television stations in 1993. South Carolina has one of the most highly regarded educational television systems in the nation. In 1993, eight large cable systems provided television programming.

36 PRESS

Of the leading morning newspapers published in South Carolina, the *Charleston Post and Courier* had a paid daily circulation of 112,000, and 122,383 on Sunday, in 1994; the *Spartanburg Herald-Journal* had 64,136 daily and 66,332 on Sunday; and the *Greenville News* had 96,500 daily and 145,000 on Sunday. Overall, as of 1994, South Carolina had 10 morning newspapers, 6 evening dailies, and 19 Sunday newspapers.

37 TOURISM, TRAVEL, AND RECREATION

Domestic tourists spent $4.8 billion in South Carolina during 1993. About 75% of tourist revenue is spent by vacationers in Charleston and at the Myrtle Beach and Hilton Head Island resorts. The Cowpens National Battlefield and the Fort Sumter and Kings Mountain national military sites are popular tourist attractions. State parks attracted a total of 7,970,000 visitors in 1991.

38 SPORTS

There are no major league professional sports teams in South Carolina. Several steeplechase horse-races are held annually in Camden, and important professional golf and tennis tournaments are held at Hilton Head Island. In collegiate football, the Clemson Tigers won the AP and UPI polls in 1981. There are two major stock-car races held at Darlington each year: the TranSouth 500 in April and the Southern 500 on Labor Day weekend.

39 FAMOUS SOUTH CAROLINIANS

Many distinguished South Carolinians made their reputations outside the state. South Carolina native Andrew Jackson (1767–1845), the seventh US president, studied law in North Carolina before establishing a legal practice in Tennessee. Identified more closely with South Carolina is John C. Calhoun (1782–1850), vice-president from 1825 to 1832.

Charles Cotesworth Pinckney (1746–1825) was a delegate to the US constitutional convention. Benjamin R. Tillman (1847–1918) was governor, US senator, and leader of the populist movement in South Carolina. The state's best-known recent political leader is J(ames) Strom Thurmond (b.1902), who was the only person ever elected to the US Senate by write-in vote, and who has served in the Senate since 1955.

Famous military leaders native to the state include the Revolutionary War General Francis Marion (1732?–95), known as the Swamp Fox; and General William C. Westmoreland (b.1914), commander of US forces in Viet Nam. Notable in the academic world are Mary McLeod Bethune (1875–1955), founder of Bethune-Cookman College in Florida and of the National Council of Negro Women; and Charles H. Townes (b.1915), awarded the Nobel Prize in physics in 1964.

South Carolinians who made significant contributions to literature include DuBose Heyward (1885–1940), whose novel *Porgy* was the basis of the folk opera *Porgy and Bess.* Entertainers born in the state include singer Eartha Kitt (b.1928) and jazz trumpeter John Birks "Dizzy" Gillespie (1917–93). Tennis champion Althea Gibson (b.1927) is another South Carolina native.

40 BIBLIOGRAPHY

Lander, Ernest M. *A History of South Carolina, 1856–1960.* Columbia: University of South Carolina Press, 1970.

Taylor, Rosser H. *Ante-Bellum South Carolina: A Social and Cultural History.* New York: Da Capo Press, 1970.

Wright, Louis B. *South Carolina: A Bicentennial History.* New York: Norton, 1976.

SOUTH DAKOTA

State of South Dakota

ORIGIN OF STATE NAME: The state was formerly the southern part of Dakota Territory; *dakota* is a Sioux word meaning "friend" or "ally."

NICKNAME: The Mount Rushmore State.

CAPITAL: Pierre.

ENTERED UNION: 2 November 1889 (40th).

SONG: "Hail, South Dakota."

MOTTO: Under God the People Rule.

COAT OF ARMS: Beneath the state motto, the Missouri River winds between hills and plains; symbols representing mining (a smelting furnace and hills), commerce (a steamboat), and agriculture (a man plowing, cattle, and a field of corn) complete the scene.

FLAG: The state seal, centered on a light-blue field and encircled by a sun, is surrounded by the words "South Dakota" above and "The Mount Rushmore State" below.

OFFICIAL SEAL: The words "State of South Dakota. Great Seal. 1889" encircle the arms.

ANIMAL: Coyote.

BIRD: Chinese ring-necked pheasant.

FISH: Walleye.

FLOWER: Pasqueflower.

TREE: Black Hills spruce.

INSECT: Honey bee.

GEM: Fairburn agate.

MINERAL: Rose quartz.

GRASS: Western wheatgrass.

TIME 6 AM CST = noon GM; 5 AM MST = noon GMT.

1 LOCATION AND SIZE

Situated in the western north-central US, South Dakota ranks 16th in size among the 50 states with a total area of 77,121 square miles (199,743 square kilometers). It extends about 380 miles (610 kilometers) east-west and has a maximum north-south extension of 245 miles (394 kilometers). The total boundary length of the state is 1,316 miles (2,118 kilometers).

2 TOPOGRAPHY

The eastern two-fifths of South Dakota is prairie, while the western three-fifths falls within the Missouri Plateau, and the High Plains extend into the south. The Black Hills occupy part of the state's western border. Harney Peak, at 7,242 feet (2,207 meters), is the highest point in the state. East of the Black Hills are the Badlands, a barren, eroded region with large fossil deposits. The Missouri River is controlled by four massive dams—Gavins Point, Fort Randall, Big Bend, and Oahe. Major lakes in the state include Traverse, Big Stone, and Lewis.

3 CLIMATE

South Dakota has an interior continental climate, with hot summers, extremely cold winters, high winds, and periodic droughts. The normal temperature is 12°F (–11°C) in January and 74°F (23°C) in July. The record low temperature, set in 1936, is –58°F (–50°C); the record high, 120°F (49°C), was set in the same year. Normal annual precipitation ranges from less than 13 inches (33 centimeters) to 24 inches (61 centimeters) in Sioux Falls.

4 PLANTS AND ANIMALS

Oak, maple, and beech are among the trees represented in South Dakota's forests, while thickets of wild plum, gooseberry, and currant are found in the eastern part of the state. Pasqueflower *(Anemone ludoviciana)* is the state flower. Other wildflowers are bluebell and monkshood. Familiar native mammals include the coyote (the state animal), porcupine, and black-tailed prairie dog. Nearly 300 species of birds have been identified; the sage grouse, bobwhite quail, and ring-necked pheasant are leading game birds. Trout, catfish, and pike are fished for sport. The black-footed ferret, interior least tern, and pearl dace are endangered.

South Dakota Population Profile

Estimated 1995 population:	735,000
Population change, 1980–90:	0.8%
Leading ancestry group:	German
Second leading group:	Norwegian
Foreign born population:	1.1%
Hispanic origin†:	0.8%
Population by race:	
White:	91.6%
Black:	0.5%
Native American:	7.3%
Asian/Pacific Islander:	0.4%
Other:	0.2%

Population by Age Group

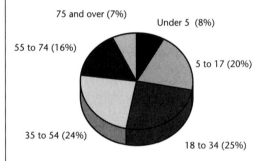

75 and over (7%)
Under 5 (8%)
55 to 74 (16%)
5 to 17 (20%)
35 to 54 (24%)
18 to 34 (25%)

Top Cities with Populations Over 25,000

City	Population	National rank	% change 1980–90
Sioux Falls	105,634	191	23.9
Rapid City	57,053	435	17.3

Notes: †A person of Hispanic origin may be of any race. NA indicates that data are not available.
Sources: Economic and Statistics Administration, Bureau of the Census. *Statistical Abstract of the United States, 1994–95.* Washington, DC: Government Printing Office, 1995; Courtenay M. Slater and George E. Hall. *1995 County and City Extra: Annual Metro, City and County Data Book.* Lanham, MD: Bernan Press, 1995.

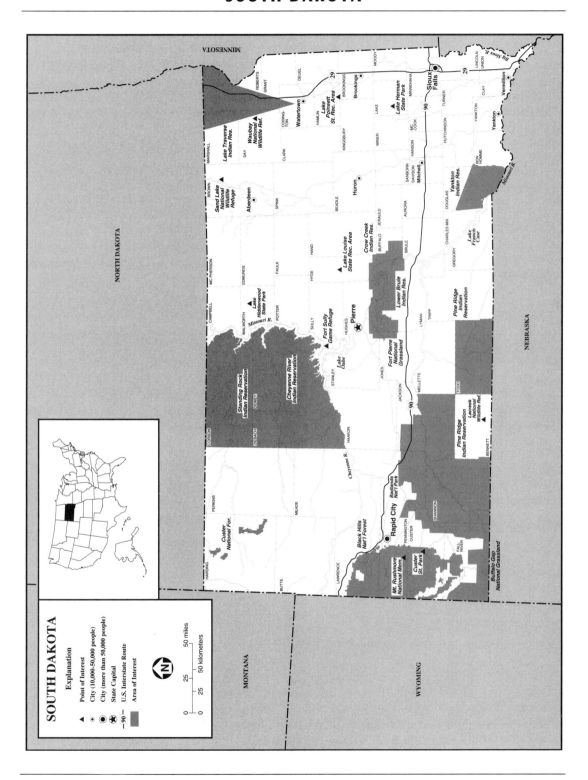

5 ENVIRONMENTAL PROTECTION

Agencies concerned with natural resources and environmental protection include the Department of Game, Fish, and Parks, and the Department of Water and Natural Resources. The Health Department deals with solid waste disposal and air pollution. South Dakota had four hazardous waste sites as of 1994.

6 POPULATION

South Dakota ranked 45th in the US with a 1990 census population of 696,004. The estimated 1995 population was 735,000. The Census Bureau projects a population of 770,000 residents in 2000. The average population density in 1990 was 9.2 persons per square mile (3.5 persons per square kilometer). About 30% of all South Dakotans lived in metropolitan areas in 1990. The leading cities as of 1992 were Sioux Falls, with 105,634 residents, and Rapid City, with 57,053.

7 ETHNIC GROUPS

In 1990, South Dakota's population included some 50,575 Native Americans. As of 1990, the state had 3,258 black Americans and 3,123 Asian-Pacific peoples. Of the South Dakotans who reported at least one specific ancestry in the 1990 census, 355,102 listed German; 106,361, Norwegian; 87,657, Irish; 68,345, English; and 36,844, Dutch.

8 LANGUAGES

South Dakota English combines the Northern and Midland dialects. In 1990, 641,226 South Dakotans—93.5% of the resident population—spoke only English at home. Other languages spoken at home, with number of speakers, included German, 17,537; Spanish, 5,033; and various Native American languages, 9,969.

9 RELIGIONS

Leading Protestant denominations in 1990 were the South Dakota Evangelical Lutheran Church in America, with 114,690 members; and Lutheran Church—Missouri Synod, 32,968. The state had 143,776 Roman Catholics and an estimated 135 Jews in 1990.

10 TRANSPORTATION

In 1994, 1,977 rail miles (3,181 kilometers) of track were utilized by ten railroads. Public highways, streets, and roads covered 83,313 miles (134,051 kilometers) in 1995. Joe Foss Field at Sioux Falls was the most active airport, with 99,110 arrivals and departures in 1994.

11 HISTORY

The Sioux, driven from the Minnesota woodlands, began to move westward during the second quarter of the eighteenth century, forcing all other Native American groups out of South Dakota by the mid-1830s. Significant European penetration of South Dakota followed the Lewis and Clark expedition of 1804–06. White men came to claim US sovereignty, negotiate Indian treaties, and conduct trade in hides and furs.

The Dakota Territory, which included much of present-day Wyoming and Montana as well as North and South Dakota, was established in 1861. The territory was

Photo credit: photo by South Dakota Tourism.

Buffalo in Custer State Park, Black Hills.

reduced to just the Dakotas in 1868. Six years later, a gold rush brought thousands of prospectors and settlers to the Black Hills. South Dakota emerged as a state in 1889, with the capital in Pierre. Included within the state were nine Native American reservations, established after lengthy negotiations and three wars with the Sioux.

State Development

Through the late 19th and early 20th centuries, South Dakotans, dependent mainly on agriculture, had limited economic opportunities. Some 30,000 Sioux barely survived on farming and livestock production, supplemented by irregular government jobs and off-reservation employment. The 500,000 non-Native Americans lived mainly off cattle-feeding enterprises and modest grain sales, mineral production (especially gold), and employment in South Dakota's cities.

The period after World War I saw extensive road-building, the establishment of a tourist industry, and efforts to harness the waters of the Missouri. Like other Americans, South Dakotans were helped through the drought and depression of the 1930s by federal aid. The economic revival brought about by World War II lasted into the postwar era. The mechanization of agriculture, dam construction along the Missouri, and reclamation of desert land all helped the rural economy. Federal programs were also organized for Native Americans on the reservations.

For 70 days in 1973, some 200 armed Sioux occupied Wounded Knee, on the Pine Ridge Reservation, where hundreds of Sioux had been killed by the US cavalry 83 years earlier. In 1980, the US Supreme Court upheld compensation of $105 million for land in the Black Hills taken by the federal government in 1877. But members of the American Indian Movement (AIM) opposed this settlement and demanded the return of the Black Hills to the Sioux.

The overall state economy showed strength in the 1980s under the direction of Republican Governor William Janklow, through the development of the state's water resources, the revival of railroad transportation, and by bringing new industry to South Dakota.

12 STATE GOVERNMENT

South Dakota's legislature consists of a 35-seat senate and 70-seat house of representatives, all of whose members serve two-year terms. Chief executive officials include the governor, lieutenant governor, secretary of state, attorney general, and treasurer, all elected for four-year terms.

13 POLITICAL PARTIES

For the most part, South Dakota has voted Republican in presidential elections, even when native-son George McGovern was the Democratic candidate in 1972. South Dakotans chose George Bush in 1988 and again in 1992. In the latter election, Bush

received 41% of the vote, Bill Clinton collected 37%, and Ross Perot earned 22%. Larry Pressler was elected to a third term in the US Senate in 1990, while Thomas Daschle won a second term in the Senate in 1992. South Dakota's US Representative, Tim Johnson, is a Democrat. As of 1995/96, there are 16 Democrats and 19 Republicans in the state senate, and 46 Republicans and 24 Democrats in the state house.

South Dakota Presidential Vote by Major Political Parties, 1948–92

YEAR	SOUTH DAKOTA WINNER	DEMOCRAT	REPUBLICAN
1948	Dewey (R)	117,653	129,651
1952	*Eisenhower (R)	90,426	203,857
1956	*Eisenhower (R)	122,288	171,569
1960	Nixon (R)	128,070	178,417
1964	*Johnson (D)	163,010	130,108
1968	*Nixon (R)	118,023	149,841
1972	*Nixon (R)	139,945	166,476
1976	Ford (R)	147,068	151,505
1980	*Reagan (R)	103,855	198,343
1984	*Reagan (R)	116,113	200,267
1988	*Bush (R)	145,560	165,415
1992**	Bush (R)	124,888	136,718

* Won US presidential election.
** Independent candidate Ross Perot received 73,295 votes.

14 LOCAL GOVERNMENT

As of 1992, South Dakota had 1,803 units of local government, including 66 counties, 310 municipalities, 971 townships, 184 school districts, and 273 special districts. Typical county officials include a treasurer, an auditor, a state's attorney, a sheriff, a register of deeds, and a clerk of courts.

15 JUDICIAL SYSTEM

South Dakota has a supreme court with 5 justices, and 8 circuit courts with 36 judges.

In 1994, South Dakota's crime index total was 3,102.2 crimes per 100,000 inhabitants (well below national averages).

16 MIGRATION

Since the 1930s, more people have left South Dakota than have settled in the state. Between 1940 and 1990, the net loss from migration amounted to almost 340,000. Between 1990 and 1994, the state gained about 10,000 residents due to interstate migration. As of 1990, just over 70% of all South Dakotans had been born within the state. By 1990, the urban population equaled the rural population (at 50%).

17 ECONOMY

Agriculture dominates South Dakota's economy. Grains and livestock are the main farm products, and processed foods and farm equipment are leading manufactured items. Mining and tourism are also important.

18 INCOME

Per capita (per person) income in 1994 was $19,630, ranking South Dakota 33d among the 50 states. Total personal income rose to $14.2 billion in 1994. In 1993, 14.2% of South Dakotans, many of them Native Americans, were below the federal poverty level.

19 INDUSTRY

Food and related products, machinery, computer equipment, and printing and publishing together account for more than 58% of all South Dakota manufacturing employment. Total reported sales for manufacturing in 1993 were $2.5 billion, with food contributing nearly 30%.

20 LABOR

The state's civilian labor force numbered 374,000 in 1994, of whom 3.3% were unemployed. Some 8.3% of all workers in the state were union members in 1994.

21 AGRICULTURE

South Dakota ranked 20th among the 50 states in 1994 in agricultural income, with receipts of $3.3 billion. In 1994, there were about 34,000 farms and ranches in the state, covering about 44.8 million acres (18 million hectares). Production of leading crops in 1994 included hay, 7.3 million tons; wheat, 95.3 million bushels; soybeans, 94.4 million bushels; and oats, 31.4 million bushels.

22 DOMESTICATED ANIMALS

The livestock industry is of great importance in South Dakota, particularly in the High Plains. In 1994 there were 4,000,000 cattle, 1,740,000 hogs, and 530,000 sheep. That year, cattle products accounted for 30.5% of all agricultural receipts; hog products, 9.4%.

23 FISHING

Nearly all fishing is recreational.

24 FORESTRY

Most of South Dakota's forest land is in the Black Hills. Three counties, Pennington, Lawrence, and Custer, account for most of the state's forest area, which totals roughly 1.7 million acres (0.6 million hectares). Forests in the Plains region consist

Photo by South Dakota Tourism.

Rodeo, a Western tradition.

primarily of tree species associated with eastern hardwood forests, such as elm, ash, and basswood. The forests in the Black Hills and at higher elevations consist principally of ponderosa pine. The Black Hills has, for nearly a century, been producing and supplying sawlogs, fuelwood, pulpwood, posts, and poles.

25 MINING

The estimated value of nonfuel mineral production for South Dakota in 1994 was $322 million. In terms of value, gold remained the leading commodity, followed by portland cement, construction sand and gravel, and crushed stone. In 1991 the major gold-mining operations

processed more than 8.7 million metric tons (9.6 million short tons) of ore.

26 ENERGY AND POWER

In 1993, South Dakota produced 5.3 billion kilowatt hours of electricity, more than half of it sold to customers in other states. Almost 50% of power output is from hydroelectric sources. Energy expenditures were $1,818 per capita (per person) in 1992. South Dakota has very modest fossil-fuel resources. The state has no nuclear power plants.

27 COMMERCE

Wholesale sales totaled $6.5 billion in 1992; retail sales were $6.3 billion in

1993; service establishment receipts were $2.1 billion in 1992. The state's exports were valued at $232 million in 1992 (49th in the US).

28 PUBLIC FINANCE

The general revenues for 1994/95 (actual) were $621,386,833; expenditures were $588,613,811. As of 1993, the outstanding debt was $1.8 billion, or $2,539 per capita (per person).

29 TAXATION

South Dakota's per capita (per person) taxation is among the lowest in the US: state and local taxes per capita were $751.4 in 1991, for a rank of 49th. There is no personal or corporate income tax, and personal property taxes have been reduced since 1978. A state sales and use tax of 4% is imposed, and taxes are also levied on gasoline sales, alcoholic beverages, tobacco products, inheritances, insurance premiums, and other items. Federal income taxes in South Dakota totaled $1.1 billion in 1992.

30 HEALTH

Death rates for heart disease, cancer, cerebrovascular disease, suicide, and accidents were above the national average in 1992. In 1993, the state had 51 community hospitals, with 4,300 beds. The average hospital expense in 1993 was $506 per inpatient day, or $5,052 for an average cost per stay. South Dakota had 1,100 active nonfederal physicians in 1993 and 6,800 nurses. Some 13% of state residents did not have health insurance in 1993.

31 HOUSING

In 1993, there were an estimated 303,000 housing units. In 1993, 3,729 new housing units valued at $242.2 million were authorized. In 1990, the median monthly costs for homeowners (with a mortgage) and for renters were $569 and $306, respectively.

32 EDUCATION

As of 1990 77.1% of South Dakotans 25 years of age or older were high school graduates and 17.2% had four or more years of college. Fall 1993 enrollment in public schools totaled 133,062: 95,367 in grades K–8, and 37,695 in grades 9–12. Expenditures on education averaged $4,367 per pupil (42d in the nation) in 1993. There are eight state-supported colleges and universities, of which the largest were the University of South Dakota (Vermillion) and South Dakota State University (Brookings). The state had 12 private institutions of higher education.

33 ARTS

Artworks and handicrafts are displayed at the Dacotah Prairie Museum (Aberdeen) and other facilities. Symphony orchestras include the South Dakota Symphony in Sioux Falls and the Rapid City Symphony Orchestra. The state of South Dakota generated a total of $4,420,322 for its arts programs from 1987 to 1991.

34 LIBRARIES AND MUSEUMS

In 1994, South Dakota had 118 public libraries with a combined total of 2,278,053 volumes and a total circulation of 5,042,183. Leading collections included those of South Dakota State University

Mount Rushmore, Black Hills.

(Brookings) and the South Dakota State Library. South Dakota has 80 museums and historic sites, including the Siouxland Heritage Museum and the Shrine to Music Museum (Vermillion).

35 COMMUNICATIONS

In March 1993, 93.5% of South Dakota's 271,000 occupied housing units had telephones. Commercial broadcasters included 73 of 90 radio stations (37 AM, 53 FM) and 22 television stations. Cable television service was mainly provided by Midcontinent Cable Company in the Sioux Falls area.

36 PRESS

In 1994, South Dakota had four morning newspapers, eight evening papers; and four Sunday papers. Leading newspapers included the *Rapid City Journal*—evenings 33,929, Sundays 35,670; and the Sioux Falls *Argus Leader*—mornings 48,072, Sundays 35,670.

37 TOURISM, TRAVEL, AND RECREATION

Visitors from other states spent an estimated $834 million in South Dakota in 1993. Most of the state's tourist attractions lie west of the Missouri River, especially in the Black Hills region. Mount Rushmore National Memorial consists of enormous sculpted heads of four US presidents—George Washington, Thomas Jefferson, Theodore Roosevelt, and Abraham Lincoln—carved in granite in the mountainside. Wind Cave National Park and Jewel Cave National Monument are also in the Black Hills region.

38 SPORTS

There are no major league professional sports teams in South Dakota. The University of South Dakota Coyotes and the Jackrabbits of South Dakota State both compete in the North Central Intercollegiate Athletic Conference. Skiing and hiking are popular in the Black Hills. Other annual sporting events include the Black Hills Motorcycle Classic in Sturgis, and many rodeos.

39 FAMOUS SOUTH DAKOTANS

The only South Dakotan to win high elective office was Hubert H. Humphrey (1911–78), a native of Wallace. After rising to power in Minnesota Democratic politics, he served as a US senator for 16 years before becoming vice-president under Lyndon Johnson during 1965–69.

Other outstanding federal officeholders from South Dakota were Newton Edmunds (1819–1908), second governor of the Dakota Territory; Charles Henry Burke (b.New York, 1861–1944), who as commissioner of Indian affairs improved education and health care for Native Americans. The son of a German-American father and a Brulé Indian mother, Benjamin Reifel (1906–90) was the first Native American elected to Congress from South Dakota. He later served as the last US commissioner of Indian affairs. George McGovern (b.1922) served in the US Senate from 1963 through 1980. An early opponent of the war in Viet Nam, he ran unsuccessfully as the Democratic presidential nominee in 1972.

Associated with South Dakota are several distinguished Native American leaders. Among them were Red Cloud (Mahpiua Luta, b.Nebraska 1822–1909), an Oglala warrior; Sitting Bull (1834–90), the main leader of the tribal army that crushed George Custer's Seventh US Cavalry at the Battle of the Little Big Horn (1876) in Montana; and Crazy Horse (1849?–77), an Oglala chief who also fought at Little Big Horn. Russell Means (b.1940) is noted for his activity in the American Indian Movement and the Libertarian Party.

Ernest Orlando Lawrence (1901–58), the state's only Nobel Prize winner, received the physics award in 1939 for the invention of the cyclotron. The business leader with the greatest personal influence on South Dakota's history was Pierre Chouteau, Jr. (b.Missouri, 1789–1865), a fur-trader after whom the state capital is named.

South Dakota artists include George Catlin (b.Pennsylvania, 1796–1872); Harvey Dunn (1884–1952); and Oscar Howe (1915–83). Gutzon Borglum (b.Idaho, 1871–1941) carved the faces on Mt. Rushmore. The state's two leading writers are Ole Edvart Rölvaag (b.Norway, 1876–1931), author of *Giants in the Earth* and other novels; and Frederick Manfred (b.Iowa, 1912–94), a Minnesota resident who served as writer-in-residence at the University of South Dakota and has used the state as a setting for many of his novels.

40 BIBLIOGRAPHY

Milton, John R., ed. *South Dakota: A Bicentennial History*. New York: Norton, 1977.

Parker, Watson. *Gold in the Black Hills*. Norman: University of Oklahoma Press, 1966.

Schell, Herbert. *History of South Dakota*. 3d ed. Lincoln: University of Nebraska Press, 1975.

Shaff, Howard, and Audrey Shaff. *Six Wars at a Time*. Sioux Falls, S.D.: Center for Western Studies at Augustana College, 1985.

Glossary

ALPINE: generally refers to the Alps or other mountains; can also refer to a mountainous zone above the timberline.

ANCESTRY: based on how people refer to themselves, and refers to a person's ethnic origin, descent, heritage, or place of birth of the person or the person's parents or ancestors before their arrival in the United States. The Census Bureau accepted "American" as a unique ethnicity if it was given alone, with an unclear response (such as "mixed" or "adopted"), or with names of particular states.

ANTEBELLUM: before the US Civil War.

AQUEDUCT: a large pipe or channel that carries water over a distance, or a raised structure that supports such a channel or pipe.

AQUIFER: an underground layer of porous rock, sand, or gravel that holds water.

BLUE LAWS: laws forbidding certain practices (e.g., conducting business, gaming, drinking liquor), especially on Sundays.

BROILERS: a bird (especially a young chicken) that can be cooked by broiling.

BTU: The amount of heat required to raise one pound of water one degree Fahrenheit.

CAPITAL BUDGET: a financial plan for acquiring and improving buildings or land, paid for by the sale of bonds.

CAPITAL PUNISHMENT: punishment by death.

CIVILIAN LABOR FORCE: all persons 16 years of age or older who are not in the armed forces and who are now holding a job, have been temporarily laid off, are waiting to be reassigned to a new position, or are unemployed but actively looking for work.

CLASS I RAILROAD: a railroad having gross annual revenues of $83.5 million or more in 1983.

COMMERCIAL BANK: a bank that offers to businesses and individuals a variety of banking services, including the right of withdrawal by check.

COMPACT: a formal agreement, covenant, or understanding between two or more parties.

CONSOLIDATED BUDGET: a financial plan that includes the general budget, federal funds, and all special funds.

CONSTANT DOLLARS: money values calculated so as to eliminate the effect of inflation on prices and income.

CONTERMINOUS US: refers to the "lower 48" states of the continental US that are enclosed within a common boundary.

CONTINENTAL CLIMATE: the climate typical of the US interior, having distinct seasons, a wide range of daily and annual temperatures, and dry, sunny summers.

COUNCIL-MANAGER SYSTEM: a system of local government under which a professional administrator is hired by an elected council to carry out its laws and policies.

CREDIT UNION: a cooperative body that raises funds from its members by the sale of shares and makes loans to its members at relatively low interest rates.

CURRENT DOLLARS: money values that reflect prevailing prices, without excluding the effects of inflation.

DEMAND DEPOSIT: a bank deposit that can be withdrawn by the depositor with no advance notice to the bank.

ELECTORAL VOTES: the votes that a state may cast for president, equal to the combined total of its US senators and representatives and nearly always cast entirely on behalf of the candidate who won the most votes in that state on Election Day.

ENDANGERED SPECIES: a type of plant or animal threatened with extinction in all or part of its natural range.

FEDERAL POVERTY LEVEL: a level of money income below which a person or family qualifies for US government aid.

FISCAL YEAR: a 12-month period for accounting purposes.

FOOD STAMPS: coupons issued by the government to low-income persons for food purchases at local stores.

GENERAL BUDGET: a financial plan based on a government's normal revenues and operating expenses, excluding special funds.

GENERAL COASTLINE: a measurement of the general outline of the US seacoast. See also TIDAL SHORELINE.

GREAT AWAKENING: during the mid–18th century, a Protestant religious revival in North America, especially New England.

GROSS STATE PRODUCT: the total value of goods and services produced in the state.

GROWING SEASON: the period between the last 32°F (0°C) temperature in spring and the first

32°F (0°C) temperature in autumn.

HISPANIC: a person who originates from Spain or from Spanish-speaking countries of South and Central America, Mexico, Puerto Rico, and Cuba.

HOME-RULE CHARTER: a document stating how and in what respects a city, town, or county may govern itself.

HUNDREDWEIGHT: a unit of weight that equals 100 pounds in the US and 112 pounds in Britain.

INPATIENT: a patient who is housed and fed—in addition to being treated—in a hospital.

INSTALLED CAPACITY: the maximum possible output of electric power at any given time.

MASSIF: a central mountain mass or the dominant part of a range of mountains.

MAYOR-COUNCIL SYSTEM: a system of local government under which an elected council serves as a legislature and an elected mayor is the chief administrator.

MEDICAID: a federal-state program that helps defray the hospital and medical costs of needy persons.

MEDICARE: a program of hospital and medical insurance for the elderly, administered by the federal government.

METRIC TON: a unit of weight that equals 1,000 kilograms (2,204.62 pounds).

METROPOLITAN AREA: in most cases, a city and its surrounding suburbs.

MONTANE: refers to a zone in mountainous areas in which large coniferous trees, in a cool moist setting, are the main features.

NO-FAULT INSURANCE: an automobile insurance plan that allows an accident victim to receive payment from an insurance company without having to prove who was responsible for the accident.

NONFEDERAL PHYSICIAN: a medical doctor who is not employed by the federal US government.

NORTHERN, NORTH MIDLAND: major US dialect regions.

OMBUDSMAN: a public official empowered to hear and investigate complaints by private citizens about government agencies.

PER CAPITA: per person.

PERSONAL INCOME: refers to the income an individual receives from employment, or to the total incomes that all individuals receive from their employment in a sector of business (such as personal incomes in the retail trade).

PIEDMONT: refers to the base of mountains.

POCKET VETO: a method by which a state governor (or the US president) may kill a bill by taking no action on it before the legislature adjourns.

PROVED RESERVES: the quantity of a recoverable mineral resource (such as oil or natural gas) that is still in the ground.

PUBLIC DEBT: the amount owed by a government.

RELIGIOUS ADHERENTS: the followers of a religious group, including (but not confined to) the full, confirmed, or communicant members of that group.

RETAIL TRADE: the sale of goods directly to the consumer.

REVENUE SHARING: the distribution of federal tax receipts to state and local governments.

RIGHT-TO-WORK LAW: a measure outlawing any attempt to require union membership as a condition of employment.

SAVINGS AND LOAN ASSOCIATION: a bank that invests the savings of depositors primarily in home mortgage loans.

SECESSION: the act of withdrawal, such as a state that withdrew from the Union in the US Civil War.

SERVICE INDUSTRIES: industries that provide services (e.g., health, legal, automotive repair) for individuals, businesses, and others.

SHORT TON: a unit of weight that equals 2,000 pounds.

SOCIAL SECURITY: as commonly understood, the federal system of old age, survivors, and disability insurance.

SOUTHERN, SOUTH MIDLAND: major US dialect regions.

SUBALPINE: generally refers to high mountainous areas just beneath the timberline; can also more specifically refer to the lower slopes of the Alps mountains.

SUNBELT: the southernmost states of the US, extending from Florida to California.

SUPPLEMENTAL SECURITY INCOME: a federally administered program of aid to the aged, blind, and disabled.

TIDAL SHORELINE: a detailed measurement of the US seacoast that includes sounds, bays, other outlets, and offshore islands.

TIME DEPOSIT: a bank deposit that may be withdrawn only at the end of a specified time period or upon advance notice to the bank.

VALUE ADDED BY MANUFACTURE: the difference, measured in dollars, between the value of finished goods and the cost of the materials needed to produce them.

WHOLESALE TRADE: the sale of goods, usually in large quantities, for ultimate resale to consumers.

Abbreviations & Acronyms

AD—Anno Domini
AFDC—aid to families with dependent children
AFL–CIO—American Federation of Labor–Congress of Industrial Organizations
AI—American Independent
AM—before noon
AM—amplitude modulation
American Ind.—American Independent Party
Amtrak—National Railroad Passenger Corp.
b.—born
BC—Before Christ
Btu—British thermal unit(s)
bu—bushel(s)
c.—circa (about)
C—Celsius (Centigrade)
CIA—Central Intelligence Agency
cm—centimeter(s)
Co.—company
comp.—compiler
Conrail—Consolidated Rail Corp.
Corp.—corporation
CST—Central Standard Time
cu—cubic
cwt—hundredweight(s)
d.—died
D—Democrat
e—evening
E—east
ed.—edition, editor
e.g.—exempli gratia (for example)
EPA—Environmental Protection Agency
est.—estimated
EST—Eastern Standard Time
et al.—et alii (and others)
etc.—et cetera (and so on)
F—Fahrenheit
FBI—Federal Bureau of Investigation
FCC—Federal Communications Commission
FM—frequency modulation
Ft.—fort
ft—foot, feet
GDP—gross domestic products
gm—gram
GMT—Greenwich Mean Time
GNP—gross national product
GRT—gross registered tons
Hist.—Historic

I—interstate (highway)
i.e.—id est (that is)
in—inch(es)
Inc.—incorporated
Jct.—junction
K—kindergarten
kg—kilogram(s)
km—kilometer(s)
km/hr—kilometers per hour
kw—kilowatt(s)
kwh—kilowatt-hour(s)
lb—pound(s)
m—meter(s); morning
m^3—cubic meter(s)
mi—mile(s)
Mon.—monument
mph—miles per hour
MST—Mountain Standard Time
Mt.—mount
Mtn.—mountain
mw—megawatt(s)
N—north
NA—not available
Natl.—National
NATO—North Atlantic Treaty Organization
NCAA—National Collegiate Athletic Association
n.d.—no date
NEA—National Education Association or National Endowment for the Arts
N.F.—National Forest
N.W.R.—National Wildlife Refuge
oz—ounce(s)
PM—after noon
PST—Pacific Standard Time
r.—reigned
R—Republican
Ra.—range
Res.—reservoir, reservation
rev. ed.—revised edition
s—south
S—Sunday
Soc.—Socialist
sq—square
St.—saint
SRD—States' Rights Democrat
UN—United Nations
US—United States

NAMES OF STATES AND OTHER SELECTED AREAS

	Standard Abbreviation(s)	Postal Abbreviation
Alabama	Ala.	AL
Alaska	*	AK
Arizona	Ariz.	AZ
Arkansas	Ark.	AR
California	Calif.	CA
Colorado	Colo.	CO
Connecticut	Conn.	CN
Delaware	Del.	DE
District of Columbia	D.C.	DC
Florida	Fla.	FL
Georgia	Ga.	GA
Hawaii	*	HI
Idaho	*	ID
Illinois	Ill.	IL
Indiana	Ind.	IN
Iowa	*	IA
Kansas	Kans. (Kan.)	KS
Kentucky	Ky.	KY
Louisiana	La.	LA
Maine	Me.	ME
Maryland	Md.	MD
Massachusetts	Mass.	MA
Michigan	Mich.	MI
Minnesota	Minn.	MN
Mississippi	Miss.	MS
Missouri	Mo.	MO
Montana	Mont.	MT
Nebraska	Nebr. (Neb.)	NE
Nevada	Nev.	NV
New Hampshire	N.H.	NH
New Jersey	N.J.	NJ
New Mexico	N.Mex.(N.M.)	NM
New York	N.Y.	NY
North Carolina	N.C.	NC
North Dakota	N.Dak. (N.D.)	ND
Ohio	*	OH
Oklahoma	Okla.	OK
Oregon	Oreg. (Ore.)	OR
Pennsylvania	Pa.	PA
Puerto Rico	P.R.	PR
Rhode Island	R.I.	RI
South Carolina	S.C.	SC
South Dakota	S.Dak. (S.D.)	SD
Tennessee	Tenn.	TN
Texas	Tex.	TX
Utah	*	UT
Vermont	Vt.	VT
Virginia	Va.	VA
Virgin Islands	V.I.	VI
Washington	Wash.	WA
West Virginia	W.Va.	WV
Wisconsin	Wis.	WI
Wyoming	Wyo.	WY

*No standard abbreviation

.

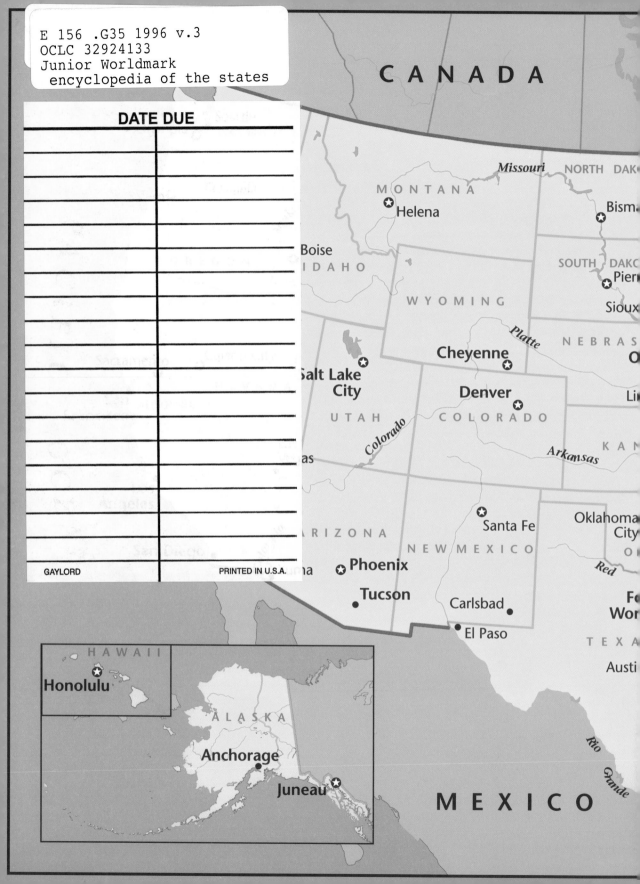

CANADA

Missouri NORTH DAK

MONTANA
Helena

Bism

Boise
IDAHO

SOUTH DAKO
Pierr

WYOMING

Sioux

Platte

Cheyenne

NEBRAS

O

Salt Lake
City

Denver

Li

UTAH

COLORADO

Colorado

K A N

Arkansas

as

Santa Fe

Oklahoma
City

RIZONA

NEW MEXICO

O

Red

Phoenix

Tucson

Carlsbad

Fo
Wor

El Paso

T E X A

Austi

HAWAII

Honolulu

A L A S K A

Anchorage

Juneau

MEXICO

Rio

Grande